An In-Fisherman®
Library Series

An In-Fisherman®
Library Series

by Wade Bourne

Published by
In-Fisherman® Inc.

Authored by Wade Bourne
Project coordinater, Bob Ripley
Edited by Joann Phipps
Photo by Wade Bourne
Layout and Design By Dan Vickerman
Typesetting by Nelson Graphic Design
Litho Prep by Quality Graphics
Printed by Bang Printing
Copyright 1988 by In-Fisherman® Inc.
Published by In-Fisherman® Inc.
P.O. Box 999, 651 Edgewood Dr., Brainerd Minnesota 56401
Printed in the United States of America
ISBN 0-929384-03-2

First Edition, 1988
Second Printing, 1989
Third Printing, 1992

Acknowledgements

Writing can be a lonely experience, just the author, his word processor, and unruly piles of notes and reference materials. But while writing FISHING FUNDAMENTALS, I didn't feel this loneliness. Instead, I was kept company by the memories of years of fishing trips, people, and places where joy reigned, and the anticipation of the next cove or stream bend pushed every worry aside. I've been fortunate in my 41 years to have experienced many fishing highlights and to have known dozens of fun-loving anglers who shared the same optimism about life that I hold.

The most important of these is my father, Joe Bourne, who took me to the water at an early age. We caught crappie like they were going out of style. But he did more than teach me how to fish. He instilled within me a great love for the outdoors, thus providing the cornerstone for my career, and ultimately my life. Thanks, Pa. I love you for it.

Thanks also to those who encouraged and helped me realize my dream of becoming a writer: Dr. Robert Drake, Tommy Akin, Glenn Sapir, Dave Precht, and Larry Teague. Special thanks go to Al and Ron Lindner for their pioneering work in fishing education and for providing the medium through which this book could be published.

Just as trees grow from seeds, books spring from ideas. The man who planted the idea for FISHING FUNDAMENTALS was Dr. Ron Whitford, who wanted to learn to fish and asked me for direction. He's since become an accomplished angler, and he's passing the traditions and pleasures of this sport on to his children.

Any book is a combined effort of several people, each of whom deserves credit for his contributions. Project leader Bob Ripley, editor Joann Phipps, and graphics designer Chuck Nelson transformed FISHING FUNDAMENTALS from raw copy into this final product, and they have my gratitude.

And what would fishing be without friends with whom to share on-water hours? I pay tribute to my fishing buddies: my brother Joe Bourne, Jr., my uncle Doug Bourne, Phil Sumner, Don Buck, Lane Lyle, Steve Fugate, David Kuykendall, Steve Swift, Scott Loxley, Mike Hall, and many others. Thanks also to the fishing pros who have shared their boats and secrets over the years.

Special recognition and love go to my mother, Lucile Bourne, for her indomitable spirit and unfailing support of her family. She's the kind of mother—fun-loving, understanding, and patient—I would wish for all anglers.

And finally, thanks and endearing love to my wife Becky, who has struggled up mountains with me, and sometimes in spite of me. She's my anchor and my inspiration, and without her this book would never have been written.

In closing, I dedicate FISHING FUNDAMENTALS to my young son Hampton, who on his first fishing trip was more interested in the cows in the pasture than catfish in the pond. My hope for the future is that we will spend many days together on the water. As the years roll by and the distractions of growing up pull you in other directions, may we always find time to slip away for a few hours, just Hamp and the old man and the fish, and the bonds which bind the two generations into one.

INTRODUCTION

It is our hope to pass on the joys and outdoor experiences that have blessed our lifetime. Fishing is an outdoor activity that can be experienced by anyone—any age, sex, race, or religion.

Bourne's FISHING FUNDAMENTALS is a handbook that leads us through various angling specifics, such as selecting equipment, locating the best fishing areas, and choosing the best methods for catching fish. After all, catching fish is part of the fun, along with all the other pleasures the great outdoors has to offer.

Families are important to our society. Whether you're a single parent, grandparent, or just a friend, joining together in a fishing experience will provide a common ground for enjoying a pleasant time together. And possibly lines of communication will be opened forever.

Bourne's book guides us on the right path to gaining angling knowledge and thus increasing the whole fishing experience. Enjoy this gem of wisdom, and then pass it on for future generations.

No one person could have researched and developed all the valuable angling information contained in this book. Hats off to all the angling pioneers: Al Lindner for the F+L+P=S system; Buck Perry for the theory of structure; Bob Murray for reservoir information; Dan Gapen for information on rivers; Bill Binkelman for Calendar Periods; Ron Lindner for lake classifications; In-Fisherman Inc. for photos, charts, and diagrams; as well as a host of other writers and teachers who paved the way to modern angling concepts.

Bob Ripley

TABLE OF CONTENTS

THE WIDE, WONDERFUL WORLD OF FISHING

"There's something magical about baiting a line, dropping it in the water, and pulling out a fish."

There's an old saying which goes, "Take a man some fish; feed him for a day. But *teach* a man to fish; feed him for *life*." I'd like to offer a sequel to this: "Take a man fishing; entertain him for a day. But *teach* a man to fish; introduce him to a *lifetime of joy*."

This is my wish for you in writing *FISHING FUNDAMENTALS*: to teach you how to experience the great pleasure of this hook-and-line sport. By learning to fish, you'll join millions of people who already enjoy the thrills, challenges, and satisfactions of angling. Indeed, fishing appeals to all ages, classes, and cultures the world over. There's something magical about baiting a line, dropping it in the water, and pulling out a fish.

Exactly what is this magic? What will you gain by taking up fishing? There are many answers to these questions, because fishing offers different benefits to different people.

For most, it's a healthy, fresh-air activity that can be enjoyed by young and old, male and female, athletic and infirm. Fishing is no discriminator of age, sex, or physical skills. Anyone who makes the effort can find a place and a way to catch fish.

Fishing provides a perfect setting for fun and togetherness with family or friends. It's amazing how fishing removes barriers between people and allows them to know and understand each other. Fishing also helps build a strong relationship between parents and children.

Fishing is a good way to make friends. Anglers share a common bond and speak a universal language. When two fishermen meet for the first time, they have something in common to talk about.

Fishing is a means of communing with nature. Outdoors, the pressures of modern life seem to blow away.

Fishing relieves the stresses of work or school. It's a way to relax and tune into the soul-soothing rhythms of the wind and waves.

Fishing offers suspense and excitement. There's intense drama in watching a bobber disappear underwater, setting the hook, and then battling the fish up to the bank or boat. When you catch the fish, you know the satisfaction of a job well done. Fishing gives feelings of accomplishment and self-esteem as you learn the tricks of the sport and how to apply them successfully.

Fishing teaches patience, perseverance, and how to work toward goals. Ponds, lakes, and streams are natural classrooms for some very important lessons in life.

And last, fishing can provide nutritious, delicious-tasting meat. There are few banquets as pleasing as fresh fish you've caught, cleaned, and cooked.

But I must forewarn you before you take up this sport! With all its benefits, fishing also carries certain liabilities. It can cause otherwise rational people to crawl out of bed well before sunrise, to travel long distances, to burn enormous amounts of energy, and even to spend large sums of money, all for the chance of tricking a simple fish into biting a bait. For many, fishing is truly addictive. I feel fortunate to be in this category.

Understand, though, that you don't *have* to go to these extremes to catch fish. This sport absolutely *is not* all hardship, effort, and expense. It can also be laid back and inexpensive, close to home and unsophisticated. This is one of the beauties of fishing. You write your own ticket. You certainly don't need a fancy boat, space age tackle, glittering baits, and the education of Einstein to catch fish. You can keep this sport as easy or as challenging as you want it to be. You decide.

The Fishing Fundamentals Master Plan

My guess is that you fall into one of two categories: (1) You've never tried fishing before, and you want to learn how. (2) Or you go fishing occasionally, and you'd like to improve your catch. In either case, this book will guide you step-by-step toward fishing success.

First, I will explain the *master plan* we'll follow as you learn to fish. It's important to be methodical and to keep this process in the right order. Then we'll learn about different types of fish, how to find good fishing spots, select tackle, tie rigs, choose the best bait, and use easy techniques in various waters and situations you might encounter. We'll also cover how to play, land, and handle fish, and how to care for them either for eating or live release.

Then we'll move ahead to a higher level of fishing knowledge. We'll cover tricks to try when fish won't bite; how to continue to grow in your new fishing skills; and how to select boats, motors, and electronic equipment. You'll learn about fishing safety and ethics. And last, I'll give you helpful hints on how to plan a successful fishing vacation.

Overall, my goal is to take you from "Point Zero" to where you have a good basic understanding of how to find and catch fish. Then you can take advantage of more advanced books, magazines, and videos to continue your fishing education. Maybe this other literature is confusing and a bit intimidating to you now, but it won't be when you finish the *FISHING FUNDAMENTALS* study course.

Before getting into the master plan, however, let's take a brief look at the world of fishing and the people who participate in this sport.

A Look at the World of Fishing

Each year some 60 million Americans and Canadians go fishing at least once. This is more people than attend all major league baseball games, all college or pro football or basketball games, all auto races, golf tournaments, and on and on. In terms of participant sports, fishing ranks second in popularity, falling only behind swimming. Altogether, fishermen spend more than $28 billion annually on tackle, boats, motors, gas, travel, etc.

But fishing isn't a high-profile activity, and it doesn't get the exposure of the big team sports. Fishermen do their thing alone or in small groups, without scores and cheerleaders, in out-of-the-way places scattered across the continent. On any weekend, North American waters are dotted with bank and boat anglers who quietly seek their own pleasures. (It's true that tournaments are a growing phenomenon in this sport, but the number of tournament anglers remains small in comparison to anglers who fish strictly for fun or food.)

There are two reasons for this large number of fishermen. There are more people and more fishing opportunities than ever before. In the last 30 years, hundreds of reservoirs have been built throughout the U.S. and Canada. At the same time, fisheries biologists have learned more about managing fish and stocking species into waters where they weren't previously found. They have literally created new fishing opportunities from east to west. In some cases popular fishing spots are receiving far more pressure than they used to. But for each of these, there are other waters and fish populations that remain relatively unaffected by angling pressure.

Fishing bridges the gap between people of all educational and economic levels. Several U.S. presidents have been avid fishermen, including Herbert Hoover, Franklin D. Roosevelt, Harry Truman, Dwight Eisenhower, and Jimmy Carter. Hoover once described fishing as a "discipline in the equality of man, for all men are equal before fish." Grandparents, parents, and children are peers in this sport. Recent research shows large increases in the number of senior citizens and single parents who have taken up fishing.

Each year the fishing tackle industry turns out increasingly better rods, reels, line, lures, and accessories. Futuristic methods and materials have been incorporated into a wide range of fishing products. Modern anglers can purchase electronic accessories that do everything from taking water temperature and measuring pH to actually showing fish swimming below the boat. Also, researchers are continually learning more about fish—where they live, what they eat, and how they react to different influences in their watery world.

Many fishermen feel these gadgets and knowledge take some of the mystery away from the sport by substituting technology for plain old know-how. I disagree with this, however, for one reason. We still don't have a way to make fish bite when they don't want to, and until we do, fishing *will* contain elements of uncertainty and chance. But I also agree with a close friend who says, "I hope we never learn all there is to know about fish." I don't think we will, and as long as we don't, the mystery and anticipation in fishing will remain.

Meanwhile, all the information and new gear will make it easier for you to learn to fish. They will reduce the amount of time it will take you to gain proficiency in this sport. You don't have to learn the old trial-and-error lessons on the water. There are many shortcuts available now to shorten your fishing apprenticeship, and I recommend that you take them.

In its most basic sense, learning to fish is a matter of stacking the odds in your favor: trying to figure out where the fish are, what they're doing, and what bait they'll hit. Then you offer that bait in the most efficient and appealing manner. You do everything possible to make it *easy* for fish to bite, and from that point on, it's up to the fish.

Sometimes they cooperate; sometimes they don't. But they *will* cooperate a lot more often if you fish with skill instead of depending on dumb luck. Sure, luck plays a big role in this sport, but day in and day out, good

5

fishermen will almost always catch more fish than "lucky" fishermen.

Teaching Children to Fish

As I mentioned earlier, fishing is an excellent way for parents and children to spend time together. If more parents took their kids fishing,

there would be fewer problems with drugs and delinquency. Fishing gives kids something constructive to do, an activity to occupy their time. Fishing provides a common bond between parents and children. It gives them something to plan, look forward to, and do together.

Parents should be careful how they introduce children to fishing, however. Those first trips should be short, simple, and with a maximum chance of catching easy fish such as bluegill, perch, or bullheads. Don't fish more than an hour or two. Don't get tense if the kids lose interest. Don't criticize them if they have trouble learning to use the tackle. Don't nag them if they'd rather throw rocks in the water than sit quietly and watch a bobber. Remember that a fishing trip should be *fun*. If you make those first trips enjoyable, your kids will keep coming back. Then, before you know it, they'll be serious about what they're doing, and you'll have fishing partners for life.

The Scope of Fishing Fundamentals

FISHING FUNDAMENTALS teaches methods for catching popular *freshwater* fish. It does not cover saltwater fish, nor does it cover Great Lakes species and tactics. While much of the information and methods in the

following chapters apply to saltwater and Great Lakes fishing, these two fisheries have distinctly different species and techniques for taking them; they'd make good subjects for two other books.

Instead, *FISHING FUNDAMENTALS* confines itself to traditional North American fishing found in inland lakes, reservoirs, streams, and rivers. This book covers species which are the most likely targets of entry-level anglers. It describes simple ways to catch them. Less popular species and more complicated fishing methods are omitted. In math, you have to learn how to add before you can work equations. In fishing, you have to master the basics before moving ahead to more difficult procedures.

The following chapters contain these basics in an easy-to-follow sequence. Study them. Digest them. Then put them into practice. And remember that the *more* you fish, the better you'll understand this sport and the more success you'll enjoy in it. If I were a "doctor of fishing" and you were my patient, I'd prescribe a concoction of water, fresh air, and fishing tackle. Mix well and take on a regular basis. I guarantee this is one medicine that will go down easily!

THE F+L+P FORMULA FOR FISHING SUCCESS

"Learning to fish is like building a house. You start with a blueprint that outlines everything step by step. Then you simply add one piece at a time."

A couple years back, a friend came to me and said he wanted to take up fishing, but he was perplexed. There was so much to learn, and he didn't know where to start. He asked if I could help, and I tried to get him started in the right direction. Eventually these efforts led to my writing this book.

It's easy to understand how fishing can intimidate a beginner. There are so many pieces to fit into the puzzle. You must learn about different species and their habits; different waters and where fish can be found in them; and various types of tackle, baits, rigs, techniques, etc.

But learning to fish is like building a house. You start with a blueprint that outlines everything step by step. Then you simply add one piece at a time. Before you know it, your "house of fishing knowledge" is complete.

This chapter will provide that blueprint for fishing success. It's a simple formula that you should memorize and apply whenever and wherever you fish. It will work for all species, on all waters, at all times. Also, by applying this formula, you'll organize your fishing approach. You'll have a starting

11

point and a charted course for figuring out where the fish are and how to catch them. Then, in succeeding chapters you'll pick up fundamentals you need to build your house of fishing skills.

The Algebra of Angling

Back in the 1950s and early 1960s, two brothers from Chicago barnstormed through the midwestern U.S., going from lake to lake and consistently catching huge stringers of walleye, bass, muskies, and other species from lakes the locals thought were "fished out." These brothers were Al and Ron Lindner, and their purpose was to sell fishing lures. They later founded In-Fisherman Inc., which continues to lead the way in teaching America to fish.

In those days, the Lindners were among the few people in North America who were scientific in their fishing. They had learned that regardless of where fish live, they behave in predictable ways under similar sets of conditions. Al and Ron could go onto a lake they'd never seen before, apply a few basic principles and techniques, and almost always load the boat.

These brothers devised a formula for fishing success and tagged it the "algebra of angling." That formula is: F+L+P = Success. Plugging in words for the letters, Fish + Location + Presentation = Success. This formula means that if you understand the habits of the fish you're after, and if you know where to find the fish in a given body of water, and if you use the best bait and fishing method for the specific situation, you'll catch the fish.

12

It's a simple three-step process.

You can plug in all the variables you'll ever encounter in fishing into this formula. It allows for versatility in methods, for new tactics when water conditions or moods of the fish change. This can happen from trip to trip or even hour to hour. The trick is recognizing these changes and then adapting to them. As you gain experience as an angler, deciding when and how to change will come easier. Still, you must have a starting point, and that's what the F+L+P = Success formula provides.

Now let's backtrack and look at each part of this formula in detail.

The "Fish" Factor: Understanding Fish's Basic Nature

Each fish species has its own special nature. Some fish like deep water, some shallow. Some chase their prey; others wait in ambush for food to swim, float, or crawl by. Some fish gather in large schools; others live by themselves. Each type fish has its own distinct spawning habits. This list of differences goes on and on.

Because each species has its own personality, you must fish for each differently. For instance, since bluegill are different from bass, you shouldn't use bass tackle, baits, and techniques when going after these smaller sunfish. This is why understanding the basic nature of the fish you're after is vital to fishing success.

How do you learn about different fish? The next chapter has brief outlines of North America's popular freshwater species. It tells the type of waters they prefer, favorite foods, spawning habits, etc. However, these outlines are necessarily brief and include only the highlights. You should do more research on fish you'll be trying for. Most libraries have books which detail life cycles of various species. Study them carefully, and learn all you can about your fish.

How Fish Sense Their Surroundings

Like humans, fish depend on their senses for survival and for satisfying daily needs. They see, smell, hear, feel, and taste. Some species depend more on certain senses than others. For instance, catfish use their sense of smell more than other fish. They can easily sniff out and find food when they can't see it (at night, in muddy water, etc.).

Most fish have excellent vision, and they depend on sight to find food and detect danger. They use hearing the same way. A quiet splash on the surface might mean food falling into the water. On the other hand, banging the floor of a metal boat is an unnatural sound to fish, and they may

TRIGGERS THAT STIMULATE RESPONSES

Both live bait and artificial lures have qualities designed to stimulate positive responses from fish. Any one or a combination of these qualities are triggers. They appeal to 6 of the 8 sensory elements of a fish's basic nature. Lure or bait choice depends on what triggers are required to cause a response from a particular species of fish at a certain time.

TRIGGERS		CONTROLS
1. Action	5. Scent	1. Depth
2. Color	6. Sound	2. Speed
3. Size	7. Vibration	
4. Shape	8. Texture	

perceive it as danger.

Fish also feel vibrations of objects moving through the water. Most species have a lateral line of vibration sensors running lengthwise down their bodies. And fish use their sense of taste to decide whether or not something that looks, sounds, smells, and feels like food actually is food. If a bait looks like a minnow, but tastes like plastic, the fish will usually spit it out in short order!

Learn which senses the fish you're after depend on most, and how they affect where the fish stay and how they collect their food. Then you'll have a better idea how to find the fish and decide on baits and techniques that seem natural to them.

Other Fish Basics

Several other factors go into defining a fish's personality. A major one is spawning habits. Different species require different water temperatures, depths, bottom content, etc. for spawning. Food preference is a second major difference from one species to the next. And a third is a particular species' "comfort zone," the combination of water temperature, sunlight level, water clarity, and other conditions that a certain species finds most comfortable.

Again, all fish don't share the same behavior patterns. Each species is different, and to catch fish consistently, you must tailor your methods to suit the personality and habits of your target species. The first step in doing this is understanding your fish's basic nature.

The "Location" Factor: Where to Find Fish

The second step in the F+L+P formula builds on the first. Once you know something about a fish's basic nature, you have a better idea where to find it.

Let's use two examples to explain this concept. Say you're after crappie, and it's the time of year when they should be spawning. If you're familiar with crappie spawning habits, you know they'll probably be in quiet, relatively shallow areas that have some type cover (brush, stumps, reeds). So you seek out such places when you're ready to start your fishing day. Another example: You're fishing for smallmouth bass in the fall, and you know that crawfish are their preferred food at this time of year. You'd be wise to fish along rocky banks where the craws are most plentiful. These are the types of things you should learn about your target species and apply them to determine where to find the fish.

Fish change locations according to needs that are part of their basic nature. In late winter and spring, spawning determines where fish will be. Through the rest of the year, food is the most important factor. Except during the spawning season, fish will normally stay close to their prey.

Fish change locations both seasonally and daily. Seasonal movements are major shifts in location—when migrating to spawning territory, or when

Understanding the predator/prey relationship is one of the keys to successful fishing.

moving to find food. These seasonal movements occur over drawn-out time periods, and they're usually predictable from year to year.

On the other hand, daily movements cover much smaller distances. They may be from deep water into adjacent shallows to feed, or from deep within a clump of weeds out to the edge. Daily movements are less predictable than seasonal movements.

So to locate fish on any given day, first you must decide where they are that time of year. Then figure out their specific location according to daily conditions.

Three Factors in Daily Fish Location

There are three main factors in a fish's environment which affect its day-to-day location: (1) structure in the body of water; (2) interaction between fish species; and (3) reaction to outside stimuli (mainly weather and man). Following are brief looks at how each of these factors figure into where to find fish.

Structure

This is one of the most important concepts in fishing. Understanding how fish relate to structure is vital to your success. Basically, fish don't just scatter at random through a body of water. Instead, they are drawn to specific locations because of some difference or attractive feature that these spots hold. These differences or features are called structure.

Let's use a simple example to explain structure. Say there's a man walking around in a desert. If there's nothing but sand, he'll wander aimlessly. But if somebody sticks up a telephone pole in the middle of the desert, he'll walk straight to it and probably stay there. The telephone pole gives him something to orient to. Or if somebody builds a fence across the desert, the man will walk to the fence and follow it. Now he has something to guide his movements. If the telephone pole is somewhere along the fence, this is a

Some structure is visable like the timber in this photo. But, underwater the creek channel is much harder to follow.

likely spot for the man to stop, since this place is different, hence more attractive, compared to the rest of the desert.

Underwater objects affect fish the same way. If the bottom is flat and without any special features, fish will swim around without any pattern. But there's *almost always* some structure that will attract them or guide their movements. Submerged stumps, trees, rocks, and weeds, are like the telephone pole. They give fish something to orient to. A sunken creek channel, gully, or roadbed is like the fence. Fish will swim along it. A stump or rock pile on the edge of a sunken channel is a likely place for fish to stop and rest as they swim along the channel.

For now, just remember that structure is anything *different* from the usual. This applies to lakes, reservoirs, ponds, big rivers, small streams, wherever. Structure may also include turns in channels, reefs, bridge foundations, boat docks, manmade fish attractors, old tires thrown in the lake, or *any-*

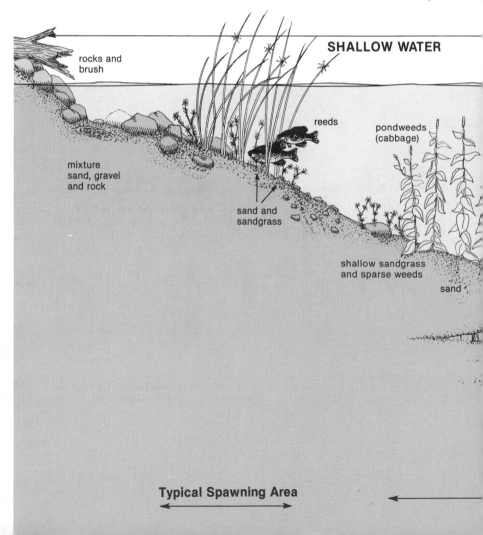

SHALLOW WATER

rocks and brush

reeds

pondweeds (cabbage)

mixture sand, gravel and rock

sand and sandgrass

shallow sandgrass and sparse weeds

sand

Typical Spawning Area

thing else that's different from a clean, smooth bottom.

Also, structure may be more subtle, such as a spot where the current shifts direction, changes in bottom makeup (for instance, where a mud bottom turns into gravel), where muddy water changes to clear, or where shadows fall onto the water surface.

The point is, think *change* or *differences*, and you'll be thinking *structure*. In Chapter 9, we'll get into a more detailed discussion of how structure affects specific fishing techniques.

The cross-section on these two pages shows the various structural elements that could be found in many but not all natural lakes. The depths are relative. The edge of the weedline, for example, could occur at 8 feet or 18 feet, depending on water clarity.

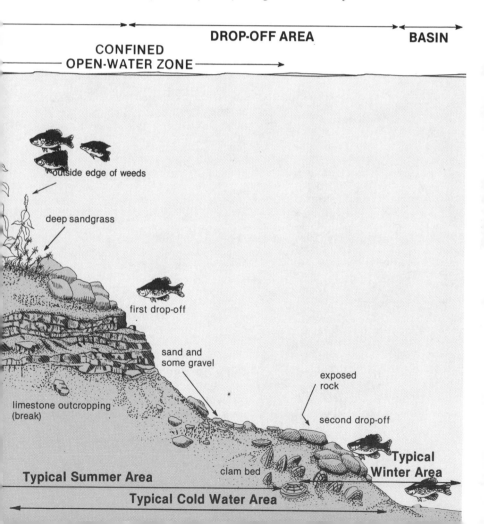

CONFINED OPEN-WATER ZONE

DROP-OFF AREA

BASIN

outside edge of weeds

deep sandgrass

first drop-off

sand and some gravel

exposed rock

limestone outcropping (break)

second drop-off

Typical Summer Area

clam bed

Typical Winter Area

Typical Cold Water Area

TYPICAL IMPOUNDMENT FEATURES

The accompanying illustrations show various impoundment features. There are so many regional variations, that we adopted or coined words or phrases to describe them. For example, we dropped the word "bay" and became more specific by using the term "cove" or "cut." The accompanying example is not meant to depict a specific type of impoundment. Note that it is divided into three sections.

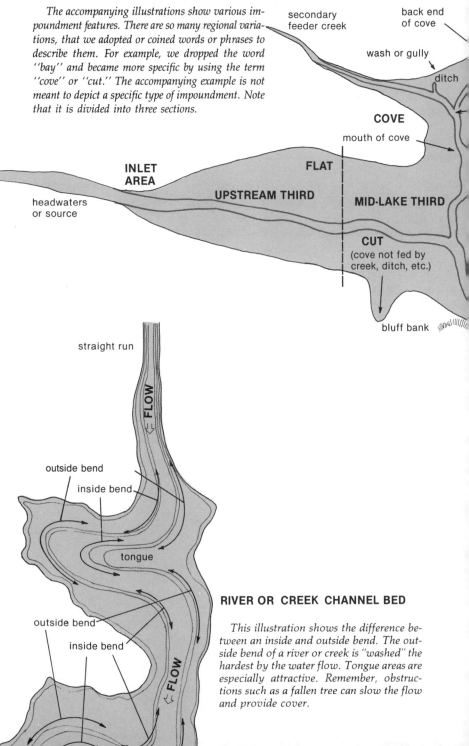

secondary feeder creek

back end of cove

wash or gully

ditch

COVE

mouth of cove

FLAT

INLET AREA

headwaters or source

UPSTREAM THIRD

MID-LAKE THIRD

CUT
(cove not fed by creek, ditch, etc.)

bluff bank

straight run

FLOW

outside bend

inside bend

tongue

outside bend

inside bend

FLOW

RIVER OR CREEK CHANNEL BED

This illustration shows the difference between an inside and outside bend. The outside bend of a river or creek is "washed" the hardest by the water flow. Tongue areas are especially attractive. Remember, obstructions such as a fallen tree can slow the flow and provide cover.

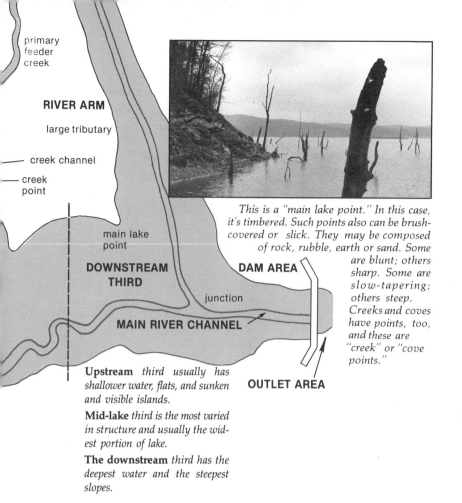

primary
feeder
creek

RIVER ARM

large tributary

— creek channel

— creek
point

main lake
point

DOWNSTREAM THIRD

DAM AREA

junction

MAIN RIVER CHANNEL

OUTLET AREA

This is a "main lake point." In this case, it's timbered. Such points also can be brush-covered or slick. They may be composed of rock, rubble, earth or sand. Some are blunt; others sharp. Some are slow-tapering; others steep. Creeks and coves have points, too, and these are "creek" or "cove points."

Upstream *third usually has shallower water, flats, and sunken and visible islands.*

Mid-lake *third is the most varied in structure and usually the widest portion of lake.*

The downstream *third has the deepest water and the steepest slopes.*

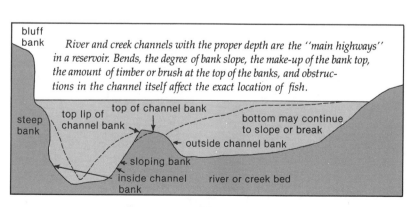

bluff
bank

River and creek channels with the proper depth are the "main highways" in a reservoir. Bends, the degree of bank slope, the make-up of the bank top, the amount of timber or brush at the top of the banks, and obstructions in the channel itself affect the exact location of fish.

steep
bank

top lip of
channel bank

top of channel bank

bottom may continue
to slope or break

outside channel bank

sloping bank

inside channel
bank

river or creek bed

21

Habitat in Rivers

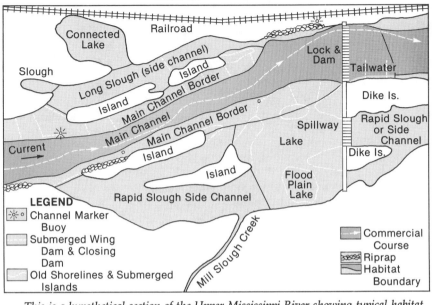

This is a hypothetical section of the Upper Mississippi River showing typical habitat areas. High and low water dictates the movement of fish from backwaters to the main channel. Side channels have reduced current and attached lakes provide very little current.

Oxbow and Flood Plain

In the lower sections of the Mississippi River, oxbow lakes are important. Some oxbows are connected to the main river; some are not. A few lie outside the levee system while others lie inside the levees included in the flood plain. Oxbows connected to the river channel and lying within the levee system usually provide the best fishing.

Interaction Between Fish Species

"Species interaction" means how different fish relate to each other in terms of population density, availability of food, and competitive species.

Basically, the more fish there are in a body of water, the more orderly and predictable their locations will be. The bass will be staying and feeding in one area. Walleye will be in another. Sunfish will be in another. There is some sharing of territory, and several species may occasionally mix if they're feeding on the same food source, but most of the time different species will stay separated. This is nature's way of maintaining order in the environment.

Typical Aquatic Food Chain

"The Game of Who Eats Whom"

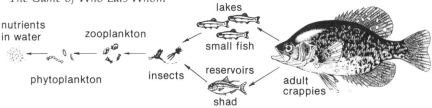

As mentioned above, after the spawning season, availability of food mainly influences where fish will be. Predator fish will stay close to baitfish. Also, the *amount* of available food determines how large predator fish populations will be and how fast and how large individual fish will grow. For instance, reservoirs with larger shad populations will have more and bigger bass and crappie.

Some species are compatible with each other; others are not. Competition between species for food and for spawning sites can have a direct bearing on fish location.

Reaction to Outside Stimuli

The third factor which affects daily fish location is "reaction to outside stimuli." Specifically, this is how fish respond to two different sets of conditions: natural, and manmade.

Natural conditions include water temperature and weather. These influence where fish will be from one day to the next. A detailed explanation of how water temperature and individual weather conditions affect fish is found in Chapter 12.

Manmade conditions can include many things: fishing pressure, boat traffic, swimmers, pollution. Also, man may alter the fish's habitat—clearing weeds or brush, draining sloughs, adding brush or other fish attractors. All of these have some bearing on where fish will be in a given body of water.

23

The Presentation Factor: Catching Fish After You've Found Them

Once you know where the fish are, you still have to figure out what bait and technique will make them bite, and when this bait and technique will work. This combination of bait, method, and timing is called presentation. Once you've located the fish, if you use the right presentation, you'll catch them. But if you use the wrong presentation, you might still strike out.

The right presentation changes frequently, depending on several factors. If the fish are actively feeding, a fast-moving bait that simulates their prey may work best. But when the feeding period ends and fish get picky, a slow, subtle bait and retrieve might still entice strikes when a fast, flashy bait and retrieve will be ignored. You have to match your bait and technique to present conditions and the fish's mood.

Presentation is broken down into two sub-categories: Position, and Working Method.

Position

Position is easy. It means how you implement your Working Method. Your presentation will either be stationary or mobile. It will be stationary if you're fishing from a fixed position on a bank, bridge, or pier; or while you're anchored in a boat. It will be mobile if you're trolling, drifting, wadefishing, floating on a stream, or moving your boat with an electric motor.

Whether you're stationary or mobile will have a direct influence on the rest of your presentation. If you're stationary, you must wait for the fish to come to you. If you're mobile, you go to the fish.

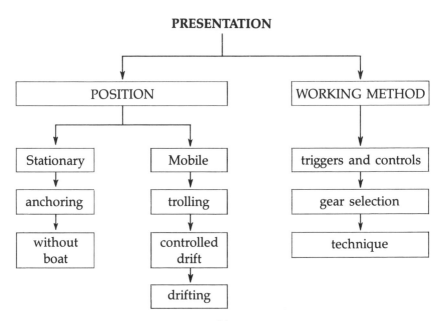

As we look over a body of water it may be confusing. But, breaking it down we can approach fishing with the best position and working method.

Working Method

The Working Method half of the presentation is a little more complicated than Position. It involves lure selection and retrieve methods. So, working method is broken down even further into Triggers and Controls.

Triggers are the eight characteristics of a bait or lure that affect a fish's decision to bite it. These triggers are: action, color, size, shape, scent, sound, vibration, and texture. Baits or lures should be selected with the right combination of triggers to match the basic nature and preferences of the target fish. For instance, bullheads are far more likely to bite a gob of night crawlers resting on the bottom than they are a topwater lure popped across the surface.

Lure and bait selection vary not only by location and species preferences, but also by the feeding attitude of the fish—positive, neutral, or negative. When fish are in a positive (active) feeding mood, they respond to many baits and methods. When they are neutral, they aren't actively feeding, but can still be tempted with *just the right* presentation. When they're negative, they're spooky and difficult to catch with any presentation.

Controls include depth and speed, the two variables of all baits and lures. Sometimes fish are shallow and want fast-moving baits. Sometimes they're deep and want slow-moving or stationary baits. Based on the fish's basic nature and its location, you must decide whether to fish shallow or deep; fast, slow, or stationary.

Gear selection and technique figure into the Controls portion of your presentation. When choosing gear (Chapter 5), you must match it to the type of structure you'll be fishing and the baits you'll use. Also, technique refers to the depth, speed, action, and vibration of your bait. These are controlled by how fast you retrieve your lure (if you retrieve it at all), how you work your rod tip, etc. For example, when fishing a jig, your technique may be to swim it along above the bottom, or you may hop it off the bottom.

Summary of the F+L+P Formula

What happened? The F+L+P formula was supposed to be simple, but all of a sudden it got complicated. Fish + Location + Presentation is easy to understand. But when you add such things as structure, interaction between species, position, and controls and triggers, the confusion factor sets in.

For now, don't worry if you don't understand all these concepts. As you continue through this book, and as you gain experience, your new fishing knowledge will clear up much of this confusion. Right now you probably don't know how to match your gear to the areas you'll be fishing and the baits you'll use, but you *will* know how when you finish Chapter 5. The same holds true for many other points in this chapter.

Here's the main idea. Successful fishing isn't hodgepodge. It's structured. To catch certain fish under certain conditions, you do specific things. You don't pick any spot at random, cast out any lure or bait, and use any retrieve method. Again, you must understand the basic nature of the fish. You have to figure out where they are. Then you have to decide which presentation will be most effective under present conditions.

So again, remember to think F+L+P each time you go fishing. This will cover the basics and provide that blueprint for all your angling efforts. Later on, you'll learn more details, and then making correct decisions will come easy.

PUTTING IT TOGETHER

The Basis For
Sustained Fishing Success

A) Edge Effect and Structure
B) Body of Water Classification
C) Calendar Periods
D) Evaluating Structural Elements

    1) Social Conditions
        a) Predator/Prey
        b) Competing Species
        c) Prey/Predator
        d) Man's Influence
    2) Water Clarity

    3) Structural Depth
    4) Bottom Content
    5) Bottom Configuration
    6) Structural Loction
    7) Water Exchange Rate
    8) Vegetation and/or Cover

POPULAR FISH SPECIES OF NORTH AMERICA

"The more you know about the fish you're after, the more likely you are to catch them."

The first step in learning to fish is learning *about* fish: the species that are available to anglers, where they live, the kinds of waters they prefer, and what they eat. Beginners should realize that the more they know about the fish they're after, the more likely they are to catch them. Many expert anglers learn even the smallest details about daily routines of their target species. This helps find the fish and select bait and a technique to make them bite.

Following are brief looks at our most popular freshwater species. Included in these outlines are the bare essentials you need for catching each of them. As your fishing skills grow, add to this knowledge until you have a broad understanding of where to find and catch individual species under varying conditions.

Black Bass

Some authorities consider black bass the most important freshwater fish in North America. Actually, this group (the genus Micropterus) includes three popular species (largemouth bass, smallmouth bass, and spotted bass) and four lesser known species (Guadalope, redeye, shoal, and Suwannee). These fish are closely related, but differ in the waters they prefer, favorite foods, spawning habits, and other life basics.

The largemouth is the most abundant bass, and it grows larger than smallmouth or spotted bass. In North America, largemouth live in lakes, reservoirs, streams, and ponds from Florida and Mexico to southern Canada, and from the East Coast to the West Coast. These fish feed and rest in quiet, relatively shallow water, usually around cover like vegetation, rocks, and logs.

LARGEMOUTH BASS

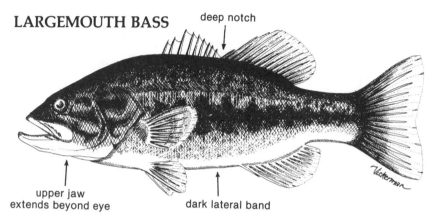

deep notch

upper jaw
extends beyond eye

dark lateral band

As with many species, largemouth bass grow bigger in southern states because warmer weather allows a longer growing season. In Florida, Georgia, Texas and southern California, largemouths over 15 pounds are occasionally boated. On the other hand, in northern states and Canadian provinces, largemouths over 7 pounds are rare. The world-record large-mouth bass was caught in south Georgia in 1932. It weighed 22 pounds 4 ounces.

Largemouth bass are predators that eat a wide range of foods. Minnows, crawfish, frogs, and insects are favorite prey, but these fish will also strike baby ducks, mice, snakes, and other creatures which are available and small enough to swallow.

Smallmouth bass prefer clearer, cooler waters than largemouth. They also like a rocky environment, and they adapt well to medium-strength currents. Because of these preferences, they thrive in the streams, lakes, and reservoirs of the Northeast, Midwest, and southern Canadian provinces. Smallmouth occur naturally as far south as northern Alabama and Georgia, and they have been successfully stocked into lakes and rivers west of the Rockies. (The world-record smallmouth bass was caught in Kentucky in 1955. It weighed 11 pounds 15 ounces.)

Smallmouths are also feeding opportunists. Their favorite prey are crawfish and minnows, but they will also eat a wide variety of other foods.

Spotted bass, also called "Kentucky bass," are the third common member of the black-bass genus. For years this fish was confused with both large-mouth and smallmouth bass. But finally in 1927, the spotted bass was recognized as a distinct species.

SMALLMOUTH BASS

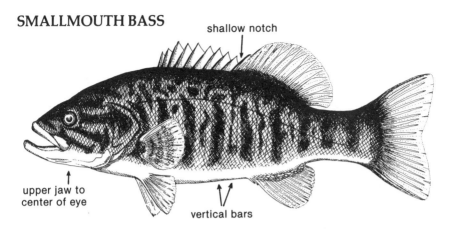

shallow notch

upper jaw to
center of eye

vertical bars

The spotted bass is sort of an intermediate fish between the largemouth
and smallmouth both in appearance and habits. Its name comes from rows
of small, dark spots running from head to tail below a lateral band of dark-
green, diamond-shaped blotches. Spotted bass occur naturally from Texas to
Georgia and north to the Ohio River valley. These fish have also been
stocked in several western states. In fact, the current world-record spotted
bass (9 pounds 4 ounces) was caught in California in 1987.

SPOTTED BASS

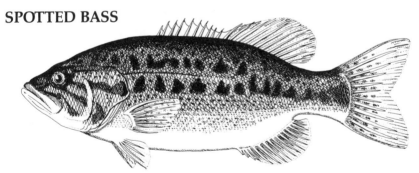

Spotted bass like some current, but not too much. They like deep water,
but not as deep as smallmouth prefer. They gather in large schools and
chase baitfish in open water. Some lakes contain these three black bass
species. Largemouth bass will often be back in the quiet coves. Smallmouths hold along deep shorelines and reefs; and spotted bass roam
through the open lake in search of prey. Sometimes these three bass species
will mix to feed on the same food source. But more often each species stays
in areas where it feels most comfortable.

Spawning habits of the black bass species are similar. When water
temperature climbs into the low to mid-60°F range, they begin to build
round nests in shallow areas. Largemouth bass typically spawn in wind-
protected spots along the sides or back of lake embayments. Smallmouth
and spotted bass usually nest on main-lake shorelines or flats.

Sunfish

Sunfish are the most numerous and widespread of all panfish. They are willing feeders, scrappy fighters, and usually easy to catch. This is why sunfish are extremely popular with beginning anglers. It's a safe bet that a sunfish was the first catch of a vast majority of North American fishermen.

Actually, there are around a dozen different species of sunfish (called "bream" in the southern U.S.). The more common ones include bluegill, pumpkinseed, redear sunfish (shellcracker), longear sunfish, redbreast sunfish, and green sunfish. Sunfish live in warm-water lakes, reservoirs, rivers, and ponds throughout the U.S. and southern Canada. They stay in shallow to medium depths, and usually stay close to cover (weeds, rocks, brush, stumps, and boat docks). They feed mostly on tiny invertebrates, larval insects and worms in the water, and sometimes insects that fall into the water.

SUNFISH

Sunfish are capable of reproducing in great numbers. One female may produce tens of thousands of eggs in a single season. Because of this, many smaller waters experience sunfish overpopulation. The result is lots of little fish that never grow large enough to be considered "keepers" by fishermen. In waters where there are enough bass and other predators to prevent overpopulation, however, some sunfish species may average a half pound in size, and these fish make excellent eating and are fun to catch.

The bluegill is the most popular sunfish. The world-record bluegill was caught in Alabama in 1950. It weighed 4 pounds 12 ounces.

Crappie

Crappies are abundantly widespread and prized for their delicious eating quality. They grow larger than sunfish and are fairly easy to catch. These are three main reasons why 20 million anglers try for these fish each year.

Actually, there are two species of crappie: black and white. Differences between these species are minor. One apparent difference is as their names imply; black crappies have darker, blotchier scale patterns than whites, which usually have dark vertical bars.

BLACK CRAPPIE

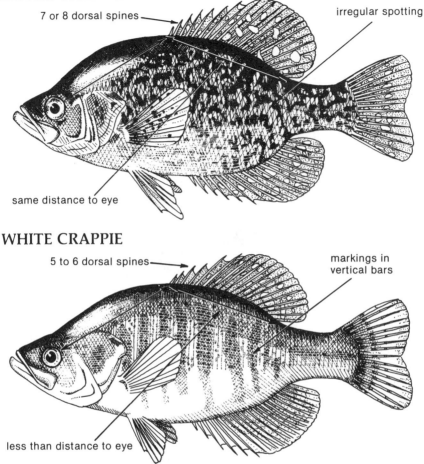

7 or 8 dorsal spines

irregular spotting

same distance to eye

WHITE CRAPPIE

5 to 6 dorsal spines

markings in
vertical bars

less than distance to eye

Both species live in natural lakes, reservoirs, larger ponds and quiet, deep pools of medium-to-large streams. Crappies occur naturally from southern Ontario to the Gulf of Mexico in the eastern half of North America. They, too, have been stocked into numerous western lakes and rivers.

Traditionally, most crappie fishing occurs in spring when these fish migrate into quiet, shallow areas to spawn. When the water temperature climbs into the low 60^{0}F range, they begin spawning in or next to cover such as reeds, brush, stumps, or "fish attractors" sunk by anglers.

After spawning, they head back to deeper water, where they collect in schools and roam along weedlines, standing timber, submerged creek channels, and other areas where the lake bottom contour changes abruptly. Such contour breaks are more likely to attract crappies if stumps, brush, or other cover is present. Expert crappie anglers know that these fish can be caught from such areas all year long, though it's more difficult than taking them in the shallows in spring.

Crappies feed primarily on invertebrates and small baitfish. In some lakes, they average a pound or more in size; crappies over 2 pounds are considered trophies. The world-record white crappie weighed 5 pounds 3 ounces and was caught in Mississippi in 1957. The world-record black crappie weighed 6 pounds and was taken in Louisiana in 1969.

Walleye
The walleye is a member of the perch family. It gets its name from its large, glassy, light-sensitive eyes. While walleyes average 1 to 3 pounds, in some waters they grow to more than 20 pounds. Many walleye experts consider fish over 10 pounds real trophies. The world-record walleye, weighing an even 25 pounds, was caught in Tennessee in 1960.

Many anglers consider walleyes the most delicious of all North American freshwater fish. Its meat is white, firm, and mild-tasting. Because of this eating quality and its elusiveness, the walleye is a favorite among anglers wherever it's found.

WALLEYE

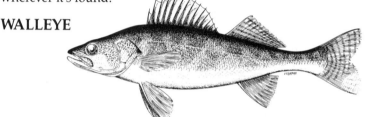

Walleyes are native to cool, clean lakes, reservoirs, and major rivers of the Central United States and most of Canada. They have also been stocked in the East and West

Walleyes spend most of their time in deep main-lake/river areas where there is good water circulation, but they also frequently feed on shallow flats and close to shore. They normally move into these areas in low-light periods such as night, dawn, dusk, cloudy days, or when weeds or muddy water shield them from bright sunlight. A walleye's main food is small fish, though it will eat insects, crustaceans, and amphibians.

Walleyes are early spawners. Spawning runs start when the water temperature climbs above 45°F. Walleyes in lakes spawn on shallow flats with hard, clean bottoms. In rivers, walleyes spawn below riffles in pools with rock or sand bottoms. One large female walleye can lay several hundred thousand eggs.

One characteristic of these fish is of special importance to beginning anglers: They have sharp teeth! Fishermen who stick a finger into a walleye's mouth get a painful surprise. Instead, they should be gripped across the back.

Sauger
Saugers are closely related to walleyes, and many people confuse them because of their similar appearance and habits. But there are two easy ways to tell them apart. Saugers have dark, saddle-like blotches on their backs and sides, and they also have rows of small, dark spots on the main dorsal fin. Walleyes lack both of these distinct markings.

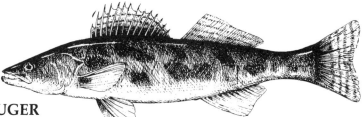

SAUGER

Saugers don't grow as large as walleyes; they seldom reach 4 pounds. The world-record sauger (8 pounds 12 ounces) was caught in 1971 in North Dakota. Saugers live in natural lakes, impoundments, and medium to large rivers. Their range includes the Mississippi valley west of the Appalachian Mountains and north to James Bay in Canada. Sometimes they're found in the same waters as walleyes, but they are also more tolerant of dingy water than walleyes. So saugers can be abundant in slow-moving silty streams where walleyes can't survive.

The sauger's feeding and spawning habits are very similar to those of walleyes. This fish is also prized by anglers for its fine table quality. And like walleyes, saugers have sharp teeth, which should be avoided by anglers.

Yellow Perch

Along with walleyes and saugers, yellow perch are members of the perch family. These fish average 6 to 10 inches long, though many lakes only have stunted "bait stealers" that are smaller than this average. Still, yellow perch are very popular since they are delicious to eat. The world-record yellow perch (4 pounds 3 ounces) was caught in New Jersey in 1865.

The yellow perch's natural range extends throughout the Northeast, Midwest and Canada (except British Columbia). It lives in all the Great Lakes and inhabits brackish waters along the Atlantic Coast. Yellow perch have also been stocked into many reservoirs in the West and Southwest. Perch thrive in clean lakes, reservoirs, ponds, and large rivers that have sand, rock, or gravel bottoms. They also abound in weedy, mud-bottomed lakes, though these are the type of spots where they tend to run small in size.

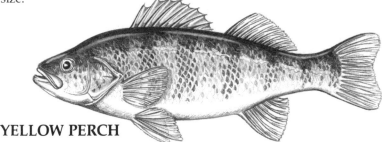

YELLOW PERCH

Yellow perch swim in schools and feed on minnows, crustaceans, snails, leeches, and invertebrates. Adults spend most of their lives in deep water, moving shallow to feed at dawn and dusk. They begin spawning when the water temperature climbs into the mid-40°F range (mid-50°F in the southern part of their range). Perch often make spawning runs up feeder streams, but they also spawn around shallow weeds or brush.

One peculiar characteristic of yellow perch is their poor vision in dark water (night). Therefore, they feed mostly during daylight hours in areas exposed to sunlight.

Muskellunge

Many anglers view the "muskie" as the supreme freshwater trophy fish. It's never very numerous in any body of water. It grows huge in size. It's hard to get to bite, but when it does, it fights savagely. Muskie anglers often cast for hours or even days without getting a strike. When they finally do get one of these fish on, however, they experience one of the most difficult and exciting challenges this sport offers. Muskies are the wild bulls of fishing, and it takes great dedication and skill to land them consistently.

The muskie is a member of the pike family. It is found in natural lakes, reservoirs, and streams in the northeastern third of the U.S. and also in southern Canada. This fish requires cool, clean water.

MUSKELLUNGE

Muskies are cylinder shaped, with long, powerful bodies. Their sides are usually yellowish and marked with dark blotches or bars. They have flat, duck-like mouths and sharp teeth. They feed mainly on fish, but they will also attack birds, muskrats, and other hapless creatures that enter their domain.

Muskies typically stalk their prey alone in shallow water, around reeds, rocky shoals, quiet eddy pools in streams, and other similar spots. During warm months, they feed more in low-light periods of dawn and dusk. On cloudy days, however, they may feed anytime. One of the best times to fish for muskies is in the fall when they go on a major prewinter feeding spree.

Muskies live many years and frequently grow beyond 35 pounds. The world-record muskie (69 pounds 15 ounces) was caught in New York in 1957.

Since the muskie is such a vicious predator, nature has a way of keeping its numbers down so other fish have a chance. The muskie is a late spawner (water temperature in the mid-50°F range). The fish that survive, however, grow to rule over their home waters. The only predator to big muskies is man.

Northern Pike

It would be fair to call pike the "poor man's muskie." Also members of the pike family, pike are much more numerous than muskies, and they're easier to catch. By nature, pike are very aggressive fish, and they often attack any bright, flashy lure pulled within eyesight.

Pike inhabit natural lakes, reservoirs, and streams throughout the northeastern and north-central U.S. and most of Canada. They thrive in warm, shallow lakes or river sloughs which have an abundance of water weeds.

NORTHERN PIKE

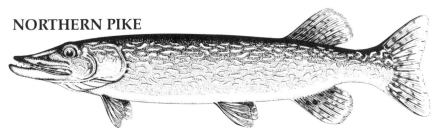

The pike's body shape is like the muskie's: long and round, with the same flat, pointed mouth and sharp teeth. Its color is dark olive on the sides with light, wavy spots; its belly is white. Pike sometimes grow over 20 pounds. Because they're so likely to be caught where there's much fishing pressure, big ones are usually found only in lakes off the beaten path. The world-record pike (55 pounds 1 ounce) was caught in West Germany in 1986.

Pike spawn in quiet, shallow areas when the water temperature climbs into the 40°F range. After spawning, they hold around weedbeds, especially those close to drop-offs. They are not school fish by nature, but they will cluster together if their food source is concentrated. Like muskies, they eat almost anything that swims, floats, or dives. Most of the pike's diet consists of other fish, and they will attack fish up to half their own body size.

When hooked, the pike is a toe-to-toe battler, rolling on the surface and shaking its head from side to side. It isn't the most desirable table fish because of its many small bones, but anglers can learn to remove these bones during cleaning. The meat of the pike is white, flaky and tasty.

Pickerel

The chain pickerel is popular with anglers throughout its range, which includes the Atlantic and Gulf Coast drainages from Nova Scotia to Texas and the Mississippi drainage from Missouri and Illinois south to Louisiana. Prime pickerel habitat includes quiet rivers and shallow weedy lakes.

PICKEREL

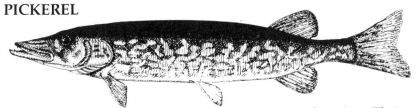

These toothy predators are a mini version of pike and muskies. Their sides are covered with a yellowish chain pattern on a green background. They're aggressive fish and give an exciting battle on light tackle. Most pickerel range from 1 to 3 pounds, but can get very large in northern and southern habitats. The world-record chain pickerel weighed 9 pounds 6 ounces; it was caught in a Georgia pond.

The grass pickerel and redfin pickerel are two small pickerels which rarely reach a foot in length. The redfin is found along the Atlantic coastal plain in small creeks and shallow ponds. The grass pickerel's range is farther west, primarily in the Mississippi and Great Lakes drainages.

Pickerel spawn in shallow weeds as water temperatures reach the high 40°F range. They do not build nests or provide parental care. Pickerel are active in cold water, and the best seasons for catching them are late fall, winter, and spring. They feed primarily on small fish, so active lures like spinnerbaits, spoons, in-line spinners, and floating minnow lures work well.

Trout

Several trout species inhabit North American waters and collectively are very important sportfish. They live in many different types of waters, from small brooks to huge lakes. Some trout are natives; others are raised in hatcheries and released into suitable waters. Trout are cold-water fish and lively fighters when hooked. They have sweet, delicate meat. Because of their wide availability, natural elusiveness, fighting qualities, and flavor, these fish are highly sought by anglers wherever they exist.

The U.S. and Canada have five major trout species: rainbows, browns, brook trout, cutthroats, and lake trout. Six other species found in localized areas are Apache trout, Arctic char, bull trout, Dolly Varden, Gila trout, and golden trout.

RAINBOW TROUT

Rainbows are so-named because of the pink streak down their sides. Native to western states, this fish has been stocked into streams, ponds, and lakes throughout much of the U.S. and lower Canada. Today the rainbow trout is probably the continent's most important cold-water sportfish. The world-record rainbow trout (42 pounds 4 ounces) was caught in Alaska in 1970.

The brown trout is a European native that has been widely stocked in suitable North American waters. These fish have dark or orange spots on their sides. They are the wariest, most difficult trout to catch, which makes them highly popular among sport anglers. Browns tolerate slightly higher water temperatures than other trout, so they can live where some of the other trout can't. The world-record brown trout (38 pounds 9 ounces) was taken in Arkansas in 1988.

BROOK TROUT

Brook trout are native to the eastern U.S. and Canada, though they have been transplanted into other areas. They are distinguishable from rainbow and brown trout by light, wormlike markings along their backs. They also have small blue and red dots along their sides. "Brookies" are probably the easiest of all trout to catch, and they are the best to eat. The world-record brook trout (14 pounds 8 ounces) was taken in Ontario in 1916.

CUTTHROAT TROUT

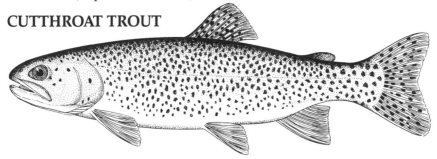

Cutthroat trout are found mainly in the western U.S. and Canada. Their name comes from the red markings behind and under the lower jaw. Their sides are dotted with small black spots. Like brook trout, they are not too hard to catch, and they're delicious to eat. The world-record cutthroat, an even 41-pounder, was caught in Nevada in 1925.

LAKE TROUT

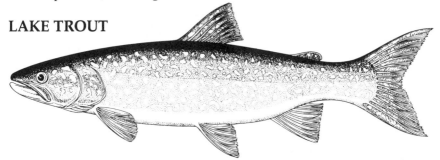

Lake trout are what their name implies: residents of large, cold-water lakes from Canada south through the Canadian Shield lakes of northern and midwestern states. Lake trout also live in western lakes where water temperatures don't exceed 65°F. Lake trout are silver-grey and have deeply-forked tails. The world-record lake trout weighed 65 pounds; it was caught in the Northwest Territories in 1970.

Trout feed on a broad variety of larval and adult insects, minnows, worms, and crustaceans. In streams, trout spawn in shallow riffles where they build nests or "redds" in gravel.

Salmon
Pacific salmon were first stocked into the Great Lakes in the late 1960s. Annual plantings have established extraordinary fishing opportunities for anglers in the Upper Midwest.

Chinook salmon is the largest species, reaching more than 30 pounds in some of the Great Lakes.

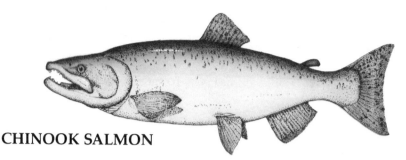

CHINOOK SALMON

Coho salmon run smaller, but 20-pounders have been taken. Sockeye and pink salmon are smaller and less common.

These open-water predators feed on huge schools of alewives and smelt that roam the cold depths, but may also feed near the surface. Coho salmon mature at age-3 and return to the stream where they were planted or hatched (Some natural reproduction takes place.). Chinooks grow for an extra year before returning to their stream of origin. Pacific salmon die after their initial spawning attempt.

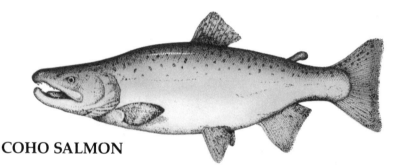

COHO SALMON

Most salmon fishing requires a large, specially equipped boat for trolling these vast waters. But during fall, adult salmon move toward tributary streams, and shorebound fishermen can make great catches with spoons or large plugs.

White Bass

White bass are natives of the Great Lakes and the Mississippi River system, but they have been widely stocked beyond this range. The white bass has silvery-white sides with dark stripes running from the gills back to the tail. Most white bass taken by anglers average about one pound. The world record, weighing 5 pounds 14 ounces, was caught in North Carolina in 1986.

Early each spring, white bass make spawning runs up river and reservoir tributaries. They lay and fertilize their eggs in pools below shallow riffles. One female may lay a half million eggs, one reason these fish often maintain high populations. During this spawning run white bass are particularly aggressive, and they can be caught in large numbers.

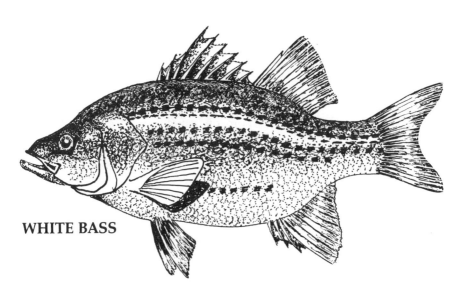

WHITE BASS

After the spawn, white bass move back into deep pools in rivers and open water in reservoirs. They gather in large schools, and they feed in a frenzy that sometimes leads them to strike anything that even vaguely resembles their prey. For this reason white bass are very popular wherever they are found.

Small shad are the white bass' main food source, though they'll also eat minnows, crawfish, and insects (particularly mayflies).

In table quality, white bass are delicious when taken from cool, clean waters. White bass caught from warm or silty waters, however, tend to have a strong flavor.

Stripers/Hybrids

"Striper" and "rockfish" are nicknames for the saltwater striped bass. Native to the Atlantic Ocean and Gulf of Mexico, this fish has been stocked into freshwater lakes and rivers throughout the mid-U.S. It does well where water temperature doesn't exceed 75°F, but natural reproduction is rare. Most of these fish are raised in hatcheries and released as fingerlings.

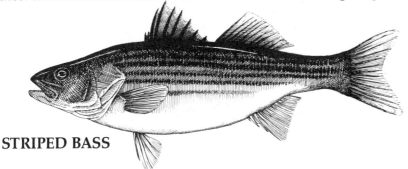

STRIPED BASS

Stripers resemble white bass, except they are more elongated, and they grow to huge size. The world record (60 pounds 8 ounces) was caught in

41

Tennessee in 1988.

Stripers are strictly open-water fish, roving in schools through main-lake and river areas in search of prey. Because of their large size and tackle-busting fighting ability, they are a favorite among thrill-seeking anglers.

"Hybrids" (also called "whiterocks" and "wipers") are a cross between stripers and white bass. They do not occur naturally, but they are easy to raise in hatcheries. Since they are more tolerant of warm water than stripers, they are now being stocked heavily in southern and midwestern reservoirs where earlier striper stockings failed. Hybrids look very much like stripers, except they are bulkier in shape, and the lines down their sides are often broken. Also, hybrids don't grow as large as stripers. The world-record striper (22 pounds 6 ounces) was caught in Georgia in 1986.

Catfish

Catfish may never win a beauty contest, but they are favorites with millions of North American anglers. These whiskered fish live in warm-water rivers, ponds, lakes, and reservoirs throughout much of the U.S. and prairie Canada. Catfish are willing biters, and they're spirited fighters when hooked. They're also very good to eat.

CHANNEL CATFISH

There are three common American catfish species: channel catfish, blue catfish, and flathead catfish. Channels have grey-blue sides that fade to silver-white bellies. They also have small dark spots on their backs and sides. Channels live mostly in rivers or lakes with slow to moderate currents. Channels are the smallest of the three catfish species, rarely exceeding 25 pounds. The world-record channel weighed 58 pounds and was caught in South Carolina in 1964.

Blue catfish look very much like channels, except they don't have spots on their backs and sides. They also grow larger than channel catfish. Blue and flathead catfish may grow to 100 pounds, though fish beyond this mark have never been officially documented. The world record blue catfish weighed 100 pounds and was caught in Kentucky in 1970. Blue catfish live mainly in big, slow-moving rivers such as the Mississippi, Ohio, and Missouri.

Flathead catfish are so-named because of their appearance. The flathead's mouth is long and flat, and its lower jaw is slightly longer than the upper. Its back and sides are mottled brown tapering to a lighter belly. Like the blue catfish, the flathead prefers larger rivers. The world-record flathead was taken in Texas in 1986. It weighed 98 pounds.

These common catfish species share certain traits. One is their slick, scaleless skin. Another is the presence of eight barbels (whiskers) around the mouth. These barbels contain highly developed smelling organs, which the fish use to sniff out and "taste" various foods, because feeding catfish sometimes depend more on smell than on sight.

Blue and channel catfish eat worms, insects, fish, crawfish, invertebrates, wild grapes, seeds, etc. Flatheads stick almost entirely to living foods. Many catfish feed more at night than during the day. They feed mainly on bottom, though they will move up to the surface or shallows if a good feeding opportunity exists there.

Catfish spawn in late spring, after the water temperature reaches 70ºF. Females lay eggs in holes, under logs, among rocks, or in other spots that offer some concealment from current and predators.

Bullheads

Bullheads are members of the catfish family, and they're often confused with small catfish. But, there is one easy way to tell them apart. Bullheads have rounded tails. (Flatheads have rounded tails like bullheads, but they're easily identified by their long, flat mouth.)

Three common species of bullheads are taken in North America: black, brown, and yellow. Their range covers most of the U.S. and southern Canada. They live in a variety of waters, from small ponds and marshes to large impoundments and rivers. Three other species (snail, spotted, and flat bullhead) are found in the Southeast. Bullheads prefer quiet, warm areas, and they usually stay close to bottom. They are highly tolerant of pollution and low oxygen content, which means they're found in many waters where other species can't survive.

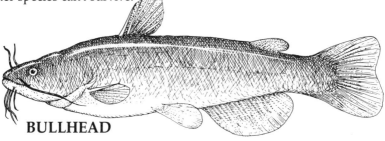

BULLHEAD

Bullheads are usually much smaller than catfish. They rarely grow larger than two pounds, and they fall well below this average in waters that have large numbers of these fish. The world-record black bullhead weighed 8 pounds 15 ounces and was caught in New York in 1951. The world-record brown bullhead weighed 5 pounds 8 ounces and was caught in Georgia in 1975. The world-record yellow bullhead weighed 4 pounds 4 ounces and was caught in Arizona in 1984.

Bullheads share many of the same feeding and spawning habits as catfish. They're favorites of many panfish anglers, since they're plentiful and usually bite when other species won't.

WHERE AND HOW TO FIND GOOD FISHING SPOTS

"These waters are now old friends which I visit as often as possible. The more time I spend with them, the more of their secrets I learn."

My favorite fishing trip is a canoe float down a stream some three-hours drive from home. This spring-fed creek is always clear and cool. It's lined by rocky bluffs and hardwood trees whose branches spread over the water to shade out the sun. This water-way is always beautiful and quiet, yet it holds some of the wildest, most terrifying smallmouth bass I've ever encountered. At any moment, a leaping bundle of brown scales and bad temper is likely to shatter the stream's tranquility.

A friend and I discovered these fish several years ago. We'd come to hunt wild turkeys in the surrounding hills, and we'd pitched camp in a meadow bordering the stream. One morning after hunting, I hiked back to camp, picked up my rod, and eased down to creekside to try my luck. (I always carry a spinning outfit and sackful of lures on such trips.) I had no idea if any fish were present, other than the sunfish that scattered out of the shallows at my approach.

I began casting a crawfish-colored crankbait into a deep pool at the edge of a riffle. On the third cast I felt a bump, so I snapped my rod tip back to set the hook. Immediately, a five-pound smallmouth rocketed out of the water, flared its gills, splashed back down, then took off downstream like a runaway mule. All I could do was hold on and hope my drag could give line as fast as the fish demanded.

The bass ran 30 yards and then burrowed under a washed-in tree stump. Saying a short prayer, I applied pressure to guide the fish out. The six-pound line snapped! I was left with a dejected feeling, but a memory that will stay with me forever.

A month later my friend and I returned with a canoe to test fish the stream, to see how good it really was. Prior to this trip, we'd called the local game warden for his opinion of the fishery, and we'd ordered topographic maps from the U.S. Geological Survey. We'd read a book written for canoeists that listed the stream's access/takeout points, float lengths between these points, and potential hazards.

On that first float we made a once-in-a-lifetime discovery: That small stream was loaded with big smallmouth and spotted bass, feisty rock bass, and a variety of other panfish. Since then we've returned to the stream at least twice each summer. We've never seen another angler, and we've always caught numbers of bass, keeping a few, but releasing most back into the currents.

Fishing spots this good are hard to find. But it's *not* difficult for beginning anglers to locate *good* spots where they can expect reasonable success. North America literally teems with fish-bearing rivers, streams, ponds, natural lakes, and manmade reservoirs. A huge number are open to the public. Others are available for either a small user fee or permission from private landowners. Everybody, even those who live in the biggest cities, can find good fishing spots within a reasonable distance from home. Many large metropolitan areas are stocking, managing, and developing their local ponds, lakes, and water resources for fishing. It's just a matter of knowing where to look, who to ask, and what information to collect.

Following is a step-by-step guide for finding good fishing spots wherever you live.

Starting the Search

Locating good fishing spots is like unraveling a mystery. Collect information from many sources. Then compare notes to decide which spots may be the best. How good are they? How easy are they to fish? How close by? The more people you contact and the more questions you ask, the more spots you'll find.

Many agencies and individuals are willing to direct you to good fishing. At the head of this list are state fish and wildlife agencies. Each state agency has an Information/Education Office or similar branch. Or

you can ask your local librarian for a list of government agencies, including addresses and telephone numbers for various departments.

When you contact your information/education officer, request four things: (1) A list of public fishing spots near your home, and available brochures, maps, and other information about these spots. (2) The name, address, and phone number of the biologist who manages these fisheries. Biologists can usually provide details about individual spots. They may also recommend the best places, the best times to fish them, and the best baits to use. (3) The names, addresses, and phone numbers of wildlife officers (game wardens) who patrol fishing spots on the list. They can often add details overlooked by the biologists. And (4) a pamphlet listing fishing seasons, license requirements, creel limits, and other regulations pertaining to your area.

Don't hesitate to contact these professionals in starting your search for good fishing spots. They spend their lives working to provide everyone with good fishing, and they enjoy helping beginners take advantage of it.

Other Government Agencies

Other agencies may also direct you to good fishing. Contact state and city park offices to see if they maintain public fishing areas. Call federal agencies, such as the Bureau of Land Management, the U.S. Army Corps of

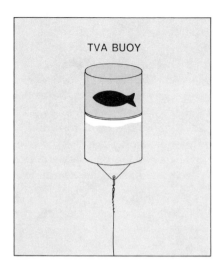

TVA BUOY

Engineers, the U.S. Forest Service, and the U.S. Fish & Wildlife Service. They all control water resources where public fishing is available. The same is true of private utility companies. Many of these agencies have recreation branches that build boat launch ramps, fishing piers, underwater fish attractors, and other facilities to make fishing easier.

Check government listings in the local telephone directory and call those that might possibly have fishing spots. Ask for the Public Information Office or someone who can provide fishing information.

By making these calls, you'll discover many fishing spots. Beginning fishermen who are good detectives may uncover spots, which get little publicity and fishing pressure, but offer great angling possibilities.

Tackle Shops, Sporting Goods Stores, and Other Information Sources

Bait and tackle shops are excellent sources of fishing information. Shop owners and clerks talk to fishermen every day, so they're aware of hot fishing spots. By helping you get started fishing, they're creating a new customer. This is why they're usually willing to share information.

Friends who already fish may have good suggestions. The outdoor writer at your local newspaper, county agricultural agents, or fishing club members will have ideas. Ask anyone you can think of who has any connection to fishing.

Also, don't overlook books, maps, or pamphlets containing information on your area. The canoeing book I mentioned earlier helped my friend and me learn more about our smallmouth stream. Look and ask for this printed material at libraries, book stores, and tackle shops. Many bait shops have maps of area lakes, guide books for lakes, or an entire book covering their region.

Fishing on Private Lands

While many fishing spots are on public property, many more are on private land. Stock ponds, watershed lakes, irrigation reservoirs, and other waters exist on many farms and ranches, and many have excellent fishing. Some landowners will allow you to fish if you ask permission in a courteous, direct manner. If fishing permission is given, you have the responsibility to show respect for the landowner and his property while you're his guest. Never litter, leave gates open, damage fences or crops, or violate in any way the trust he's placed in you. If you act responsibly and don't abuse your privilege, you probably will be welcomed to fish again. But if you fail to show proper respect and care, you'll be turned down the next time, and so will other fishermen who come after you.

Pay Lakes, Fishing Piers

Pay lakes, private fishing piers, and similar facilities run on a "for-profit" basis are another fishing opportunity. They operate two ways: (1) A flat-rate system. The angler pays an entrance fee and keeps the fish he catches at no additional charge. (2) A pay-for-what-you-catch system. Anglers are admitted free or for a small charge, and they pay for what they catch, usually by the pound.

You can locate pay lakes and fishing piers through your state fish and wildlife agency or through tackle shops. For the beginner, these spots have one advantage over many other fishing spots: They're usually well stocked and offer great fishing. Their disadvantage is the expense. In a pay-for-what-you-catch situation, you can run up a quick bill if you keep adding fish to your stringer.

Rating a Fishing Location

After compiling a list of possible fishing spots, it's time to rate them. Consider several things: How far away and how difficult to reach? How much fishing pressure? If you don't have a boat, is good fishing available from the bank? What facilities are present (bait shops, public piers, boat ramps)?

The last and best step in the process is actually fishing the top prospects. You have to test them the way my friend and I tested our smallmouth stream. I recommend test fishing a spot at least three times before giving up on it. The first time you try, the fish may not be biting. But when you

return, they may be actively feeding. If a particular lake, stream, or pond is highly recommended by biologists, game wardens, or other fishermen, don't give up on it too soon.

As you gain more experience, you'll add to your list of fishing places. When you discover better spots, discard the ones that haven't produced as well and eventually settle on a few favorites. Besides my smallmouth stream, I regularly fish two major reservoirs within an hour's drive from home, a pair of nearby farm ponds, and another river which is closer, though not as good as my smallmouth spot.

All six of these waters are now old friends that I visit as often as possible. The more time I spend with them, the more of their secrets I learn, and the better I become at fishing them. I still enjoy the excitement and mystery of trying new places. But day in and day out, I'll take the old proven spots where memories flow with the currents and the past and future are joined in the next cast.

SELECTING TACKLE

"A good overall way to think about tackle is as 'fishing tools.' You wouldn't choose a hammer to saw a board in two. . ."

A basic fishing outfit consists of four components: a pole or rod and reel, line, a terminal rig (hooks, sinkers, floats), and a bait (artificial or live). Various combinations of these four elements can be used to take any of the fish listed in Chapter 3. The trick, however, comes in selecting the *right* combination or balance for the type and size fish you're after and the presentation you will use.

When you shop for tackle, you'll find a wide variety of poles, rods, lines, rig components, etc. Knowing which ones to buy and how to match different tackle items can be confusing. But making good choices is easy once you understand the differences in various poles, rods, reels, lines, rigs, and the purposes for which each was designed. This chapter will look at the first four of these. Chapter 7 will explain basic fishing rigs, and Chapter 8 will cover baits.

A good overall way to think about tackle is as "fishing tools." You wouldn't choose a hammer to saw a board in two; and you don't want a heavy-duty bassin' outfit to go after bluegill or perch. Beginning anglers who select the right tackle will find fishing easier, more fun, and much more effective than those who use the wrong "tools."

Component #1: The Pole or Rod

I remember my dad cutting cane from the creek bank, stripping away the leaves, attaching some string, and using these poles to catch crappie and catfish. They worked well, and they provided for many family fish fries.

But over the years, I've become more sophisticated in the tackle I use. Today I have specific rods for big and small fish and for different baits and techniques. The tackle industry sells many rods for special-purpose fishing, and some anglers view rods the way most kids look at baseball cards: the more, the better.

As a beginner, however, you may start with one multipurpose fishing rod that can be used for a wide range of situations. In the months and years ahead, you will probably want more specialized tackle as your skills increase. But, you don't have to spend a fortune for a lot of fancy tackle while you're learning to fish. You can start out easy, keep the expense down, and still have capable tools for catching many different fish species.

Differences Between Poles and Rods

A pole or rod is a simple lever which acts as an extension of the fisherman's arm. By using either, you get more leverage for casting or placing a bait, for setting the hook when a fish bites, and for fighting the fish once it's hooked.

Even today, the bamboo pole is effective for some fishing situations. Rods are made of many different materials and sizes for specialized presentations.

Rods are usually shorter than poles, and they're normally used with reels to cast baits out away from the angler. Poles are longer, and they aren't used for casting. They are used to fish no farther away from the angler than the length of the pole and line combined.

Therefore, how you want to fish determines whether you need a rod or pole. If you're casting for bass away from shore, or if you're fishing on bottom in deep water for catfish, a rod and reel are required. But if you're going after panfish in brush or weeds right next to the shoreline, a pole may be more effective.

Rods and reels are much more versatile than poles because they can be used in more fishing situations. Also, many times a rod and reel can substitute for a pole for close-in fishing. That's why today, probably 90% of all fishing is with rods and reels.

Poles

Poles come in natural cane, fiberglass, and graphite. Fiberglass/graphite poles are more durable, and most are collapsible, making them easier to carry. But these poles are also more expensive. Natural cane poles cost approximately $1.50 to $5.00, while fiberglass/graphite poles may cost from $8.00 to $40.00.

The more expensive fiberglass/graphite poles come with simple reels or "line keepers" which are attached onto or near the butt of the pole. These simple reels are not for casting or reeling in fish, however. Reels or line keepers allow anglers to vary the length of line extending from the end of the pole. Line is run through the center of the pole and out a small hole in the tip, or it's threaded through line guides spaced down the length of the pole.

Rods

Buying a rod is more complicated than buying a pole, since there are more factors to consider. Rods come in different lengths, actions, materials, and a broad range of prices. Rods are designed for use with different types of reels, and they have different handle styles. These variables can bewilder a fisherman shopping for his first outfit.

There is no simple way to avoid making a bad decision, however, so seek the advice of an experienced angler. Sales personnel in tackle stores can usually help you select a suitable beginning outfit. Inform the salesman what type fish you intend to try for and, if you know, where and how you will do this. With this information, he should be able to advise you. If he can't, ask for someone who can.

Rod Features

Here are brief looks at the different features of a fishing rod. Having a general understanding of them will help you select the rod which best suits your needs.

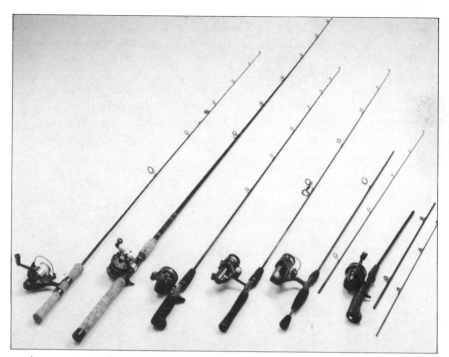

As your can see there are unlimited choices to be made when chosing a rod.

Rod Type—Rods are designed to be matched with specific types of reels that serve different purposes. Casting rods are meant to be used with bait-cast or spin-cast reels. Spinning rods are meant to be used with spinning reels. Fly-rods require the use of fly-reels. Each different rod type has advantages and disadvantages, special purposes and pleasures. Deciding whether to use a casting, spinning, or fly-casting outfit is the first and most important decision you must make when buying tackle. The following section of this chapter explains the different types of rod/reel combinations and the fishing methods to which each is best suited.

Length—Most fishing rods are 5 to 7 feet long. Longer rods can cast farther, but are awkward for the novice angler (particularly the young angler). Short rods are better for close-in casting, but they are poor for long casts. For general fishing, beginners should stick to rods that are 5½ to 6 feet long.

Action—Action refers to the stiffness (strength) of the rod. Action therefore determines the size baits a rod can cast effectively and the size fish it can handle. Standard rod actions are *ultralight, light, medium,* and *heavy.* There are also combinations of these standard actions, such as medium-light, or medium-heavy.

Ultralight rods are very limber; heavy-action rods are extremely stiff. (Many manufacturers list rod action in fine print just above the handle. Rods may also show recommended lure sizes and line weights.) The stiffer the rod, the more difficult it is to cast small, light baits. On the other hand, a limber rod is suited for casting lightweight baits, but it performs poorly with heavy baits.

The middle actions (light and medium) are the most versatile and usually suit a beginner's needs. With a 6-foot medium-action rod, you can land everything from average-size bass, walleye, and trout to perch, crappie, catfish, and white bass. You need a heavy-action rod only when you're fishing for muskies, trophy pike, or the largest bass hiding in the thickest cover.

One-Piece/Multipiece—Most rods are made in one long piece; others come apart in two or more sections which can be joined together. One-piece rods are stronger and more sensitive, though multipiece rods provide adequate strength and sensitivity for most fishing situations. The main advantage of multipiece rods is carrying convenience.

Materials/Rod Costs—Most modern fishing rods are made from either fiberglass or graphite, or a combination of both. Fiberglass rods are durable, and fairly inexpensive. Graphite rods are stronger than fiberglass, much lighter, and more sensitive to faint bites; however, they're more expensive than fiberglass rods.

A good compromise is a fiberglass/graphite-composite rod. These are fiberglass rods with varying amounts of graphite fibers added. This blend brings together the best qualities of both materials. They're tough, yet sensitive; light, yet inexpensive.

When it comes to rod materials, you get what you pay for. Most professionals use top-line graphite rods, which may cost more than $100. These are obviously superior to the lowest cost fiberglass rods, which may cost as little as $10.

That's not to say that lower-priced rods don't offer good value. Most beginner rods are very adequate for learning to fish. If you can afford a better rod, go ahead and buy one. But if you prefer to start out with an inexpensive model, don't worry about being handicapped by your choice. I still have several of my early, inexpensive rods, and I use them without hesitation when the need arises.

Handles—Handles come in a wide variety of designs and materials. Some handles are straight; others have a pistol-grip design. Some are long enough to require two hands for casting, while others are one-handed models. Materials vary from natural cork, to plastic, to padded foam.

My advice is: If it *feels* okay, it *is* okay. If it's easy to grip and feels comfortable in the tackle store, it will be satisfactory for fishing.

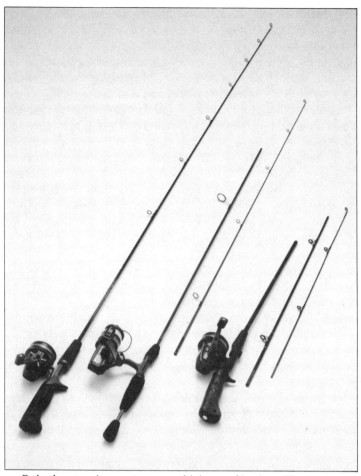

Rods also come in one, two, or multipiece combinations. The two or multipiece rods are picked because of storage or travel limitations.

Casting, Spinning, or Fly Tackle

Casting rods are mated with baitcast or spincast reels. As you hold the rod in your hand, these reels rest *on top* of the rod. baitcast reels are also called open-face or revolving-spool reels. As the bait is cast, its weight pulls line off the exposed turning spool.

Spincast reels have spools that are covered by a hood on the front of the reel, and line plays out through a small hole in the middle of this hood. Spincast reels are also called "push-button" reels. The angler pushes down on the casting button with his thumb, releases the button as he makes the cast, and then pushes down again to stop the cast. In contrast, with a baitcasting reel, line play-out is controlled by direct thumb pressure on the exposed spool.

Casting rods and these two reel types are normally stronger than spinning rods/reels, and they are used with larger baits and heavier lines for bigger fish. A spincast reel is easier to learn to use than a baitcast reel, so I recommend it for beginners. Later, however, you'll probably want to shift to a baitcast reel. In experienced hands, a baitcaster is more accurate and versatile than a spincast outfit.

Spinning reels hang *under* the rod on a straight handle. The line is wrapped around a circular open spool, and it's guided onto the spool by a wire bail. The angler catches the line with his forefinger, trips the bail out of the way, and as he casts, releases the line off his finger. The line coils off the spool with virtually no restriction. This means that it doesn't take as much lure weight to pull line off this reel as it does with a baitcast reel. This is why spinning tackle is the choice of many anglers who desire to cast small baits to species such as panfish, smaller trout, bass, walleyes, etc. Larger, heavier spinning outfits may also be used interchangeably with baitcast tackle to cast bigger baits for larger fish.

Fly-rods/reels are used almost exclusively by experienced anglers. Fly-rods are longer than most casting or spinning rods (7 to 9 feet). Rather than depending on the weight of the bait to make the cast, the weight of the line provides casting distance. The angler "false casts" the rod and waves the line back and forth over his shoulder, feeding more line through the rod's guides. When he has enough line out to reach his target, he completes his cast by driving forward with the rod and allowing the line to settle to the water.

Tied to this heavy fly-casting line is a "tippet" (length of light monofilament line) with an extremely lightweight artificial fly on the end. Most flies are meant to look like insects; others resemble larvae, small minnows, and other natural foods.

Fly-fishing will sometimes catch fish when other tackle and techniques fail. Because it's more difficult to learn, however, beginning anglers should learn the basics of casting and spinning tackle before they consider fly-fishing.

The Concept of Balanced Tackle

One of the most important things to remember in tackle selection is to balance all the components in your outfit. For instance, some reels are larger and designed for use on heavy-action rods. To achieve the right casting performance, don't mix these. Use light-action reels with light-action rods, heavy-action reels with heavy-action rods, etc.

The same advice holds true with line and baits. Light line and smaller lures work well on light-action rods, but they perform poorly on heavy tackle. The reverse is true for heavy line and large baits. They're great on heavier tackle, but they're hard to cast with light tackle.

Again, the best advice is to check with an experienced salesman to make sure your new outfit is balanced. If it isn't, you will be handicapped from the start.

Fishing Line

Line is the next component in the basic fishing outfit. Your line is the link that joins you to the fish. Choosing proper line and maintaining it in good order is critical to fishing success.

The two basic types of fishing lines are: monofilament and braided nylon or dacron. Braided lines have very little stretch, which is important when setting the hook in such bony-mouthed fish as muskies or pike. But in almost all other cases, monofilament is preferred and used by most anglers.

Monofilament comes in two grades: *premium* and *bargain* basement. My advice is to stick with the premium brands. While they cost more, they're still inexpensive enough for all fishermen to afford, and they more than make up the price difference by providing top quality. Premium-grade monofilament is extremely durable. It's smaller in diameter, which makes it easier to use. It's strong and resistant to abrasion from rubbing against rocks, logs, and other cover where fish hide.

Monofilament line comes in several colors. The most commonly used colors are clear, green, and fluorescent blue. Many anglers use clear line in extremely clear water, so the fish won't see the line and be scared by it. Green is a camouflage color for slightly stained water, again to keep from scaring the fish. Fluorescent blue is for dingy water, and when anglers want to watch line movement to detect subtle bites. This movement is much easier to see with fluorescent-blue line than with clear or green line.

Many experts swear that fish are scared by line that's visible; others feel line visibility makes no difference. They believe that fish don't know that line represents danger. Nobody really knows who's right, but I don't take a chance. Unless I'm using a technique where I need to watch for line movement, I use clear line in clear water and fluorescent blue in all other water conditions.

Selecting the Proper Line Size

Fishing line is sold in different pound tests (6-pound test, 12-pound test, etc.) This line weight represents the amount of stress under which the line will break. In other words, 10-pound line will snap when put under 10-pound strain.

Lighter lines have a number of desirable qualities. They are easier to cast. They offer better swimming action with both live and artificial baits. They provide less resistance when retrieving a bait, and they are less likely to be seen by fish. Therefore, for all practical purposes, choose the lightest line that has enough strength to land the fish you're after. For instance, a bass fisherman can get by with light line when he's casting where there are no logs, snags, heavy weeds, or rocks. But when he's casting around heavy brush, vegetation, or rocks, he needs strong line to power fish out of cover without breaking them off.

Traditionally, anglers after small panfish (sunfish, bullheads, crappies, perch, trout) use light line (4-, 6-, or 8-pound test). Those after medium-size fish (bass, walleyes, catfish) use line in the medium weights (10-, 12-, or 14-pound test). And anglers after big fish (trophy bass and pike, stripers, muskies) use heavier line (17-, 20-, 25-, 30-pound test).

These recommendations are *general* guidelines. There are certain times when they don't apply, like using light line when fishing for big, spooky fish in clear water. This and other exceptions will be discussed in Chapter 12. But for now, for most fishing conditions, these line suggestions hold true.

Spooling Line Onto the Reel

Spooling new line onto a reel must be done correctly. Improper spooling can lead to backlashes, line twist, a loss of casting distance, and other problems.

When filling a bait-cast reel, start at the tip of the rod and run the line back through all the line guides down to the reel. Next, feed the line through the reel's level wind (small guide which directs line onto the spool). Loop the line around the reel spool, and tie it on with a line end knot (see Chapter 6). Snug the line down onto the reel spool and use clippers to clip the tag end of the line close to the knot. Now have a friend hold the spool vertically in front of the rod tip with a pencil through the middle. Then reel the line off the filler spool and onto the reel while holding slight tension on the line. Fill a bait-cast reel to within 1/4 inch of capacity, or to the level indicated in the reel instructions.

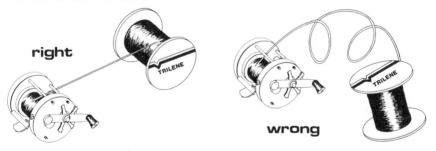

right

wrong

With spin-cast and spinning reels, again run the line through the rod guides down to the reel. With a spin-cast reel, unscrew the reel hood, pass the line through the hole in its center, tie it onto the reel spool with a line end knot, and replace the hood.

With a spinning reel, flip the wire bail open and tie the line to the spool. Now, with either type reel, lay the filler spool on the floor so line will coil off in the *same direction* the reel spool turns when you crank the handle. If the reel turns counterclockwise, make sure line is coiling off the filler spool counterclockwise. Otherwise the line will wind onto the reel with a twist,

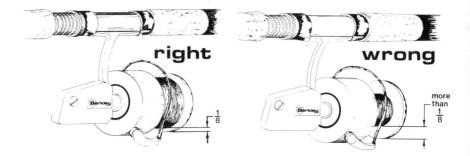

and this will cause casting problems. Fill both spin-cast and spinning reels to within 1/8 inch of full-spool capacity, or to the level indicated in the reel instructions.

Tying Line Onto a Pole

Poles are easy to rig with line. If a pole is fitted with a reel or line keeper, simply run the line through the guides or the center of the pole and out the tip. The line is already secured to the reel/line keeper. Adjust the length as desired.

If the pole doesn't have a reel or line keeper, tie the line onto the pole two feet from its tip end. Then wrap the line around the pole to the tip, and tie it again. This wraparound method provides greater strength than just tying the line directly to the tip. Stretch the line to whatever length is desired, and clip it off. Normally, the line should measure about the same length as the pole, or slightly shorter.

Tips for Proper Line Care

Modern monofilament line is tough and requires very little care. But there are a few tips that beginning anglers should follow to keep their line in the best possible condition.

Sunlight weakens monofilament. Don't leave your line in direct sunlight when you're not using it.

Prolonged exposure to heat also weakens monofilament. Never store your line (or your rod) in hot areas like car trunks and rear windows, attics, etc. The best place to store your fishing rod and excess line is in a dark, cool room or closet.

Don't let your line come in contact with gasoline, oil, suntan lotion, or other chemicals. These cause monofilament to break down or become brittle.

Even with proper care and normal use, monofilament line ages. It's a good idea to periodically strip old line off your reel and replace it with new line. Two line changes a year should be sufficient—at the beginning and middle of the fishing season.

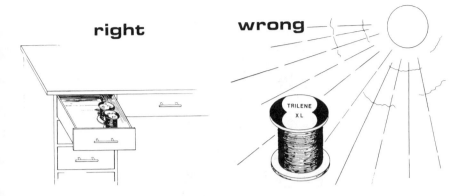

right   **wrong**

Last, while you're fishing, be on constant guard against nicks, abrasions, or other weak spots in your line. You can detect these by running the line between your thumb and forefinger. If you feel a rough spot, clip off the line above this spot and retie your bait. It's better to sacrifice a few feet of line than to break off a fish in the heat of battle.

Summary on Rods, Reels, Line

If asked to pick one fishing outfit for a beginning angler, I would select a 5-, 5½-, or 6-foot casting rod (length depending on the beginner's age and size). It would be a medium-action fiberglass/graphite composite rod, and I'd match it with a spin-cast reel loaded with 10-pound-test line. I would expect to pay $20 to $30 for this combination. Then, if I could afford a second outfit, I'd choose a 5½- or 6-foot light-action fiberglass/graphite spinning rod and matching reel, and I'd spool on 6-pound-test line. The price of this outfit will also be about $20 to $30. With these two rods, a beginner would be properly equipped to go after everything from medium-sized gamefish to the smallest panfish.

Again, as you progress in this sport, you will undoubtedly increase your skills and develop needs for more specialized tackle. But when starting out, keep your fishing tools simple, inexpensive, and versatile. You can't run before you walk, and you won't need fancy tackle until you master fishing fundamentals.

CHAPTER 6

FISHING ACCESSORIES

"Beginning anglers are the ones most likely to be looking for a short-cut to success. Save your money and forget the shortcuts."

Fishermen are gadget people, and if you don't believe it, just walk through a tackle store. The shelves will be lined with dozens of accessories, ranging from practical to outlandish, from very cheap to very expensive. As the old saying goes, some are designed to catch fish, while others are designed to catch fishermen!

In Chapter 5 we looked at the basic fishing outfit: rod, reel, and line. Beyond this, beginning anglers need several additional items to get started in this sport. Of the gadgets offered, which are necessary and which aren't?

Fortunately, there are very few accessories you absolutely must have, and they're not expensive. You probably already have some of them, and if not, all the essentials can be purchased for less than $50.

That's not to say that many of the other accessories in the tackle store won't help you be a better fisherman. Some will, or they'll make your fishing easier or more enjoyable. But they're luxuries that you can do without, at least until you gain some experience in fishing and learn for yourself what you need and what you don't need.

Following are two lists: Accessories that *are* essential and which beginning anglers should take on each fishing trip; and accessories that *aren't* absolutely necessary, but are recommended. Items on this second list can be purchased later as your finances allow and needs dictate.

Essential Fishing Accessories

Tackle Box—This is the main accessory which you will carry every time you go fishing. The tackle box holds terminal tackle (hooks, sinkers, floats, etc.), artificial lures, extra line, and other small items. A tackle box is like a country doctor's medicine bag. It's your "organizer" that allows you to carry all needed items in one handy package.

I've fished with anglers who carried tackle in paper sacks or small cardboard boxes. You should have seen the mess when the sack or box got wet! Buying a hard plastic tackle box is an excellent investment. All bait and sporting goods stores sell tackle boxes in a wide range of designs and prices.

Only when you are out fishing do you realize what accessories you really need. Make a list of the essential items and keep them together.

I recommend a medium-size box with fold-out lure trays or compartments rearranged as you wish. Also, make sure the box has a deep, roomy area for larger items like a spare reel, spool of line, insect repellant, and other extras. Several companies offer such tackle boxes in the $10 to $20 range.

Avoid the bigger tackle boxes with many drawers, or the specialized tackle boxes made for one particular type bait. As your involvement in fishing grows, you may desire these boxes later. But to start with, keep your tackle box simple and inexpensive.

Instead of having one giant tackle box, I use several smaller ones, and I stock them according to fish species. I have two boxes with bass-fishing tackle, one for panfish, one for walleye and sauger, and one for stream fishing for smallmouth and trout. When I'm going fishing, I choose the tackle box that fits my target species. This way I'm not overburdened with extra tackle I don't need.

Fish Stringer—If you'll be fishing from the bank or from a boat that doesn't have a live well, you'll need a chain or rope stringer to keep your fish. A chain stringer has safety-pin snaps that hold fish at spaced intervals. On a rope stringer, fish slide down on top of each other. Chain stringers are better for keeping fish alive. They cost slightly more than rope stringers, but neither type is very expensive.

Hook Sharpener—This is one item that belongs in *every* tackle box, and it should be used frequently. One major mistake many beginners make is not having sharp hooks. Hook companies are making sharper hooks than they used to, but most hooks, especially larger ones such as plastic worm hooks, spinnerbait hooks, or treble hooks on artificial lures, can stand some touching up. Having sharp hooks will make a big difference in the number of fish you catch.

There are several types of hook sharpeners which do a good job. I carry a small file in my tackle box, and I use it several times each fishing day. Also, one gadget that's not essential but which is a nice luxury is the Hook-Hone-R, an electric hook sharpener which is the quickest, easiest way to sharpen hooks I've ever seen. The Hook-Hone-R is available through leading tackle stores and mail order houses. It's expensive, but if you can afford it, it's worth the money.

Needle-Nose Pliers—I never go fishing without my needle-nose pliers. There are many uses for them: prying hooks out of a fish's mouth, rebending hooks, tuning a lure, repairing a reel, etc. Some tackle companies make special fishing pliers with such extras as a can opener, bottle opener, fish scaler, and crimper. These are extremely handy, but they're also more expensive than regular needle-nose pliers. Regardless of which you select, always take your pliers when fishing. They'll come in handy.

Nail Clippers—Clippers are used to snip or trim line when changing rigs or lures. I wear a large pair of nail clippers on a string loop around my neck. They're always handy, which makes it easier and faster to clip and retie my

line.

Polarized Sunglasses—Some might consider these nonessential, but I've put them on the essential list for three reasons. (1) Polarized sunglasses help you see below the water surface. They make it easier to spot underwater stumps, rocks, holes, and other places where fish like to hide. (2) Doctors are learning that prolonged exposure to the sun's reflection off water can hurt the eyes. Wearing sunglasses protects vision. (3) Sunglasses shield the eyes from flying objects, especially hooks.

Inexpensive plastic polarized sunglasses are available in most tackle stores.

Fishing Cap—A mesh cap keeps you cool in summer; a heavy cap or hat provides warmth in winter. Also, a cap with a long bill shades your face, which protects against sunburn and makes it easier to see through the sun's glare.

Sunscreen—More and more, doctors are warning against too much exposure to direct sunlight. Radiation from the sun can eventually lead to skin cancer. When fishing, always use a strong sunscreen (at least protection level 15) on exposed body areas such as hands, nose, ears, etc. A more complete discussion of this hazard follows in Chapter 15.

Fishing Towel—A small fishing towel is good for wiping your hands after handling fish or messy baits. I wear one clipped onto a belt loop at my side. It's out of the way, but quickly available.

Nonessential But Recommended Accessories

Life Jacket—Most fishermen don't wear life jackets when fishing from shore, piers, or bridges, but they're still a good idea, especially if you're not a strong swimmer. Also, they are an *absolute necessity* (required by law) when fishing from a boat. I recommend the vest type life jacket. It's not as bulky as other types, and it won't interfere with your fishing.

Rainsuit—Fishermen get wet from rain or spray. A rainsuit is also a good windbreaker in breezy weather. Rainsuits can be cheap (polyvinyl) or expensive (Gore-Tex). For light duty or emergency use, I recommend a polyvinyl suit folded into a small carrying pouch.

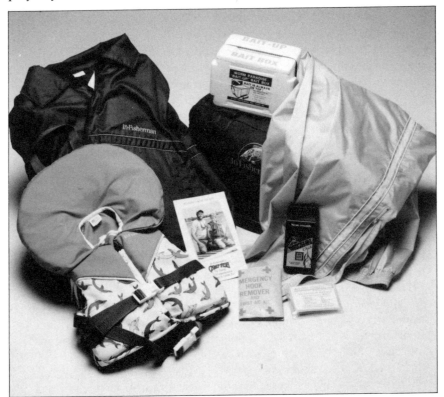

Fishing is a recreation to be enjoyed and relaxing. Too many toys distract from this goal.

Fishing Vest—I wear a fishing vest when I fish streams or from shore. It's a wearable tackle box with pockets for sunglasses, pliers, a rainsuit, and snacks. I keep my vest stocked and ready to go. Then I can pick it up, along with my tackle box and rod, and head out knowing I have everything I need.

Tote Bag—I use a tote bag when I boat fish. In it I carry my life vest, rainsuit, extra clothes, lunch, and other items that won't fit into my tackle box. By bundling all these accessories into one package, they're much easier to carry, and I'm not as likely to forget something.

Live-Bait Holder—Different baits and how to care for them will be covered in detail in Chapter 8. So right now, suffice it to say that if you'll be using live bait, you need a minnow bucket, cricket cage, or some other box or container to keep your bait alive and healthy.

De Liar—This is a registered brand name for a small spring-operated scale and tape. I use it to weigh and measure fish before releasing them alive. The De Liar is inexpensive and fits into any tackle box.

Reel Repair Kit—Another handy tackle-box item is a small reel-repair kit consisting of miniature screwdrivers (standard and Phillips head), a tiny adjustable wrench, and a container of reel oil. My kit came packaged in a plastic envelope. I bought it for a dollar from a tackle store bargain bin. I use it dozens of times each fishing year, both to work on reels and to handle other small, miscellaneous chores.

Lure Retriever—This gadget is for anglers casting artificial lures from a boat. If you hang your lure on an underwater object and you can't pull it

free, a lure retriever will recover it for you.

Lure retrievers come in two types: a heavy weight on a string, or a collapsible pole. The pole works better, but it's bulkier and more expensive. With either type, however, it only takes a few lures saved to recover the cost of the retriever. So a lure retriever is a good investment.

Which Accessories Not To Buy

Every year I see new fishing products that make outlandish claims about how many fish they produce. My warning flag goes up. Usually these products are aimed at beginning anglers, since they're the ones most likely to be looking for a shortcut to success.

Save your money and forget the shortcuts. This isn't to say that all new gadgets are hoaxes. Many are legitimate. (The depthfinder changed fishing forever.) But other new products are designed to catch fishermen instead of fish.

My advice is: If it sounds too good to be true, it probably is. Don't buy these gadgets on impulse. If they're legitimate, they'll still be around in a few months. Wait until the jury, more experienced anglers, returns a verdict. Watch for product reviews in fishing magazines. Don't expect to buy your way to fishing success. In some cases you can buy knowledge (books, videos, magazines), but you can't buy experience. And it takes *both* of these to become a good angler.

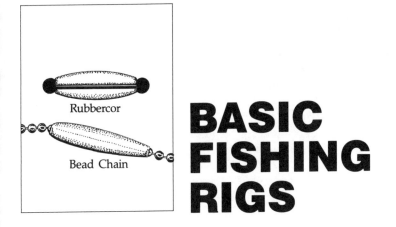

Rubbercor

Bead Chain

BASIC FISHING RIGS

"Rigs will vary from one fishing situation to the next, depending on size and strength of fish, water depth, bottom type, amount of current, and other variables."

A few years back I fished below a dam on the Ohio River for white bass and sauger. I was casting a diving lure across the current and simply reeling it back in. Periodically a fish would load on, so I thought I was doing well, except for the angler in the boat anchored just upstream.

He was catching a fish on every cast! I watched enviously as he filled his cooler. Besides white bass and sauger, he also boated a couple catfish; one weighed at least 10 pounds.

His technique was obviously different from mine. He was baiting with live minnows, casting upstream, and allowing his rig to sink to bottom. Then he kept his line tight as the current bumped his bait downstream. It never bumped far before a fish nailed it.

When this angler began stowing away his gear, I idled my boat over to see if he would share his secret. "There's not much secret to it," he said. "I've been using shad minnows. I caught 'em right here with a cast net before you came. You can't do better than the exact bait the fish are feeding on.

"I used a light slip-sinker rig to let the current wash the minnow downstream," he continued. "This seemed natural to the fish, since they're used to watching upcurrent for their food."

So he did have secrets, three of them! One was his bait. The second was his rig, and the third was his method of using it. Think back to Chapter 2 and the F+L+P formula. These are the three elements of presentation. This angler had satisfied this portion of the formula to the letter, and he'd loaded his boat with fish. My presentation was far less effective, and I'd caught only a few. Even though you're in the right spot, you can still scratch if you're not using the right rig, bait, and technique.

We'll cover baits and techniques in the following two chapters. But for now, the subject is "rigs": how to select components and tie various rigs used in basic fishing techniques.

Elements of a Fishing Rig

A fishing rig is whatever you tie on the end of your line to hold and present your bait. It's your combination of hooks, sinkers, floats, snaps, swivels, leaders, and the knots that bind everything together.

Fishermen use many different rigs for special fishing situations. There are rigs for live bait and artificial lures. There are rigs for fishing on bottom, on the surface, and at depths in between. There are rigs for trolling, drifting, fishing in current, and for fishing more than one bait at a time. This list could go on and on.

However, as a beginner, you don't need to learn a lot of complicated rigs. You may do this later as your fishing becomes more specialized. But for now, a few basic rigs will provide the means for catching most popular species in a wide variety of settings.

Fishing Knots: The "Ties that Bind"

One thing all fishing rigs have in common is knots, so learning how to tie knots is a logical way to begin a chapter about rigs. You will have to tie knots several times on each fishing trip, so pay special attention to this section.

Tying a knot in a fishing line weakens it. An improperly tied knot can reduce line strength by more than 50%. But a good knot that's properly tied will retain up to 95% of the full strength of the line. Strong knots that won't slip or break will produce more fish. This is why it's very important to learn to tie knots properly. It's fun to do, and you can satisfy almost all rigging needs by mastering a few basic knots.

Following are instructions for tying six fundamental knots. The first three are my picks for tying line to hooks, lures, sinkers, swivels, etc. The fourth knot is used to tie a loop in a line. The fifth knot is the one

I use to join two lines together when I'm adding line to my reel. The sixth is a good one for adding line to an empty reel spool.

When tying any of these knots, I always follow two rules: Before snugging a knot tight, I always spit on it to lubricate it. This moisture reduces line-weakening friction and heat buildup as the knot draws tight. And I always leave 1/8 inch of line when I clip the tag end. This allows for some slippage in the knot without its coming undone.

Trilene Knot—This is the knot I use in 90% of my fishing. I tie it almost every time I need a line-to-hook or line-to-lure connection. It's a very strong knot, and it takes only a small amount of practice to master. I highly recommend it.

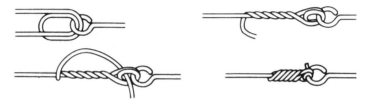

To tie the Trilene knot, run approximately 4 inches of line through the hook eye, loop it around, and run it through the eye again. Pull on the end of the line to draw the loop down to a small diameter (approximately 1/4 inch). Now hold this loop between your thumb and forefinger to keep it open. Next, wrap the end of the line around the standing line 5 times. Last, guide the end back through the double loop just above the hook eye. Snug the knot by pulling the standing line and the hook in opposite directions, and trim the tag end.

Palomar Knot—This is another general-purpose knot which also offers maximum strength and versatility. The palomar knot is very dependable, but it requires more line to tie. Regardless, the palomar is a proven knot that is a good alternative to the Trilene knot.

To tie the palomar knot, bend the line back on itself to form a double strand 6 inches long. Next, pass this double strand through the hook eye and tie a loose overhand knot, leaving a loop deep enough so the hook (or lure) can pass through it. Pass the hook through the loop. Then tighten the knot by pulling on the hook with one hand and the double strand of line with the other. Trim the tag end.

Improved Clinch Knot—This is a third general-purpose knot which is an old standby in fishing. It's slightly weaker than the Trilene or palomar knot, but it's still strong enough to be the choice of many expert anglers.

To tie the improved clinch knot, thread the line through the hook eye 3 or 4 inches. Wrap the end of the line around the standing line 6 times. Then run the end back through the opening between the hook and the first wrap. Last, turn the end upward and thread it through the long loop between the wraps and the downturned line. Hold onto the end and snug the line by pulling the standing line and hook in opposite directions. Clip the tag end. (Note: Many experts double their line and tie this knot the same as if their doubled line were a single strand. This adds to the knot's strength.)

Surgeon's Knot—When you want to form a loop in your line, this is the knot to use. The surgeon's knot is easy to tie, and it won't slip.

To tie the surgeon's knot, bend the line back to double it. Then tie a simple overhand knot. Instead of snugging up this knot, make another wrap in the overhand knot. Now snug the knot tight and clip the tag end.

Blood Knot—The blood knot is good for adding new line to old line on your reel. This knot requires a fair amount of practice to learn, because it's easy to get the twists and ends confused. But once you master it, you can splice two lines together quickly and securely.

To tie the blood knot, overlap the two lines 4 or 5 inches end to end. Wrap one line around the other 5 times. Next, wrap the other line around the first one 5 times in the opposite direction. Last, insert both ends back through the center opening in opposite directions. While holding these tag ends, snug the line up tight. Then trim the ends.

Line End Knot—This knot is used when tying line onto an empty reel spool. It's simple and allows the line to slide down snug against the spool so it doesn't slip.

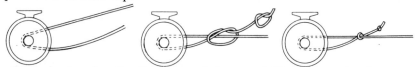

Begin by looping the line around the spool. Then tie a simple overhand knot around the standing line to form a slip knot. Last, tie another simple overhand knot in the end of the line to anchor the slip knot. Now snug the line tightly around the spool and trim the tag end.

Hooks, Sinkers, Floats

Hooks, sinkers, and floats are basic components in fishing rigs. Different combinations of hooks, sinkers, and floats can be used to take everything from the smallest panfish to the largest gamefish. Obviously, these items of terminal tackle come in many different sizes and designs. Beginning anglers must understand these differences, and they must learn to select and assemble the right terminal tackle for the species they're after.

Hooks: Getting to the Point of the Matter

Hooks can be confusing to expert anglers, much less beginners. One major manufacturer makes hooks in more than 40,000 designs, sizes, and finishes. They run the gamut from tiny wire hooks for trout to giant forged (strengthened) hooks for such saltwater brutes as sharks and marlin. Different styles bear different family names: Aberdeen, O'Shaughnessy, Sproat, Kirby, Carlisle, Limerick, etc. Modern hook making originated in the the British Isles, where these styles of hooks were named.

Hooks also come in different thicknesses, temper (springiness), barb configurations, and other features. It's easy to understand how beginners can be intimidated when faced with buying just the right hook for a particular species and situation.

Don't think, though, that you must become a hook wizard to be a successful angler. Making good hook selections is easy if you follow only a few basic guidelines.

First of all, buy *quality* hooks, not the bargain-basement variety. Stick with popular brands that are most widely advertised and distributed. Quality hooks cost only a fraction more than inferior ones, and they're well worth the price when it comes to strength and reliability.

Next, pay special attention to hook size. The general rule is to use small hooks with light tackle and bigger hooks with heavier gear. In the same vein, use small hooks for small fish and big hooks for big fish. As logical as this seems, it's one of the most common mistakes beginners make. They use bass-size hooks when fishing for small panfish, and the little guys can't get the hook in their mouths.

You'll need to understand the system manufacturers use to label hook sizes. Smaller hooks are size-numbered, and the smaller the hook, the larger its number. For instance, a #32 hook is extremely tiny and used in very small dry flies. A #10 hook is considerably larger and might be suitable for bluegill or perch. A #1 hook is larger still and a good size for crappie, walleye, and small bass and catfish.

At this point, numbering switches over to the "aught system" and heads in the other direction. After the #1 hook, the next largest size is the 1/0 (one aught), followed by 2/0, 3/0, and so forth. These larger hooks are used for bigger bass and catfish, pike, muskies, stripers, etc.

The adjacent chart will guide you in selecting hooks for specific fish. Also, some manufacturers are now selling hooks prepackaged and labeled for various species: panfish hooks, catfish hooks, etc. This eliminates confusion when buying hooks.

Hook Selection Chart

Following are recommendations for hook sizes and styles for popular fish species. In each case, a range of sizes is given which will work for the fish in question. For general purpose use, the best selection for each species would be the medium-sized hook in the appropriate category. However, if you know that your fish are likely to be on the small size, or if you're fishing strictly for trophy fish, adjust your hook choice down or up appropriately.

Bass	Sizes #2-4/0. When using live bait, choose smaller wire hooks. When using plastic worms or other artificial lures, use 1/0-4/0 forged steel hooks.
Sunfish	Sizes #10-#6 light wire hooks. Hooks with a long shaft are preferred, since they are easier to remove when a sunfish swallows the live bait.
Crappie/White bass	Sizes #4-2/0 light wire hooks.
Walleye/Sauger	Sizes #8-#1 light wire hooks. Many experts prefer "baitholder" hooks when using minnows, nightcrawlers or leeches.
Yellow perch	Sizes #8-#4 light wire hooks.
Muskellunge/Pike	Sizes 1/0-6/0 forged steel hooks.
Stream Trout	Sizes #10-#1 Aberdeen or "baitholder" styles are popular.
Salmon	Sizes 1/0-7/0 forged steel hooks.
Striped Bass/Hybrids	Sizes 1/0-6/0 forged steel hooks.
Large Catfish	Sizes 1/0-7/0 forged steel hooks.
Small Catfish/Bullheads	Sizes #8-#1 light wire hooks.

(Thanks to Tru-Turn Hook Company for providing recommendations for this chart.)

One special note should be made about camshaft hooks, which are offered under various names. These hooks have offset bends in the shaft. When a fish bites down on the offset, the hook's point rotates to a better penetrating angle, making it easier to get a good hookset. I've used camshaft hooks in recent years, and they work. I highly recommend them when fishing with live bait, plastic worms, and in other single-hook situations.

Overall, don't worry about the different names and styles of hooks.

Again, many different hooks will serve the same purpose. Just find one design and size for the type fishing you'll be doing. If it works, stick with it. Later in your fishing career you might want to learn more about hook styles and the subtle advantages of each. But for now, stay with the basics, and you'll be okay.

Sinkers: A "Weighty" Consideration

Sinkers are lead weights that pull the bait down to the fish's level. Sinkers are molded in many different designs and sizes. The type sinker you use and how you use it depends on what rig and technique you select for the species you're after. In terms of size, use a sinker heavy enough to do the job, but no heavier than it has to be. In most cases, the lighter the sinker, the more sensitive and natural the rig will be.

The most common sinkers are those which clamp directly onto the line. Split shot are small round balls that are pinched onto the line

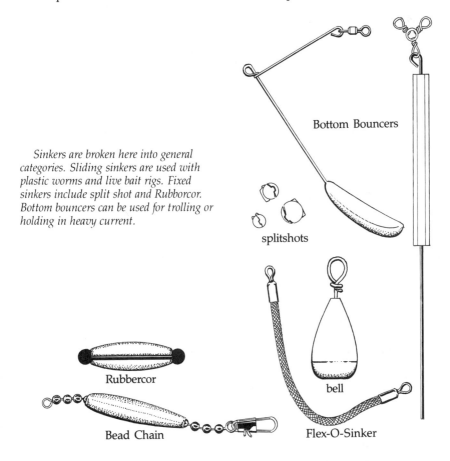

Sinkers are broken here into general categories. Sliding sinkers are used with plastic worms and live bait rigs. Fixed sinkers include split shot and Rubbercor. Bottom bouncers can be used for trolling or holding in heavy current.

Bottom Bouncers

splitshots

Rubbercor

Bead Chain

bell

Flex-O-Sinker

along a slit through the middle of the sinker. Clincher sinkers are elongated weights that pinch onto the line. Rubbercor sinkers resemble clinchers, but have a rubber strip through the center. Line is simply looped behind this rubber to hold the sinker in place.

Sliding sinkers have holes through the middle so the line can slide freely through them. Three common examples are the egg sinker and the bullet sinker, both named for their shape, and the walking slip sinker, named for the special way it's used. Egg sinkers are used with stationary live-bait rigs. The most common use for bullet sinkers is with Texas-rigged plastic worms. And slip sinkers are used with slip-sinker rigs to crawl live bait across the bottom.

Various other sinkers are used with bottom-bumping or stationary rigs. Bell swivel sinkers are bell-shaped and have a brass swivel molded in. The line is tied to the swivel, which prevents line twist when you're drift-fishing or bottom-bouncing. Bank sinkers are general-purpose bottom sinkers which cast well, slide easily along smooth bottoms, and hold well in strong current. Pyramid and inverted pyramid sinkers have flat sides for gripping into soft, smooth bottoms.

There are many other sinkers for such special techniques as trolling and drifting. But the sinkers listed above are the ones used in the rigs outlined later in this chapter and also in the fishing techniques desribed in Chapter 9.

Floats: Staying on Top of the Situation

Most fishermen start out in the sport by bobber fishing. That's watching a float and waiting for a fish to yank it under. This is a simple yet effective and exciting way to fish. When the float starts bobbing or moving away, suspense builds in a hurry.

Actually, floats serve two purposes. They tell you when you're getting a bite, and they also control the depth of your bait. A float holds the bait as deep or as shallow as you wish. It allows you to dangle the bait just above bottom or suspend it over the top of brush, sunken weeds, or other submerged cover.

Also, if you want to fish close to the bottom or cover, and you don't know how deep it is, the float will tell you. If the bait's resting on bottom, there's no pull on the float, so it lies sideways on the surface. But when you shorten the length of line between the bait and float so the bait is no longer touching bottom, the pull will cause the float to ride in an upright position.

Floats come in many different materials, shapes, and sizes. Most floats are made from hard plastic, foam plastic, buoyant wood, cork, or porcupine quills. Float designs include round, tubular, barrel-shaped, pear-shaped, quill-shaped, and combinations of these designs.

Long, slender floats are more sensitive to light bites than round floats. Also, slender floats cast better since there less wind resistant. I

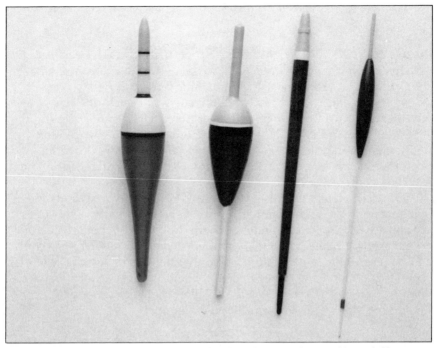

Bobbers can be divided into two classes: Fixed or slip types. Longer thinner bobbers are more sensitive. Larger rounder ones hold up heavier baits or rigs.

recommend them over the ever-popular round floats for most small-bait, light-tackle situations. If you're fishing for larger fish and using larger baits, the round floats work fine. And a good compromise for general use is the combination of a round or barrel float with a quill-like stem running through the middle. The thick part provides plenty of buoyancy for the sinker/hook/bait, while the quill adds sensitivity to indicate that you're getting a bite.

Most floats clip onto the line with a small, spring-loaded hook. Others are pegged onto the line. A third family of floats slides up and down the line freely. This sliding float is used with the popular "slip bobber" rig, explained later in this chapter.

Many beginning anglers make the common mistake of fishing with a float that's too large. Select a float that is the *smallest possible size* considering the weight of your sinker, hook, and bait. You want the float to ride high on the surface, but the slightest tug should pull it under. If a float is too large, smaller fish will have trouble swimming down with the bait. This unnatural resistance may alert them to danger. So keep several different-size floats in your tackle box to match different fishing conditions and rigs.

Snaps, Swivels, Snap Swivels, Split Rings, and Leaders

Snaps, swivels, snap swivels, split rings, and leaders are additional types of terminal tackle for use with various lures and rigs.

A snap is a small wire bracket with a safety-pin catch. It's simply a convenience device for changing lures or hooks faster and easier. Tie the line to one end and snap the lure on the other end. To change lures, simply unsnap the catch, take the old lure off, put the new one on, and fasten the catch back. With a snap, you don't have to cut and retie line each time you change lures.

There are tradeoffs for this convenience, however. A snap adds more weight, more drag, and more hardware for the fish to see. Also, snaps occasionally bend or break under pressure from hard-fighting fish. For these reasons, I rarely use a snap. Instead, I prefer to tie my line directly to the eye of the hook or lure. The only time I use a snap is when I know I'll need to change lures frequently, and these situations are rare. When I do use a snap, I choose the smallest, lightest one possible, considering the size and strength of the fish I'm after.

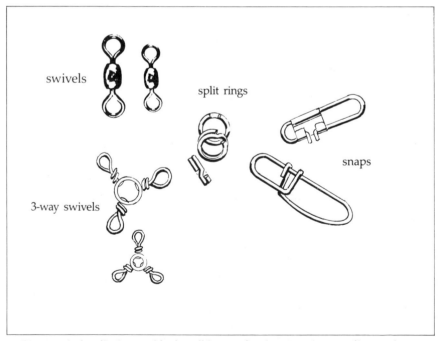

Snaps, swivel, split rings and leaders all have a place in connecting your line to a lure or bait.

A swivel is a small revolving metal link that's often tied between the main line and other components of the terminal rig. A swivel prevents line twist caused by rotating lures or baits.

Like snaps, swivels also have drawbacks. One main drawback is poor design or material that keeps the swivel from rotating freely. Simply put, cheap swivels should be avoided. The best and most expensive swivels are ball-bearing swivels that revolve under far less pressure than swivels without ball bearings. I recommend them.

The "three-way" swivel is an important specialty swivel. As its name implies, it has three tie-on rings instead of two. This swivel is used in the bottom-fishing rig explained in the next section of this chapter.

A snap swivel is a combination of a snap and a swivel. Many fishermen use snap swivels with all types of rigs and artificial lures. In most cases, however, they're unnecessary and even ill-advised. Snap swivels add weight, which can deaden the action of a lure. They can be a weak link between line and hook. And they increase the chance of fouling on brush or weeds. The only time I use a snap swivel is for casting revolving spinners with spinning tackle. The rest of the time I tie my line directly to the hook or lure.

The split ring is a small overlapping wire ring threaded into the eye of a lure, and then the line is tied to the ring. The idea is to allow more freedom of movement in the lure, which gives a more lifelike action. Many lures come from the factory with split rings already installed.

If a lure doesn't have a split ring, I don't add one. Some lures perform better with the line tied directly into the eye. Also, I never clip a snap swivel into a split ring. Such a connection hampers lure action instead of enhancing it.

A leader is a length of fishing line or thin wire tied or fastened between the main line and the hook/lure. Leaders serve either of two main purposes. (1) They increase line strength next to the hook, or (2) they provide a low-visability connection between a highly visible main line and the bait. This keeps the visible line from scaring fish, and it also makes the bait look more natural.

The term "leader" also means an additional length of line tied into a terminal rig for adding extra hooks. This is the most common use of leaders for beginning fishermen.

Most leaders are monofilament. Thin wire leaders, however, are used by anglers trying for toothy fish like pike or muskies who can bite monofilament in two. These wire leaders normally come prerigged and are available in most tackle stores.

Rigs for Everyday Fishing

Now we get to the heart of the matter. You know enough about hooks, sinkers, floats, knots, and other terminal tackle to start assembling different rigs for specific fishing situations. Following are explanations and sketches of 9 basic rigs, including how to tie them and where and how to use them. Sizes of hooks, sinkers, floats, and lines in these rigs will vary from one fishing situation to the next, depending on size and strength of fish, water depth, bottom type, amount of current, and other variables.

Fixed-Bobber Rig—This is the old standby float/sinker/hook rig that catches almost anything that swims. It's used mainly in calm water (ponds, lakes, rivers, and pools of streams). It adapts both to poles and casting tackle, although it's awkward to cast with more than three feet of line between the bobber and hook. There's no backcast with a fixed bobber rig. Simply hold the rod behind you with the line hanging down, and then make an easy lob-type cast to your fishing spot.

To assemble this rig, first tie the hook to the end of the line. Next, fasten a split shot, clincher, or Rubbercor sinker 6 inches up the

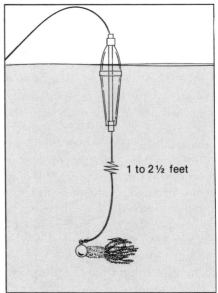

1 to 2½ feet

line. Clamp or wrap the sinker tightly onto the line so it won't slip down. Needle-nose pliers do a nice job of clamping. Last, attach a bobber onto the line at the desired distance above the sinker. The bobber can be adjusted up or down the line to float the bait at whatever depth you desire.

The fixed-bobber rig is extremely easy to use. When a fish is nibbling, the bobber will twitch on the surface. When the fish takes the bait, the bobber will move away fast or be pulled underwater. That's the time to set the hook with a sharp yank.

Slip-Bobber Rig—The slip-bobber rig is so-named because the bobber slides freely up and down the line. It allows you to cast from shore or a boat and present the bait at any desired depth.

The slip-bobber rig is similar to the fixed-bobber rig, with the exception of the free-sliding bobber. The bobber is run up the line first. Next, the sinker is attached six inches from the end of the line. The bobber will slide down and rest atop the sinker. Then the hook is tied onto the end of the line. Last, a short piece of thread or thin rubber band is tied tightly around the line at the depth you want to fish. (For instance, to fish 5 feet deep, tie the thread 5 feet up the line.)

When casting, all the weight of the bobber, sinker, and baited hook is near the end of the line, which makes casting easy. When the rig hits the water, the sinker and hook fall toward bottom, pulling line through the bobber. Since the thread is too big to pass through the hole in the bobber, it stops the line and leaves the bait dangling at the preset depth. This depth may be altered by raising or lowering the thread on the line.

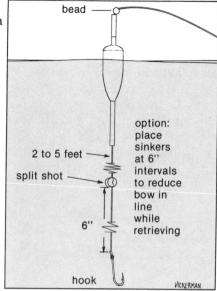

Slip-bobber rigs can be tied from individual components, or they can be bought at tackle stores in preassembled packages. These packages have instructions for tying and using this rig.

Bottom Rig—This is the basic rig for fishing on bottom without a bobber. Bottom rigs are usually used for catfish and bullheads, but they also work for bottom-feeding bass, walleye, trout, and other species. They can be used in quiet water or in current.

This rig is built around a three-way swivel. Tie the main line on one ring of the swivel. Tie a 12-inch leader on the second ring of the swivel, and on the other end of the leader tie a bank or bell swivel sinker. Last, tie an 18-inch leader on the third ring of the swivel. The hook and bait go on the end of this leader.

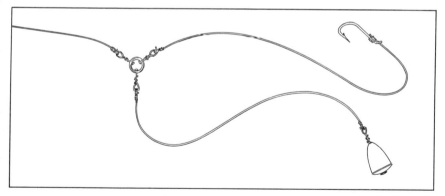

The bottom rig is highly versatile. It can be used from shore or boat, with light or heavy tackle. Length of the sinker and hook leaders may be altered as desired. Generally, however, the hook leader should be longer than the sinker leader.

When fishing from shore, many veteran anglers rig two or more rods with bottom rigs and prop them on forked sticks stuck into the ground.

Then they sit back and watch all their lines at once, waiting for a bite. Be sure to check your state fishing laws to make sure how many lines are legal.

Since you're not using a float, how can you tell when you're getting a bite? With the rig resting on bottom, reel up slack until the line is tight. Then, if you're holding the rod, you'll feel the bite. If the rod is propped, you'll see the rod tip jerk. Some fishermen attach small bells to their rod tips to alert them to bites. Also, your line may start moving as the fish swims off with the bait. The key to using the bottom rig is to keep slack out of the line so you'll notice these things.

Live-Bait Rig—This is a stationary rig that allows natural action from live bait. It can be used in any type water and for a wide variety of fish.

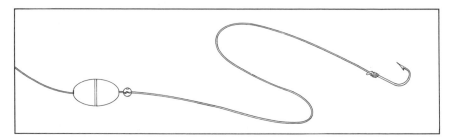

To tie this rig, run a sliding egg sinker up the line. Now clamp on a BB-size split-shot sinker below the egg sinker and 18 inches from the end of the line. This small split shot serves as a stop to keep the egg sinker from riding down on the bait. Last, tie the hook to the end of the line and bait it with a minnow or crawfish. Now the bait can swim freely off bottom and pull line through the sinker. Also, when a fish takes the bait, it can swim off without feeling the unnatural weight of the sinker.

Slip-Sinker Rig—The slip-sinker rig is used to pull live bait across bottom, either by trolling or casting and slowly cranking in line. This rig is highly effective on walleye, but it can also be used for many other species.

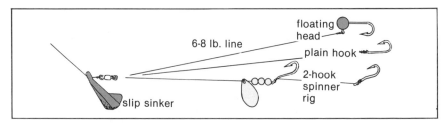

floating head
6-8 lb. line
plain hook
2-hook spinner rig
slip sinker

Most slip-sinker rigs are sold in packages, but they can also be assembled from individual components. First, slide a walking-type slip sinker up the line; then tie on a small barrel swivel. Tie a 3-foot monofilament leader onto the other end of the barrel swivel, and add the hook at the end of this leader. Bait with a night crawler, leech, crawfish, or minnow.

Most experts troll or drag slip-sinker rigs with spinning tackle. When a fish takes the bait, line is quickly released to allow the fish to run. When the run stops, reel in slack line until you feel pressure on the line. Then set the hook.

Bottom-Bouncing Rig—Bottom bouncers are weighted wire devices used to troll baits along snaggy bottoms. Thin steel wire is bent into an "L" shape. A lead weight is molded into the center of the long arm; the short arm has a ring for tying on a 3-foot leader and hook. The main line is tied to the bend between the two arms.

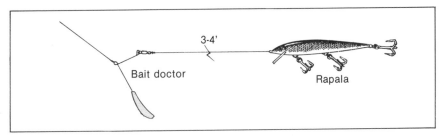

The bottom bouncer is mainly used when fishing from a boat. It is lowered to the bottom and then pulled slowly through likely structure. The wire holds the weight up off bottom where it won't hang up, and the leader and baited hook float behind, just above the bottom.

The bottom bouncer is used mainly for walleye, but it's also extremely effective on bass, crappies, catfish, and other structure-oriented species.

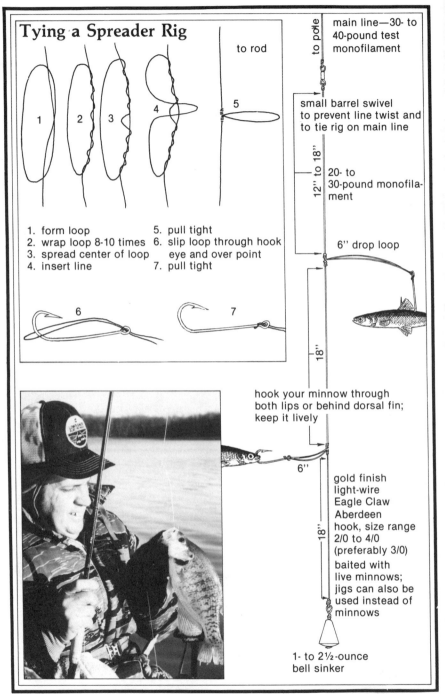

Tying a Spreader Rig

to rod

1
2
3
4
5

1. form loop
2. wrap loop 8-10 times
3. spread center of loop
4. insert line
5. pull tight
6. slip loop through hook eye and over point
7. pull tight

6
7

to pole

main line—30- to 40-pound test monofilament

small barrel swivel to prevent line twist and to tie rig on main line

12" to 18"

20- to 30-pound monofilament

6" drop loop

18"

hook your minnow through both lips or behind dorsal fin; keep it lively

6"

18"

gold finish light-wire Eagle Claw Aberdeen hook, size range 2/0 to 4/0 (preferably 3/0) baited with live minnows; jigs can also be used instead of minnows

1- to 2½-ounce bell sinker

The entire, double-hook rig is tied from one piece of monofilament. The drops are "double loops" where a hook can slide on by putting the line through the hook's eye. Hooks can be changed without cutting the line.

Two-Hook Panfish Rig—This is a deep-water rig used primarily for crappie and catfish. It is fished "tightline" fashion (no float) from a boat. The sinker is on the bottom of this rig, and it's jigged slowly off bottom while two baited hooks dangle above it. Minnows are the usual bait for this rig, though small crappie jigs are sometimes substituted.

The first step is to tie a bell swivel sinker to the end of the line. Eighteen inches above the sinker, use a surgeon's knot to tie a loop in the line. When stretched out from the line, the loop should be 4 to 6 inches long. Now tie an identical loop 18 inches up from this first loop. Last, add hooks to the loops in the following manner. Pinch the sides of the loop together as one line, and push it through the eye of the hook, from the back to the front. Then open the loop and pull the hook up through it. Cinch the hook tight at the end of the loop and add bait.

Texas-Rigged Plastic Worm—Plastic worms are popular among bass fishermen, and the Texas-rigged worm is the favorite way to use this bait. A Texas-rigged worm is weedless and can be crawled through the thickest cover where bass like to hide.

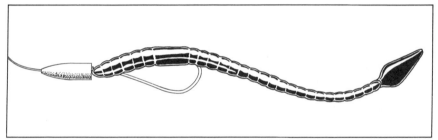

Start by running a bullet sliding sinker up the line; then tie on a plastic worm hook. Insert the point of the hook 1/2 inch into the head of the worm. Now pull the point out the side of the worm, and slide the worm up the shank of the hook until the eye is pulled into the head of the worm. Last, rotate the hook and reinsert the point into the side of the worm, completely covering the barb. Done correctly, the worm will hang straight with the hook in place.

Rigged in this manner, the sinker will slide freely along the line. Many anglers prefer to peg the sinker directly over the head of the worm. This can be done by pushing the small point of a flat toothpick through the hole in the sinker, from the back of the sinker toward the pointed front. When the toothpick can be pushed no further, break it off even with the bottom of the sinker. Then slide the sinker down the line to the head of the worm, and it'll stay in place.

A special section on how to fish plastic worms is included in the following chapter.

Carolina-Rigged Plastic Worm—Where the Texas-rigged worm is meant for fishing in heavy cover, the Carolina-rigged worm is designed for open structure fishing, for covering long distances of a bar, bank, river, or creek channel. It's very similar to the live-bait rig, except it uses a plastic worm for bait. It's also a very easy rig to use. You simply cast it out, allow it to sink to bottom and then crank it back in very slowly with small lift/drop hops with your rod tip.

To make a Carolina-rigged worm, run a heavy bullet slip sinker up the line; then tie a barrel swivel on the end of the line. Next, tie on a 3-foot leader with a hook and plastic worm on the end. With this rig, the worm is usually fished with the point exposed. Do this by inserting the point of the hook into the head of the worm and then threading the worm around the bend of the hook and up the shaft. Last, pull the point out the side of the worm, and pull the worm down to straighten it. Properly done, the worm should hang straight on the hook.

Summary

Entire books have been written about fishing rigs, so it's difficult to cover them in a single chapter. You can use these 9 basic rigs, however, in probably 90% of all the freshwater fishing in North America. These rigs are versatile and productive! Pick the ones that apply to the type fishing you want to do, and then practice tying and using them until they become second nature.

In the next chapter you'll learn about baits, and in Chapter 9 we'll cover easy fishing techniques for different spots and situations. These three chapters, 7, 8, and 9, are the heart of *FISHING FUNDAMENTALS*. Study them carefully, and follow their tips. If you use the right rig, bait, and methods in a location where fish exist, you'll catch some almost every time. You'll also have learned the basics, and you'll be ready to progress to a higher level of fishing knowledge and skills.

NATURAL BAIT AND ARTIFICIAL LURES

"There's no better teacher than experience. Lakes and streams are your laboratory. This is where you'll carry out your experiments with various tools."

One of my best fishing memories is of a Sunday afternoon in spring when I was in grade school. After church and a big family meal, I decided to go fishing in a large pond on a neighboring farm.

My father raised tuffy minnows in our own smaller pond, so I caught some for bait by dropping a biscuit into our wire minnow trap, tossing the trap into the water, and waiting an hour. When I hauled in the trap, two dozen minnows were flopping inside. I dumped them into my bucket, grabbed my cane pole, and headed for my fishing hole.

As I slipped up to the pond bank, I spotted a large bass finning lazily in the shallows below me. I crept backward, unwound the line from my pole, and baited my hook with the biggest minnow in the bucket. Then I eased up to the pond's edge and lowered the minnow right in front of the bass' eyeballs.

It was like a tornado had suddenly been tied on my line. The bass instantly struck the minnow and hooked itself in the process. Then the fish went wild, jumping and thrashing. I held on for all I was worth and finally dragged it out on the bank. That was enough action for one day. I ran straight home to show my catch. In less that a half hour after I'd left, I was back with a 5-pound largemouth and a memory to keep forever.

In this case the big minnow did the trick. At other times it was worms, crayfish, other live, or artificial lures. Bait is a part of every fishing story. This is why beginners must learn different bait types, which are good for which species, and how to use various baits. Simply put, if you aren't savvy about baits, you won't catch many fish.

Natural and Artificial Baits

There are two broad categories of baits: natural and artificial.

Natural baits are organic. They include worms, minnows, insects, crayfish, leeches, cut bait (fish pieces)—a wide variety of living or once-living baits.

Artificial baits include a vast range of lures. Some mimic natural bait. Others bear no resemblance to any natural food, yet they have some attraction which causes fish to bite. (Besides being hungry, fish strike artificial lures because they're mad, greedy, curious, or impulsive.)

The list of *categories* of artificial baits includes topwaters, spinners, crankbaits, soft plastics, jigs, spoons, and flies. Each of these categories can be broken down into individual types of baits. For example, soft plastics include plastic worms, grubs, eels, lizards, crayfish, and minnows.

Choosing Between Natural Bait and Artificials

Which should you use? Natural bait or artificials? Fishermen have faced this decision since the first artificial lures were invented. Basically, this is a matter of personal preference, convenience, and bait capabilities. Each has certain advantages over the other.

Fish usually prefer natural bait over artificials. A bluegill will eat a real earthworm before it will a plastic one. If a live crayfish is retrieved next to an artificial crayfish, a bass will recognize and take the live one. These are examples of why a majority of fish caught in North America are taken on natural bait.

So why even bother with artificial baits? There are several reasons. First, many anglers enjoy the challenge of using artificials. Since fish are harder to catch on artificials, these anglers feel there's more reward in fooling the fish with them. They're fishing more for sport than for meat.

Second, artificial lures are more convenient. You don't have to dig or trap them, and you don't have to keep them alive or fresh. Most can be kept in a tackle box indefinitely and fished with no advance preparation.

Third, artificials have certain capabilities and attractions that natural baits don't have. While natural baits are normally used with a stationary or slow-moving presentation, artificials may be retrieved fast to cover a lot of water.

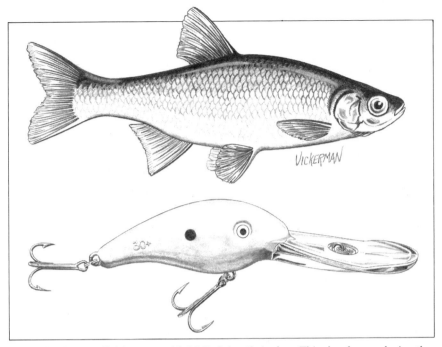

Which is best, artificial or natural bait? Each has their place. This also changes during the year. Experience and learning from others helps develop a pattern or guide.

They can cause inactive fish to strike out of impulse or anger as the bait runs by, whereas, this same fish might ignore a minnow under a bobber.

So when deciding which to use, weigh the advantages of natural bait versus artificials as they relate to your particular fishing situation. Which is more important? Making a good catch, or enjoying a sporty challenge? How difficult is it to get natural bait? Which type bait is more likely to suit your fish's mood and location and the technique you'll use to try for it?

Using Natural Bait

To use natural bait, you have to get it, keep it fresh, hook it on properly, and offer it with the right presentation. Following are guidelines for fishing with several popular natural baits.

First, however, a note on obtaining bait. Although these outlines tell how to catch your own bait, in many cases it's more practical to buy bait from a bait dealer. True, catching bait can be almost as much fun as catching first, but I usually buy my bait to save as much time as possible for fooling the fish.

One other note: Fish normally prefer fresh, active bait to old, lifeless bait. This is why I always keep fresh bait on my hook.

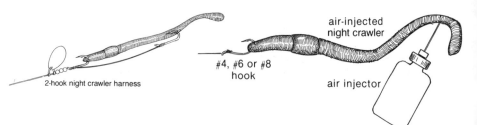

air-injected
night crawler

#4, #6 or #8
hook

air injector

2-hook night crawler harness

Worms—Worms are the most popular of all natural baits. They include large night crawlers and a variety of smaller earthworms. Worms can be used to catch all panfish and smaller sportfish. They're especially good on catfish, bullheads, bass, small sunfish, walleye, trout, and yellow perch.

Worms are easy to collect. You can dig for them in moist, rich soil in gardens, around barnyards, and under rotting leaves or logs. Night crawlers can be collected on a grassy lawn at night following a warm rain. Place them in a small container partially filled with loosely crumbled dirt. If you put a top on the container, make sure it has holes so the worms can breathe.

Keep the worm can or box out of the sun so the worms won't overheat and die. Many fishermen keep their worms in a cooler. If you have leftover worms, they can be kept for several weeks in a refrigerator.

There are a number of methods for using worms. With a stationary rig such as a bobber rig or bottom rig, gob one or more worms onto the hook, running the point through the middle of the worm's body several times with the ends dangling free. When fishing for small sunfish or yellow perch, don't put too much worm on the hook, since these fish have small mouths. But when fishing for catfish, bass, and other large fish, the more worms on the hook, the better.

If you're fishing for walleye or bass with a walking slip-sinker rig or a bottom bouncer, hook the worm (normally a night crawler) once through the head so the body can trail out behind. When driftfishing in a stream for trout, hook the worm through the middle of the body and allow the two ends to dangle.

Minnows—These small baitfish come in many different species. Shiners, tuffies (fatheads), and goldfish are popular species sold in bait stores. Also, many other small baitfish can be caught from ponds, streams, and lakes. Fishermen regularly use minnows to catch crappie, bass, walleye, sauger, catfish, white bass, stripers, and other species.

One of the easiest ways to catch minnows is with a wire basket trap found in most tackle stores. Just bait the trap with bread and drop it into water for a few hours. Also, minnows may be seined or caught with a cast net. However, seines and nets are expensive, and both take fair amounts of know-how to use. For these reasons, I don't recommend them for beginning fishermen.

Minnows must receive proper care, or they'll quickly die. Keep their water cool and fresh. I use styrofoam buckets instead of metal or plastic,

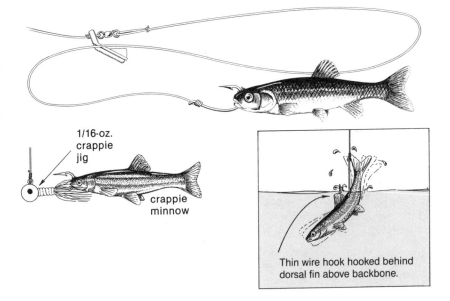

1/16-oz. crappie jig

crappie minnow

Thin wire hook hooked behind dorsal fin above backbone.

because styrofoam keeps the water cooler. I never put more than 4 dozen minnows in a bucket to avoid overcrowding.

If the water in the bucket becomes too warm or stale, the minnows rise to the surface, and you must take quick action to save them. Exchange the old water for fresh. On extremely hot days, add chunks of ice to keep the water cool. And you might consider buying a small battery-run bait aerator to spray water into the bucket to maintain a good oxygen supply.

Minnows may be kept several days between trips. Store them in the refrigerator and change their water as often as needed.

When I fish with minnows, I put them on the hook two ways. If I'm using a stationary rig, I hook the minnow through the back under the main fin. This allows it to swim naturally. But if I'm using a moving rig like a bottom bouncer, walking slip sinker, or two-hook panfish rig, I hook the minnow through both lips, from bottom to top. And again, I frequently replace battered or dead minnows with fresh ones. New minnows always attract more bites than used ones.

Crickets/Grasshoppers—Crickets and grasshoppers are excellent baits for bluegill, bass, other small sunfish, catfish, and trout.

You can catch grasshoppers in grassy or weedy fields either by hand or with a butterfly net. Or better yet, you and a partner can open a fuzzy wool blanket and run through a field into the wind. The grasshoppers will try to fly away, but the wind will blow them into the blanket, and their legs will stick in the fuzz. To catch crickets, look under rocks, planks, or logs, and grab them by hand or with a net. (Watch out for spiders and poisonous snakes.)

Place grasshoppers or crickets in a cricket box from a tackle store, or make your own container by punching holes in a coffee can that has a plastic lid. Cut a small round hole in the lid, and keep it covered with masking tape. Peel the tape back to deposit grasshoppers or crickets as you catch them. When you want to get one out, peel the tape back, shake an insect out of the hole and place the tape back over the hole.

Grasshoppers and crickets should be stored in a cool, shady place. Each day add a damp paper towel for moisture and a tablespoon of corn meal for food.

Grasshoppers and crickets are normally used with bobber rigs or bottom rigs. They are hooked by inserting the point behind the tail, running it down the length of the body and out the head.

Crayfish—Crayfish are found in most freshwater lakes and streams. Many anglers think of them as bass bait (smallmouth love them!), but they are also good on catfish. Pieces of crayfish tail are irresistible to small sunfish.

The best way to gather crayfish is to go wading in a shallow stream and slowly turn over flat rocks. When you see a crayfish, ease a tin can with holes punched in the bottom up behind it, and then poke at its head with a stick. Crayfish swim backward to escape, so it should back up into the can. Then lift the can quickly.

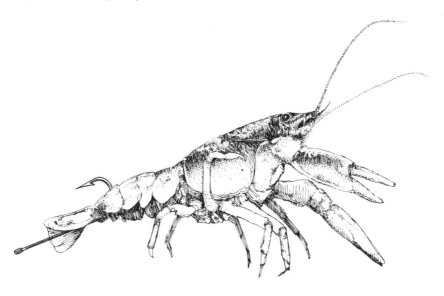

Keep crayfish in a styrofoam minnow bucket half-filled with water. They can be kept for several days if refrigerated.

When handling crayfish, be careful to avoid their pinchers, which can cause painful injury. Hold them by the body just behind the pinchers.

Live crayfish are hooked in the back section of the tail, from the bottom through the top. They are usually fished on or near bottom with a standard bottom rig or a live-bait rig. They can also be trolled slowly along bottom with a slip-sinker rig or a bottom bouncer. And once in awhile, crayfish should be fished just above bottom with a bobber rig.

For smaller panfish like bluegill or pumpkinseeds, cut a fresh crayfish tail into several small pieces and apply one to a small hook or jig dangled under a bobber.

Leeches—Several kinds of leeches inhabit North American waters, but only ribbon leeches are widely used for bait. These leeches squirm actively when held; less desirable leeches are lifeless when held. Ribbon leeches are used primarily for walleye and bass.

To trap leeches, drop dead minnows, liver, beef kidney, or bones into a large coffee can and mash the top of the can almost shut. Sink the can in leech-infested waters overnight, and the next morning pull the can up

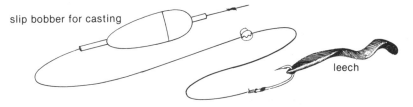

slip bobber for casting

leech

rapidly. Leeches keep for a long time in a water-filled styrofoam minnow bucket placed in the shade.

Leeches work well suspended under a bobber, since they squirm continuously. They may be trolled or crawled across bottom on a live-bait rig, slip-sinker rig, or a bottom-bouncer rig. They are also frequently used with a leadhead jig. To hook a leech, run the point of the hook through the head.

Cut Bait—Pieces or entrails of baitfish are excellent for catfish. Larger shad, herring, smelt, and other oily baitfish are best. These can be netted, cut into chunks an inch square, and hooked onto bottom rigs. Since catfish are scent feeders, they home in on the oil and blood from cut bait.

Also, a small slice of panfish meat adds to the attraction of a small jig for small sunfish, white bass, crappie, and yellow perch.

Other Natural Baits—Baits listed above are the most popular natural baits, but by no means the only good ones. Many others are extremely effective on various species of fish. Mealworms, waxworms, waterdogs, frogs, mayflies, salmon eggs, hellgrammites, grubs, catalpa worms, spring lizards, and clams are all excellent baits for different species of fish.

Fishermen wanting more information on collecting, keeping, and using natural bait should obtain a copy of *Fishing With Live Bait*, published by the Hunting and Fishing Library of Minnetonka, Minnesota. This book covers the subject in detail and is well illustrated and easy to understand.

Using Artificial Baits

Live worms and leeches wiggle on the hook. Live minnows swim. Live crayfish scoot across rocks or mud. But artificial baits hang motionless in the water until the angler gives them life by casting and retrieving. In most cases, the more skillfully this is done, the more fish the angler will catch. This is why many fishermen consider artificial baits more challenging than natural baits.

Following are brief descriptions of various artificial lures and how to use them.

Topwaters—Topwaters are the oldest category of artificial baits and one of the best. Bass, muskies, pike, stripers, white bass, and trout feed on the surface, normally in warm weather and during low-light periods of early morning, late afternoon, or night. Sometimes, however, fish will hit topwater baits in the middle of a bright day. Basically, if you see surface-feeding activity, give topwaters a try.

Topwater baits include wood and plastic lures in a wide variety of shapes and actions.

Poppers (also called chuggers) have scooped-out heads which make slapping sounds when pulled with short, quick jerks.

Propeller baits have propellers on one or both ends; the props churn the water when you pull these baits in short jerks.

Crawlers have concave metal lips; they wobble back and forth and make popping noises on a steady retrieve.

Buzzbaits have revolving metal or plastic blades which boil the water on a steady retrieve.

Floating minnows rest motionless and then swim with a quiet, subtle side-to-side action when reeled in.

Stickbaits resemble cigars with hooks attached; they dart across the surface in a zig-zag pattern when pulled with short, quick snaps of the rod tip.

If fish are actively feeding on the surface, use a lure that works fast and makes a lot of noise. But if fish aren't active, select a quieter lure and work it slowly. When casting a topwater bait, be ready for a strike the instant it hits the water. Sometimes fish see it coming through the air and take it immediately. When a fish strikes a topwater lure, wait until the lure disappears underwater before setting the hook. This takes steel nerves, since the natural tendency is to jerk the instant the strike occurs. But a short delay will give the fish more time to get the hooks in its mouth.

Spinners—This bait category includes spinnerbaits and in-line spinners.

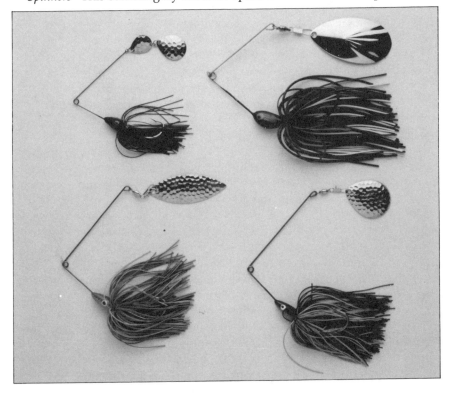

101

Spinnerbaits are shaped like an open safety pin. A rotating blade is attached to the upper arm; a leadhead body, skirt, and hook are on the lower arm. This design makes these baits semi-weedless, so they can be used in vegetation, brush, timber, and stumps, as well as open water.

Spinnerbaits come in a wide variety of sizes and blade configurations. Some have one blade, while others have two. Single-blades run deeper and slower than double-blades. Also, spinnerbaits are frequently dressed with pork rind or plastic trailers to give the bait more action and attraction.

Spinnerbaits are normally associated with bass fishing, but they're also good on muskies and pike. Very small spinnerbaits are effective on small panfish like crappie and bluegill.

The blade on *in-line spinners* is attached to the same shaft as the body, and it revolves around it. Because of this compact design, these lures work well in current. So in-line spinners are usually preferred for fishing smallmouth bass, rock bass, trout, and other stream species.

Spinners are a good artificial for beginning fishermen. In most cases, all you have to do is cast them out and reel them in. As your skills grow, you'll learn to vary retrieves and crawl spinnerbaits through cover or across bottom. In any case, when you feel a bump or see your line move sideways, set the hook immediately!

Crankbaits—This is another good lure family for beginners to try. Crankbaits are so-named because they have built-in actions. All you have to do is cast them out and then crank the reel handle. The retrieve causes these baits to wiggle, dive, and come to life.

Crankbaits are used mainly for largemouth and smallmouth bass, white bass, walleye, sauger, muskies, and pike. They are effective in reservoirs, lakes, and streams; around rocks, timber, docks, bridges, roadbeds, and other structure. Generally they're *not* effective in vegetation, since their treble hooks foul in the weeds. However, crankbaits can be effective retrieved next to weedlines or isolated patches of vegetation.

There are two subcategories of crankbaits: floater/divers and vibrating. Floater/divers are usually fat-bodied plugs with plastic or metal lips. They float on the surface, and when they're retrieved they wobble and dive. Usually, the larger a bait's lip, the deeper it will run.

One of the secrets to success with floater/divers is to keep them bumping bottom or cover objects. To do this, you must retrieve them so they dive as deeply as possible. Maximum depth may be achieved by (1) using smaller line (6- to 12-pound test is perfect), (2) cranking *slowly* instead of fast, (3) retrieving with your rod tip pointed down toward the water, and (4) making long casts. Once the bait hits bottom, vary the retrieve speed or try stop-and-go reeling to trigger strikes. Sometimes a floater/diver crankbait gets "out of tune," and won't swim a straight course back to the rod tip. Instead, it veers off to one side or the other. To retune a lure, bend the eye (where you tie the line) in the direction *opposite* the way the lure is veering. Make small adjustments and test the lure's track after each adjustment.

to fix
left hand
sidewinder

bend
eye
slightly
right

to fix
right hand
sidewinder

bend
eye
slightly
left

Vibrating crankbaits are used in relatively shallow water where fish are actively feeding. These are sinking baits, so the retrieve must be started shortly after they hit the water. They should be reeled fast to simulate bait-fish fleeing from a predator. This speed and tight wiggling action excite larger fish into striking.

Soft Plastics—This family of baits includes plastic worms, eels, grubs, minnows, lizards, crayfish, and other live-bait imitations. These baits are lifelike and natural-feeling to fish. They are used mostly on bass, white bass, and stripers, though very small, soft-plastic lures are great on smaller panfish.

Soft plastics are versatile lures. They can be fished without weight on the surface, or they can be weighted with a sinker or jighead and hopped along bottom. They can be rigged weedless and fished through weeds, brush, rocks, and stumps.

Plastic worms are the most popular of the soft plastic lures. The most common way to use them is to crawl or hop them through bottom structure. To do this, rig the worm according to the instructions under "Texas-Rigged Plastic Worms" in Chapter 7. Use a small slip sinker for fishing shallow

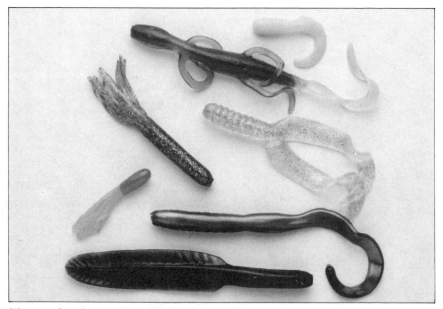

Worms and grubs come in multitudes of sizes and colors. Size is generally dictated by the food base fish are utilizing at that time. Color is picked by water clarity and light reflection. Local favorites provide a starting point.

water and larger sinkers for deeper water. A good rule of thumb is to use a 1/8-ounce slip sinker in depths up to 6 feet; a 1/4-ounce sinker from 6 to 12 feet; and a 3/8- or 1/2-ounce sinker in water deeper than 12 feet.

Cast the worm toward the structure, and allow it to sink to bottom. You'll feel it hit, or you'll see slack in your line. Hold your rod tip in the 10 o'clock position and reel up the slack. Now quickly lift the rod tip to the 11 o'clock position without reeling. This lifts the worm off bottom and swims it forward a short distance. Then allow the worm to fall back to the bottom again and repeat the process until the worm is through the target area.

When using this lift/drop retrieve, be alert for any taps or bumps, and always watch your line for unnatural pulses or sideways movements. Sometimes strikes are strong and easy to detect. Other times they are very light and subtle. If you know you've got a bite, don't delay in setting the hook. But if you're not sure, reel up slack line and hold the bait still for a few seconds. If nothing happens, tug on the bait ever so slightly. If you feel any life, anything pulling back or moving, set the hook.

When you feel a bite, quickly reel in slack line, drop the rod tip to the 9 o'clock position, and then set hard and fast with your wrists and forearms. If you don't feel that you have a good hookset, set again. This method applies to tackle spooled with line above 10-pound test. When you're using lighter line, set with less force, or you may break your line.

Virtually all soft plastics can be fished with the same lift/drop technique described above. Also, grubs can be hopped along bottom, down drop-offs or bluffs, etc. Eels or lizards can be slithered through weeds and brush. Minnows can be swum through sunken flats and timber. Crayfish can be bumped through rocks. Experiment with various baits to see which the fish prefer.

Jigs—If there's such thing as a universal bait, the leadhead jig is it. These balls of lead with hooks running out the back can be used in a wide range of circumstances to catch almost all freshwater fish. Jigs are basic baits which all anglers should learn to use.

Jigs come in a wide range of sizes. The 1/32-ouncers are for small panfish in shallow water. A 1-ounce jig might be used to bump bottom in heavy current for walleye or sauger. The most popular jig sizes are 1/16, 1/8, and 1/4 ounce.

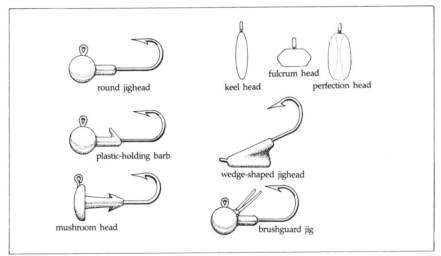

Jigs are an all time fish producer. Use plain, tip with live bait, add plastics to them, or just use your imagination.

Many veteran fishermen keep different-size jigs in their tackle boxes and then select the right size for a particular fishing situation. This selection is based on the size of the target fish, depth of water, and amount of wind and current. The bigger the fish, the deeper the water, and the stronger the wind and current, the heavier the jig should be.

Jigs are almost always dressed with an artificial trailer or live bait. Some jigs are made with hair, feather, or rubber skirts wrapped around the hook. Others come pre-rigged with plastic grubs. But the majority of jigs are sold without any trailer, leaving this choice up to the angler. You may install your own trailer (plastic grub, worm, pork rind), or you may prefer hooking on a live minnow, leech, or night crawler. Also, in addition to trailers, some jigs have small spinners attached to the head of the lure to add flash.

There are several effective jig retrieves. The basic one is the lift/drop: Allow the jig to sink to bottom, then hop it along bottom with short lifting jerks of the rod tip.

Another popular retrieve is the steady pull, swimming the jig in open water or just above bottom, sometimes grazing stumps, rocks, or other structure.

A third retrieve is bottom-bumping. Lower the jig straight to the bottom; lift it with the rod tip, and then allow it to sink back down. Appropriately, this vertical, deep-water presentation is called "jigging."

As with plastic worms, strikes on jigs may be very hard or very light. An angler using a jig will usually feel a bump or tick as a fish sucks in the bait. The key to detecting this is keeping a tight line at all times. If you feel a bump or see unnatural movement, set the hook immediately. There's no waiting with jigs.

Spoons—Metal spoons are the "Old Faithfuls" of artificial lures. They've been around a long time, and they're still producing. They are excellent baits for taking bass, walleye, pike, muskies, and white bass.

Some spoons are meant to be fished on the surface, while others are designed for underwater use. In both cases, the standard retrieve is a slow, steady pull. Sometimes, however, an erratic stop/go retrieve may trigger more strikes.

One special use for spoons is for fishing around or through weeds and grass. Topwater spoons ride over the thickest lily pads, moss, etc. Spoons retrieved underwater will flutter and dart through reeds and grass with a minimum of hang-ups. In this situation, a spoon with a weedguard over the hook is recommended.

Trailers are frequently added to a spoon's hook for extra attraction. Pork strips or plastic or rubber skirts are standard trailers. When adding a skirt to a spoon's hook, run the hook's point through the skirt from back to front so the skirt will fluff out during the retrieve.

Choosing Lure Color

Lures come in every color, shade, and pattern imaginable. Manufacturers use colors to capture the fancy of anglers who buy their lures. Less-experienced anglers almost always ask what color lure another fisherman used to make a good catch. We're *tuned in* to colors, and in the process I think we give lure color more credit than it deserves in fishing success.

I'm not saying that I don't pay attention to color. I do, but I don't think it's critical to making a good catch. It's just like lure size. Years of fishing has taught me that the type and action of my lure and the place and depth I'm using it are much more important than color. Nor do I use color selection devices. They may have some basis in fact, but I don't feel they are necessary for proper color choices.

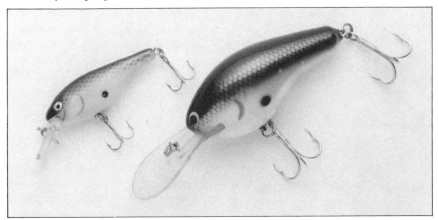

Lures come in many colors to match any color combination. The two keys to remember are bait and water clarity. Match the bait size and color, then adjust the color for muddy or clear water.

When selecting colors, I normally stick to what's natural to the fish. If they're feeding on shad, I'll use a lure that's shad-colored. If they're feeding on crayfish, I want a bait with an orange belly and a brown or green back.

There are exceptions to this rule. If the water is muddy, I prefer bright lures that show up better in the murk: chartreuse, yellow, hot pink. If the water is clear, I favor white or chrome crankbaits and spinners or a translucent-colored soft-plastic bait: smoke, motor oil, strawberry red, or salt-and-pepper.

Again, seek advice about lure colors for particular lakes or reservoirs. But don't be misled into believing that only one color will work. Several colors will usually catch the same fish. Stick with the basic colors, and concentrate more on fish location and depth than on lure color.

Making Sense Out of Fish Scents

One of the latest trends in fishing is the use of scents on lures. Do they really work? I'm not sure, and I don't think anyone is 100 percent certain if they do or don't. Biologists know that some fish have a well-developed sense of smell. Also, testing by independent laboratories indicates that scent application sometimes increases the chance that fish will bite and hold onto a lure.

I *am* certain that scents *aren't* magic potions that will cause inactive fish to suddenly go into a feeding frenzy. A scent may persuade a borderline fish that's inspecting a bait to bite it. But scents won't work miracles.

I use scents on slow-moving artificial baits like plastic worms and jigs. I don't use them on fast-moving baits like spinners or crankbaits. I can't say for certain that scents have ever helped me, but I think they have. So you have to decide this one for yourself. The fishing-scent industry is built on the basis that scents *may* help anglers increase their catch. If you experiment with scents and you *think* they help you, this will build your confidence and concentration, which will make you a better fisherman, whether the scent works or not.

Summary

In Chapter 5, I described rods, reels, and line as "tools" for fishing. Baits are also tools in the truest sense. They are objects designed to help you catch fish. Different baits serve specific purposes. You must learn what various baits are designed to do and then how to apply them where they work best.

You start to do this by reading, but then you must apply what you read on the water. There's no better teacher than experience. Lakes and streams are your laboratory. This is where you'll carry out your experiments with various fishing tools.

Now we're ready to put the entire package together. We've learned the F+L+P formula. We've covered types of fish, where to fish, tackle, accessories, rigs, and now baits. We're finally ready to actually go fishing, to learn simple ways to catch fish from different types of waters. Let's go forward into what's probably the most important chapter in *FISHING FUNDAMENTALS*.

CHAPTER 9

EASY FISHING TECHNIQUES

"Regardless of where you go and what species you're after, you must first study your water to determine where the fish are."

efore becoming a writer, I was a pilot in the U.S. Air Force, so I know, in an odd sort of way, how flying and fishing are alike. You can read books about flying for years, but that doesn't mean you know how to take off and land a plane. You have to get up in the clouds before you'll feel what flying is really like.

It's the same with fishing. You can study, but you'll never be a fisherman until you put your book knowledge to practical use. That's what we'll do in this chapter: learn how to catch fish from ponds, lakes, streams, and rivers. This is where we get specific. You'll learn practical, step-by-step techniques for taking fish from each kind of spot.

In essence, then, this chapter is the heart of *FISHING FUNDAMENTALS.* Now we'll talk mechanics of fishing, not theories. We'll cover exactly how to fish different situations. You've already learned about various species, how to find places to fish, select tackle and accessories, tie rigs, and choose baits. This was all background material to prepare you for what's in this chapter. Now it's time to get your line wet!

Obviously, though, it's impossible to cover all techniques for all fish. Instead, we'll look at the best opportunities and the easiest techniques. Also,

I'll help you identify the best fishing locations in different types of waters and then tell you how to make them pay off.

Study the following methods, and then get out on the water and practice them. You'll learn by trial and error, and you'll also change and refine techniques as you gain experience. But the basics will remain the same from one location and set of conditions to the next.

Where Fish Live

The first step in catching fish is knowing where to find them. On each outing, regardless of where you go and what species you're after, you must first study your water to determine where the fish are.

It would be a good idea to go back to Chapter 2 and review the section entitled "Structure." This is the key to determining where fish live. Remember that most fish gather in predictable places, and these places fall into what we call structure.

Various types of waters have different types of structure. In sections of this chapter, I'll identify structure specific to ponds, lakes, streams, and rivers. Next, I'll tell how to fish them. This is the proper order. First figure out where fish most likely will be found. Then decide which presentation will most effectively catch them.

You should go through this process each time you fish, on the smallest ponds and streams, or on the largest lakes and rivers. This is the F+L+P formula explained in Chapter 2. This formula will make your fishing orderly, rather than haphazard.

HOW TO FISH PONDS AND SMALL LAKES

Ponds and small lakes, scattered throughout North America, are the most numerous of all fishing spots, and they offer some of the most consistent action. A few ponds are formed naturally by beavers, mud slides, etc. But most ponds and small lakes are manmade to provide water for livestock, irrigation, and to prevent erosion. Other ponds and small lakes were built strictly for recreation.

Small bodies of water are excellent places to start fishing, for two reasons. First, many of them have healthy fish populations, but not much angling pressure, so the fish aren't too spooky. They usually bite. And second, since these waters are small, the fish are more confined, so they're easier to locate. It doesn't take as long to test different locations and techniques. For this reason, I like to think of ponds and small lakes as "training grounds" that prepare you to fish larger, more sophisticated waters.

Analyzing Ponds or Small Lakes

When you get to a pond or small lake, your fishing starts before you wet your line. First you should study the pond to determine its characteristics. Some ponds have flat basins, while others have a shallow end with ditches feeding it, and a deep end with an earthen dam holding the water back. Many ponds have brush, weeds, trees, logs, rocks, cattails, or other structure. Take note of all the combinations of depths and structure. It's your job to figure out the right combination.

Again, think of the F+L+P formula and the factors that determine where fish will be. One is the fish's basic nature. The type of fish found in certain areas will vary according to the time of year and water conditions. For instance, bass might stay in the shallows all day in spring, but move to deeper water during summer. However, they may still feed in the shallows at night. These are things you must learn before you can make an educated guess about where to find fish.

Don't worry if you don't know the specifics of fish behavior. You can learn them as you go. For now, you'll be fishing effectively if you follow the directions in the next section. These are the basic, tried-and-true methods that produce fish consistently from one season and set of conditions to the next.

Techniques for Fishing Ponds and Small Lakes

Most ponds and small lakes support what biologists call "warm-water fisheries": bluegills and other species of small sunfish, crappies, bass, catfish, and bullheads. Some spring-fed ponds hold trout. Let's take these species one at a time and look specifically at how to catch them.

Bluegill

Bluegills are my choice for anybody just starting to fish, since they're usually the most plentiful fish in ponds and small lakes, and they always seem willing to bite. The following information also applies to pumpkinseeds, redear sunfish, longear sunfish, and green sunfish.

In spring, early summer, and fall, sunfish stay in shallow to medium-deep water (2 to 10 feet). In hottest summer and coldest winter, they normally move deeper, though they may still occasionally feed in the shallows.

Bluegills hold around brush, logs, weeds, rocks, piers, stumps, or other similar cover. On cloudy days or in dingy water, bluegills usually hang around edges of such structure. This is also true early in the morning and late in the afternoon. But during the part of the day when the sun is brightest, especially in clear-water ponds, these fish swim into brush or vegetation, under piers, or tight to stumps. On sunny days, they like to stay in shade.

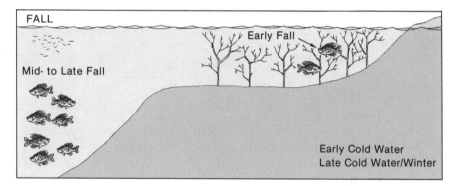

If possible, get out early for bluegills in a pond or small lake. Take a long cane pole, a fiberglass panfish pole, or a light-action spinning or spin-cast rod and reel spooled with 4- or 6-pound-test line. Tie a fixed-bobber rig. Use a long-shank wire hook (#6 or #8), a little split shot, and a bobber. You'll catch far more bluegills with a lightweight bobber rig than with a heavy one.

For bait, try earthworms, crickets, or grasshoppers. You don't need a large bait. Thread a small worm up the shank of the hook, or use only a small piece of night crawler, not a whole worm. A whole cricket or grasshopper is the perfect-size bite for a bluegill.

Next, adjust the bobber so your bait hangs midway between the surface of the water and the bottom. If you can't see bottom and you don't know how deep the pond is, begin fishing 2 to 4 feet deep. If you don't catch fish, experiment with different depths.

Now you're ready to begin fishing. Let's say you think bluegills may be holding around weeds sticking out of the water close to the bank. Lower or cast your bait next to the weeds. The bobber should be floating upright. If it's lying on its side, the bait is probably on bottom. You need to shorten the distance between the bobber and hook so the bait will hang above the bottom.

Be careful not to stand right over the spot you're fishing, especially if the water's clear, because the fish can see you, and they'll spook. Sometimes it's better to sit on the pond bank rather than stand, so your profile's lower. Also, wear natural-colored or camouflage clothes instead of bright colors. Avoid making any commotion that might scare the fish.

If bluegills are present and you haven't spooked them, they'll usually bite with no hesitation. If you don't get a bite in a couple minutes, twitch your bait to get the fish's attention. If you don't get a bite in 3 to 5 minutes, try another spot.

Carefully select locations to place your bait. Keep it close to cover, and if the fish aren't biting well, look for openings in the cover where you can drop the bait without getting hung up.

Fishing is a game of experimenting, so if you're not getting bites, try something different. Fish around another type of structure. If you've been fishing in shallow water, try a deeper area. (Don't forget to lengthen the distance between your bobber and hook.) If the pond has a dam, drop your bait close to it.

Most anglers who pond fish walk the banks, but you have two other options. You can fish from a small boat to cover more water. Be quiet, however, as you move around the pond.

Your second option is wadefishing. This technique is especially good in ponds with a lot of brush, cattails, or similar cover. You can wadefish in old pants and tennis shoes. Don't try this, however, if you're not a good swimmer. You could step in a hole and be in trouble.

Remember to "think structure." Don't drop your bait at some random spot in the middle of the pond and then sit and watch your bobber for an hour. Keep your bait where there's higher potential for getting bites. This type of fishing is like playing around a golf course, except you pick the holes. Keep moving until you begin catching fish. Then slow down and work the area thoroughly. Once you find a productive spot, stay with it as long as the fish keep biting.

One special fishing opportunity exists during spring when bluegills are spawning. They fan nests in only 1 to 4 feet of water, usually in the shallow end of the pond. Many times you can see these nests. They're about the size of a dinner plate, and they're light against the pond's dark bottom.

Many nests are usually clustered in the same area. When you see these bluegill "beds," set your bobber shallow and drop your bait right into them, but try not to spook the fish. You're probably better off casting into the beds, rather than sneaking in close with a long pole. Then get ready to catch some fish! Spawning bluegills are super aggressive, and they bite with little hesitation.

Crappie

Fishing for crappies in ponds and small lakes is similar to fishing for bluegill. Always fish close to structure and stay on the move until you find fish. The primary difference is the bait you use. Crappies prefer minnows over other natural baits, and they also readily attack small jigs and spinners.

Long poles are a favorite with crappie fishermen. Many crappie experts quietly skull a small boat from one piece of structure to the next and use a panfish pole to dangle a minnow or jig in beside the cover. They ease their bait down beside a tree or piece of brush, leave it momentarily, pick it up, set it down on the other side, and then move to the next spot. In ponds and small lakes, crappies scatter throughout shallow structure, and this "hunt-and-peck" method of fishing is very effective. This is especially true in spring, when the fish move into shallow cover to spawn. You can also use this method while wadefishing or fishing from shore, if structure is within reach.

Another good crappie technique is to use a slip-bobber rig with a spinning or spin-cast outfit. Hook a live minnow through the back on a plain hook (#4) or through the lips on a lightweight (1/32 or 1/64 ounce) jig. Then cast this rig next to a weedline, brush pile, or log that is likely to attract crappies.

Slip Bobber Rig

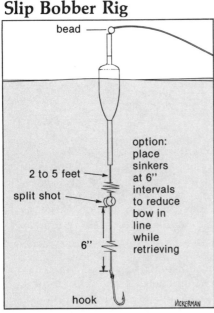

bead

2 to 5 feet
split shot
6"
hook

option: place sinkers at 6" intervals to reduce bow in line while retrieving

VICKERMAN

If you don't get a bite in 10 minutes, try somewhere else. If you get a bite, don't yank if the bobber is just twitching. Wait for the bobber to start moving off or disappear underwater before setting the hook. Crappies have soft mouths, so don't set too hard, or you'll rip out the hook. Instead, smoothly lift up on your pole or rod, and you should have the fish.

If you don't catch fish shallow, try deeper water, especially during hot summer months or on bright, clear days. Adjust your bobber up the line and drop your bait right in front of the dam or off the end of a pier. Or cast into the middle of the pond and see what happens. With this method of fishing, 6 to 12 feet is not too deep to try. There is more uncertainty in this technique, however, because you're hunting for crappies in a less definable area.

But keep trying different locations and depths, and one combination might be the right one.

Another method that allows you to cover a lot of water in a hurry is

116

Jig Tip

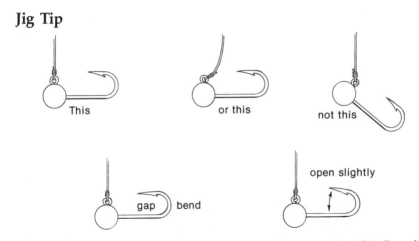

Simply position the knot in the center or slightly back of the jig's eyelet. This allows the jig to remain in a horizontal position and not just hang at an off angle. Remember to re-adjust the knot after catching a fish. An additional tip that will help you hook more crappies is to open the bend of the hook slightly to increase the gap and hooking ability.

casting a 1/16-ounce jig or a small in-line spinner. After casting either lure, count slowly as it sinks. Then after several seconds, begin your retrieve. Experiment with different counts (depths) on succeeding retrieves. If you get a bite, let the bait sink to the same count next time. You may have discovered the depth where crappies are holding. This technique is called the "countdown" method of fishing a sinking bait.

When retrieving the jig, move it slowly, and alternate between a straight pull and a rising/falling path back through the water. With the spinner, a slow, straight retrieve is best. Crappies will usually bite if you pull either of these baits past them.

Bass

Bass fishing is more complicated than fishing for bluegill or crappie because of all the different types of bass tackle and lures. Bass, however, are still members of the sunfish family, and they share certain behavior characteristics with bluegill or crappie. Anywhere you're likely to catch these fish, you're also apt to find bass because they all hold around the same types of structure.

Let's start with the simplest technique. You can catch bass on a long cane or fiberglass pole, but you need a stronger pole than you used on bluegill, and your line should be at least 15-pound test.

Tie on a slip-bobber rig with the bobber set at around 3 feet. Use a 1/0 or 2/0 steel hook. Add a light split shot or Rubbercor sinker 6 inches up from the hook. Then bait this rig with a gob of night crawlers or a live minnow hooked through the back.

Drop your line close to likely fish-holding spots, but don't leave it in one place more than 2 or 3 minutes. If a bass is there, it'll usually take the bait.

117

When you get a bite, wait until the bobber completely disappears underwater before setting the hook. Then pull the fish quickly to the surface and land it.

When using this long-pole method, work your way around the pond, being careful not to let the fish see you. They are extremely skittish and will spook at the first hint of danger.

While this long-pole method is a good one, most fishermen go after pond bass with casting or spinning tackle and artificial lures. Casting allows you to reach targets farther away and to cover more water.

Many artificial lures will catch pond bass, but my three favorites are topwaters, spinnerbaits, and plastic worms.

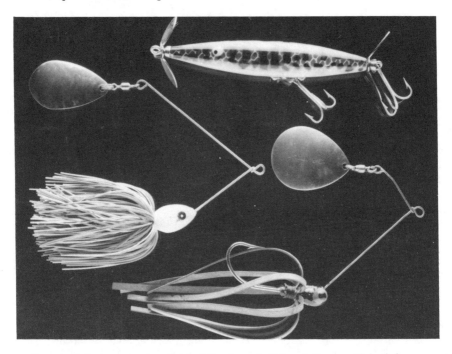

Topwater baits can trigger explosive strikes (upper). Spinnerbaits are mid-depth lures (lower) and both long and short arm styles are good—note ball bearing swivel on blade of short-arm spinnerbait.

Try topwaters early in the morning, late in the afternoon, or at night (during summer) when the surface is calm. In warmer months, I prefer poppers and propeller baits that make a lot of noise and attract bass from a distance. In early spring, I like the quieter floating minnows.

Cast topwaters close to weeds, beside logs or stumps, along dams, or anywhere you think bass might be holding and where your lure won't hang up. Cast past a particular object. Then work the bait up to where you think the fish are. Allow the bait to rest motionless for several seconds, and then twitch it with your rod tip, just enough to cause the slightest ripple on the water. This is usually when the strike comes!

If a spot looks good, but you don't get a strike, cast back to it several times. Sometimes you have to agitate inactive bass into striking. They may not be feeding, but they may strike if a lure keeps invading their territory.

Sometimes, though, bass just won't strike a surface lure. If you don't get any action on a topwater lure in 15 minutes, switch to a spinnerbait and work the same area, running your lure underwater. Usually, keep your retrieve steady, although sometimes it pays to flutter the bait or allow it to sink after it runs past a log, stump, treetop, or other high-percentage fish-holding piece of structure. Spinnerbaits will swim through brush, weeds, and other cover that'll hang up a topwater.

Don't be afraid to cast a spinnerbait through this structure. Just keep the bait moving during the retrieve. You'll hang up occasionally—use strong line with these baits so you can pull them free—but you'll also get more strikes by fishing the thick stuff. An occasional lost bait is a small price to pay for more action.

Plastic worms are what I call "last-resort baits." Bass can usually be coaxed into striking worms when they won't hit other lures, and plastic worms can be worked slower and through the thickest cover. They're also good for taking bass in deep water. Plastic worms are good for mid-day fishing in hot weather, or any time the fish aren't actively feeding.

For pond bass, use a 4- to 7½-inch plastic worm rigged Texas-style with a 1/8- or 1/4-ounce slip sinker. (The heavier sinker is for deeper water.) Cast the worm right into cover rather than close to it. Then crawl it slowly through the cover, lifting it with the rod tip, then allowing it to settle back to the bottom.

When you're fishing moss, lily pads, brush, or other thick vegetation, cast to openings and pockets. Also, cast to points, ends of weedbeds or riprap, and corners of piers.

If you don't get action in the shallows, and you suspect the bass are deeper, it's time to change tactics. Since you can't see underwater to locate structure, you have to do some interpreting based on what you *can* see above the surface. Find a gully feeding into the shallow end of the pond. Then try to imagine how this gully runs along the pond bottom, and cast your plastic worm along it. This could be prime bass-holding structure.

A second deep-water strategy is to cast a plastic worm into the deep end or along the dam and then crawl it back up the bank. And the third option is to simply walk along the bank and cast at random, hoping you'll locate bass along some unknown structure. In smaller ponds, this is likely, since it won't take long to cover the whole pond. In all these cases, however, it's very important to allow your plastic worm to sink to bottom before starting your retrieve.

When casting to deep spots, if you get a bite or catch a fish, throw several more casts, because bass often school together in deep water. There are likely to be more fish where the first one came from.

There are other baits you might use in special situations. Many ponds have heavy weedbeds. You can fish them with a topwater spoon that wobbles over plants and attracts bass lying underneath. Leadhead jigs tipped with pork rind or a plastic trailer can be hopped rapidly across bottom when searching deep-water areas. Diving crankbaits are also good for random casting into deep spots.

Wadefishing or skulling a small boat are good alternatives to fishing from the bank. If a pond or small lake is too large to cast to the middle, a boat let's you move within range of midpond structure. Wadefishing lets you sneak close to thick structure and be precise in dropping your bait into tight spots.

A third way to fish ponds is with a tube float, a large inner tube with a sewn-in seat. (Tube floats are explained in detail in Chapter 14.) In a tube float, you can cover a pond or small lake thoroughly, quietly, and with little effort.

Catfish/Bullheads

Catfish and bullheads are bottom dwellers, so this is where you should fish for them. Although they normally prefer deep water, they may move up and feed in the shallows. In either location, you should fish directly on bottom without a float or just above bottom with a float.

While you moved a lot searching for bluegill, crappie, and bass, fishing for catfish and bullheads is more of a pick-one-spot-and-wait-'em-out method. Since these fish find their food by smelling, you have to leave your bait in one place long enough for the scent to spread through the water and for the fish to home in on it. In essence, when you're fishing for bluegill, crappie, and bass, you have to find the fish. Catfish and bullheads will find you.

You can fish for these species with long poles, but I prefer spin-cast or spinning outfits so I can cast farther off the bank. I take at least two rods for this type of fishing. I pick a spot on the bank close to deep water (the dam, a point, etc.). Then I cut a forked stick for each rod and push it into the ground next to the pond's edge. I toss out my lines, prop my rods in the forked sticks, and wait for something to happen.

When I'm using two rods, I tie a bottom rig on one and a slip-bobber rig on the other. This gives the catfish or bullheads a choice of a bait lying on bottom or hanging just above it.

Catfish grow much larger than bullheads, so if catfish are your main target, you need larger hooks. I'd recommend a #1 or 1/0 sproat or baitholder hook. But if you're fishing mainly for bullheads, select a smaller hook, say a #6. If you're trying for both species, use something in between, either a #2 or #4.

Catfish and bullheads will eat the same baits. Earthworms or night crawlers are two favorites. Chicken livers, live or dead minnows, grasshoppers, and a wide variety of commercially-prepared stink baits also work well. With all these baits, load your hooks. The more bait on them, the more scent you have in the water, and the more likely you'll attract fish.

Cast your baited lines into deep water. With the bottom rig, wait until the sinker is on bottom, then gently reel in line until all the slack is out. With a slip-bobber rig, set the bobber so the bait is suspended just above bottom.

Now all you have to do is wait for a bite. Sit down, relax, read a book, let your mind wander. Keep a steady watch for a bite, however. When a fish takes the bottom-rig bait, the rod tip will jump. When there's a bite on the slip-bobber bait, the bobber will dance nervously on the surface.

If you get a bite, don't set the hook until the fish starts swimming away with the bait. Pick up the rod and get ready to set the hook, but don't exert any pull until the line starts moving steadily off or the bobber goes under and stays. Then strike back hard and begin playing your fish.

If you're not getting bites, how long do you stay in one place before moving to another spot? Probably the best answer is "as long as your patience endures." The best catfishermen are usually the ones who wait the longest. But at the minimum, you should fish in one spot at least 30 minutes before moving somewhere else.

Catfish like to feed in low-light periods of dawn, dusk, or at night. If you'd like to try night fishing, buy a small metal bell and fasten it to the end of your rod. When you get a bite, the bell will ring, indicating that a fish has your bait.

Trout

Trout are generally thought of as fish of streams and large lakes. But they can also live in ponds with cool water year-round. Northern beaver ponds are great places for wild brook trout, and spring-fed manmade ponds can sustain stocked rainbows.

Trout don't relate to structure the way warm-water fish do. They'll roam a pond or small lake at random, and they're likely to be at any depth. So the best way to locate them is walking the bank and fishing different areas.

You can catch trout on either natural bait or artificials. Use spin-cast or spinning tackle and 4- or 6-pound-test line. For fishing natural bait, you can either use a bobber rig or a very lightweight slip-sinker rig. Bait with a night crawler, grasshopper, commercially preserved salmon eggs, whole kernel corn, or small marshmallows. Use a #8 short-shank hook, since trout have small mouths. Move around and experiment with different depths and presentations until you find a combination the trout like.

If you prefer to use artificials, stick with very small crankbaits, sinking spoons, in-line spinners, or minnow lures. Again, walk along the bank and cast at random. If you're casting a lure that sinks, use the countdown method to fish different depths until you find the level where trout are holding.

HOW TO FISH LARGE
LAKES AND RESERVOIRS

Large lakes and reservoirs are some of North America's most popular, most accessible fishing locations. Most large lakes are public and have piers, boat ramps, and other facilities to accommodate fishermen. They usually support many different species of fish, so they offer many opportunities for beginning anglers.

It's necessary to distinguish between lakes and reservoirs. A lake is natural, while a reservoir (or impoundment) is manmade. Natural lakes are plentiful in the northern U.S. and Canada, in Florida, and southern Georgia, along major river systems, in western mountains; and they're scattered sparsely through the rest of the continent.

Natural lakes take several forms. Some have rounded, shallow basins with soft bottoms. Others are very deep with irregular shapes and bottoms that include reefs, islands, drop-offs, and other structure. In many natural lakes, abundant vegetation grows in shallow areas.

Natural lakes vary in age and fertility—measures of their ability to support fish populations. Some are young (relatively speaking) and infertile, while others are much older and more fertile.

Reservoirs throughout the U.S. and Canada are created by building a dam across a river or stream and backing up water behind it. Dozens of reservoirs, built since World War II, provide water and electrical power and control floods.

In most cases, the bottoms of reservoirs once were farmlands or forests. As the water rose, it covered fields, woods, creeks, roads, buildings, and other features which, when submerged, became structure. Where man once lived and worked, fish now swim.

Reservoirs are divided into two basic categories: upland and mainstream. Upland reservoirs are built in highlands and canyons. Their shape is deep and irregular. A map of an upland reservoir might look like an octupus with arms running in all directions. In contrast, mainstream reservoirs are built in lowlands, where larger rivers run straighter courses through broad, flat valleys. These reservoirs are wider and shallower than upland reservoirs. They typically have a long lake stem with numerous smaller tributary bays running off to the sides of the main body.

The fertility of a reservoir often depends on how fertile the area was before it was flooded. Mainstream reservoirs impounded over river-bottom farmland are highly fertile, especially if trees are left standing when the water is backed up. As the trees rot, they release nutrients that support fish life. On the other hand, highland or canyon areas usually are less fertile, so it follows that upland reservoirs are also less fertile. This is why upland reservoirs seldom support fish populations as large as those in lowland reservoirs.

Analyzing Large Lakes and Reservoirs

It's easy for a beginning angler standing on the bank of a large lake or reservoir to feel overwhelmed. There's so much territory, so many places where fish can be. Where and how do you start?

Begin by adjusting your attitude. Since there's more water, there are more fish, so your odds for success are roughly the same as when you're fishing a pond or smaller lake.

And that's exactly how you treat this situation. It's impossible to fish an entire large lake or reservoir. So choose one small part of it, approach it like a pond or small lake, and use the same tactics explained in the previous section. Whether they live in big or small waters, fish react the same to similar conditions in their environment. The basics still apply, and the same tactics work in small *and* large waters. It's almost that simple. The main difference is that, since they aren't confined in small ponds, fish in large lakes and reservoirs have more freedom to roam, and they may migrate from one area of the lake to another, depending on the season, food supply, and other factors. Therefore, when deciding where to fish on a big lake, you have to pick the right small part.

How do you do this? Ask in a nearby tackle store where the fish are biting. Notice where other anglers are fishing. Try to determine if the fish are shallow or deep. Learn the depth where they're biting. Use whatever information you can gather to get an overall picture of where the fish are, and then key in on these locations.

Typical Shallow Spawning Bay

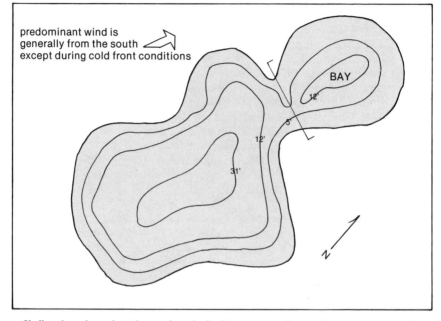

predominant wind is generally from the south except during cold front conditions

BAY

Shallow bays located at the north end of a lake are typically the first areas to warm in early spring. Such bays generally draw the first, shallow-spawning movements of spring crappies.

Also, one aid that all anglers should learn to use is a topographic map. A "topo" map shows water depth and changes in the lake bottom. You can look at a topo map and find structure—drop-offs, reefs, flats, sunken islands, etc. Then you can use this map to locate the types of spots where you've learned the fish are. For instance, if the tackle store operator tells you that crappie are spawning around shoreline in shallow bays, you can locate shallow bays on your topo map, see how to get to them, and then fish them.

As you progress in fishing, you'll learn just how much information these maps offer. In essence, they are road maps to the hot spots. Get one for the lake where you plan to fish and begin studying it.

Techniques for Fishing Large Lakes and Reservoirs

Large lakes and reservoirs support many different fish species. Some have only warm-water fish, some only cold-water fish, and some a mixture of the two. When you go fishing, single out which species you'd like to catch, and then tailor your efforts around it.

Obviously it's not possible in this section to discuss *all* places and methods for catching different types of fish from large lakes and reservoirs. Instead, I'll give you the best, easiest big-water opportunities for beginning anglers. I'll identify *key* areas and times, and then I'll explain how to fish them. Once you've mastered these basics, you can learn more complex methods.

Bluegill

There's little difference in fishing for bluegills in small ponds or in large lakes. Catching them is a simple matter of figuring out their locations and then placing a bait in front of them.

In spring, bluegills migrate into the shallows to spawn, so look for them in bays along wind-protected shorelines. Before spawning, these fish hold around brush, stumps, weeds, rocks, or other structure in 2 to 8 feet of water. Then as the water temperature climbs into the high 60°F range, bluegills will move up 1 to 4 feet deep and spawn in areas that have firm bottoms—gravel, sand, clay.

Long poles or light-action spinning or spin-cast tackle will take these fish. Use fixed or slip-bobber rigs with worms or crickets. Keep your bait right beside cover. When fishing a spawning area, drop the bait right into the "beds"—lighter, dish-shaped ovals on darker bottoms.

After spawning, bluegills head back to deeper water. Many fish will still hold around visible cover, but they prefer to be close to deep water. Two classic examples are a weedline on the edge of a drop-off and a steep rocky bank. Many bluegills linger right along the edges of these weeds and rocks.

A-Just-A-Bubble Rig

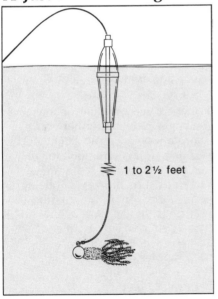

1 to 2 ½ feet

Besides a bobber rig, another good way to take these fish is "jump-jigging," which involves casting a 1/16-ounce tube jig into the weeds or rocks. Use a very light spinning outfit. Slowly pull it away from the weeds or rocks and let the jig sink along the edge. Set the hook whenever you feel a bump or tug. This technique requires a boat, since you have to be over the deep, open water casting into the weeds. If you try jump-jigging from the bank, you'll have to pull your jig back through thick cover, and you'll snag every time.

Docks, fishing piers, or bridges are good locations to catch post-spawn bluegill. The water may be deep, but usually the fish will be up near the surface, holding under or close to this manmade structure. Don't stand on a dock, pier, or bridge and cast far out into the water because the fish are likely under your feet. Set your bobber so your bait will hang deeper than you can see it, and then keep it close to the structure.

Sometimes you may have to experiment with different depths to find where bluegill are holding, and change locations if you're not getting bites. But once you find the fish, work the area thoroughly. Bluegill collect in big schools after spawning, so you can catch several in one place.

One special bluegill opportunity exists when insects are hatching. Mayflies hatch by the millions on my home lake in the summer. They swarm around shoreline trees and bushes, and hordes of hungry bluegill collect just under the surface to eat flies that fall into the water. If you can find insects swarming over the water and fish swirling beneath them, get ready for some hot action! Just thread one of the flies onto your hook, and drop it into this natural dining room. You're almost guaranteed fish.

Crappie

Crappies follow the same seasonal patterns as bluegills, except slightly earlier. When spring breaks, crappies head into bays and quiet coves to get ready for spawning. When the water warms into the mid-60°F range, they fan out into the shallows to spawn. They spawn in or around brush, reeds. stumps, logs, roots, submerged timber, or artificial fish attractors. Crappie spawning depth depends on water color. In dingy water, they may spawn only a foot or two deep. But in clear water, they'll spawn deeper, even as far down as 15 feet. A good starting point is 1 to 2 feet below the depth at which your bait sinks out of sight.

Minnows or small plastic jigs are the best baits. Drop them next to or into potential spawning cover. You can do this from the bank, from a boat, or by wadefishing the shallows. Lower the bait down, wait 30 seconds, then pick it up and move it. When fishing a brush pile, tree top, or reed patch, try moving the bait around in the cover. If you catch one fish, put the bait back into the same spot to try for another.

Stay on the move until you find some action. With this technique, you go to the fish. Don't wait for the fish to come to the bait.

After the spawn, crappies head back toward deeper water, where they collect along sunken ledges, old creek channels, and other types of sharp bottom-contour breaks. This is where a topo map can help. Study the map to find these breaks. If you're fishing from shore, look for spots where deep water runs close to the bank.

Then go to these areas and look for treetops, brush, logs, or other cover. Fish these spots with minnows or jigs. Or if there is no visible cover, cast jigs randomly from shore. Wait until the jig sinks to the bottom before starting your retrieve. Then use a slow, steady retrieve to work the bait back up the bank. Set the hook when you feel any slight bump or when you see your line twitch. Crappies can hit very lightly, so you have to be alert.

Fish attractors offer another good deep-water crappie opportunity. Many state fish and wildlife agencies sink brush, stakes, or similar cover into prime deep-water areas to draw fish. These attractors are marked to show their location. They may be out in a bay or around fishing piers

Crappie-Go-Round

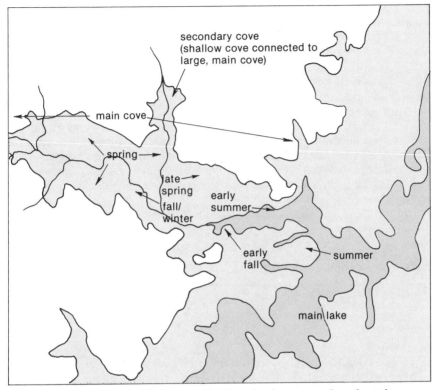

Flatland-reservoir crappies display a predictable cycle of movement throughout the year. The accompanying map shows a portion of Kentucky Lake along the Kentucky/Tennessee border.

The spring spawning season finds large numbers of crappies in the mid- to back- sections of shallow, secondary coves. After they spawn, the fish begin slowly dropping back toward the main lake. They don't race to deeper water; rather, they gradually migrate toward their summer habitat.

Summer crappies relate primarily to the drop-offs along deep creek channels and the main river channel, so you should concentrate your efforts in the main portion of the lake. Then, as the water cools in early fall, the crappies begin moving back toward the large coves again.

Fall and winter finds huge schools of crappies gathering along channel edges in the center to outer portions of the coves. They don't move as far back into the coves as they did in spring, largely because the drawdown has typically lowered the lake level 3 to 5 feet.

or bridges. These are always high-percentage crappie spots. Dangle minnows or jigs around the edges and into the middle of cover. You'll hang up once in awhile, but you'll also catch a lot more fish.

If you hang on underwater cover, don't break your line. Instead, pull up with light, quick jerks, allowing the line to go slack once you feel the snag. Keep trying to jiggle or bump your hook free. If it won't come, then pull it with slow, steady pressure. This may straighten your hook rather than break your line.

Bass

Spring, early summer, and fall are the three best times for beginning anglers to try for bass. This is when the fish are aggressive and shallow. When they're deep, they may be tough even for the pros to find.

Bass spend most of their time in or around cover like brush, weeds, lily pads, and timber, or under docks and logs, and beside stumps, rocks, and bridge pilings. By casting around structure, you've always got a chance for a strike.

In spring, bass spawn in shallow, wind-sheltered coves and shore-lines, especially the ones with hard bottoms of sand, gravel, or clay. During the spawning season, try top-water minnows, spinnerbaits, and plastic lizards in these areas and around the structure listed above. Bass love to position their nests next to logs, rockpiles, or other cover that provides security from egg-eating sunfish.

After spawning, bass may stay shallow for several weeks. Try casting the shallows, but if you don't get bites, work your way toward deeper water.

Bass On Points

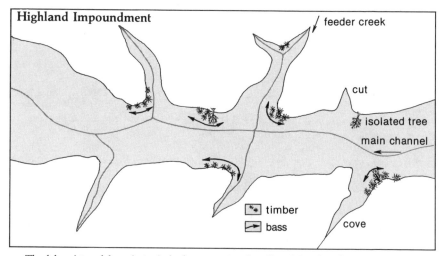

The lake pictured here is typical of many natural walleye lakes found across the north country. It's part of a chain of lakes, has a feeder stream for a water source, and a spiller dam to regulate the water level.

This is a good time to fish points—a ridge of land that runs off into the water. Stand on the tip of the point and fancast crankbaits, plastic worms, or noisy top-water lures around the point. Pay special attention to any additional structure, such as brush, stumps, rocks, or weeds. If you don't get a strike the first time through such a high-potential spot, cast back to it several times. Sometimes you have to rile bass before they'll hit.

Despite the warm water temperatures of summer, good bass fishing can be found. Early and late in the day are best times. Some will still be in the shallows, especially if baitfish are present. Other bass will be along deeper areas, or shallow flats that border deep water. Fish along reefs, weedlines, channel drop-offs, edges of standing timber, or even around boat docks. Also, cast to any isolated piece of structure, such as a log, brush top, or rock pile.

Crankbaits and spinnerbaits are good lures for hot-weather bass, since you can fish them fast and cover a lot of water. If you go through a likely area without getting a bite, try a plastic worm. The fish may be in an inactive mood, and it'll take a slower presentation to get them to hit.

Still, don't spend much time in one area if you're not getting any action. Move around and try to find where fish are concentrated. Be especially alert for minnows. At this time of year, you'll find bass where you find baitfish.

In fall, concentrate on shorelines and shallows in coves. Water temperature cools off here first, and the bass move in and feed heavily on baitfish. Use the same tactics and baits you did in spring. Pay special attention to the cover spots and the presence of baitfish. Also, in reservoirs, try the extreme backs of major bays, where feeder creeks empty into the reservoir. Sometimes bass gang up in unbelievable numbers in these locations.

Catfish/Bullheads

Big lakes can hold big catfish, and best action is in late spring during the spawn. These fish move into the banks and look for holes and protected areas to lay their eggs. When they're up shallow, they're vulnerable to savvy anglers.

Banks with big rock bluffs, riprap, etc. are hot spots during the spawn. Fish around these areas with fixed or slip-bobber rigs baited with gobs of worms or night crawlers. Set your float so the bait hangs just above the rocks. Use medium strength line (10- to 17-pound test) and a steel hook (1 to 3/0), since the possibility of hooking a big fish exists.

After the spawn, catfish head back to deep water flats and channels. Normally, they spend daylight hours deep, and they move up and feed in adjacent shallows at night. Find a point, causeway, or some other spot where the bank slopes off into deep water; and fish here from late afternoon well into the night.

Use a bottom rig for this technique, and bait with worms, cut bait, liver, commercial stink bait, or any of many other popular catfish baits. Set up more than one rod where allowed, propping them in forked sticks stuck into the ground, and tie a small bell to the end of each rod. When a catfish bites, the bell will ring.

One other easy and productive method for taking catfish is called "jug fishing." This method requires a boat and 25 or more milk or bleach jugs. Tie strong lines of 4 to 6 feet onto the jug handles. Tie a 2/0 steel hook on the end of the line, and add a split shot or a clincher sinker 6 inches up from the hook. Bait these lines with minnows or some other catfish bait and throw the jugs overboard on the upwind side of a lake or bay. The wind will float the jugs across the water, and catfish will be drawn to the bait. When a jug starts bobbing on the surface, move the boat in and retrieve your fish.

Bullheads normally stay in warm bays which have silty or muddy bottoms. Like catfish, they stay deep during the day, but they move up shallow and feed from late afternoon through the night.

The technique for taking bullheads is the same as for night-feeding catfish, except you need lighter tackle. A spinning rod, 6-pound line and a #3 hook are a good combination. A small split shot should be clamped on the line a foot up from the hook so the bait will sink. Worms are good bait for bullheads.

Walleye

Walleyes are among the nation's most popular gamefish. They're plentiful throughout the middle and upper regions of the U.S. and in the lower half of Canada. These traditionally deep-water, bottom-hugging fish frequently feed in the shallows. The determining factor seems to be light penetration into the water. Walleyes don't like bright sunlight. But on overcast days, at night, when shallow areas are muddy or wave-swept, or when heavy weed growth provides shade, they may feed in water no deeper than a couple feet.

Walleyes may be the ultimate structure fish. They hold along under-water humps, reefs, and drop-offs on hard, clean bottoms, such as rock or sand. They also prefer water with good circulation. They rarely concentrate in dead-water areas like sheltered bays or coves. Walleyes move

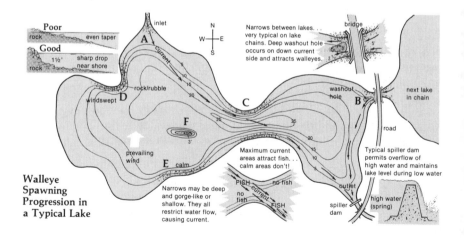

Here's a map that Al Lindner uses to explain some of the fine points of spring walleye location. You'll be surprised at how many subtle factors are involved.

The lake pictured here is typical of many natural walleye lakes found accross the north.

in and out of feeding areas, causing problems for fishermen trying to locate them.

Walleyes spawn when water temperatures climb into the mid-40°F range and this is a good time for beginning anglers to try for these fish. (Check local regulations because many states maintain a closed season until after the spawn.)

Look for shallows or shoal areas with gravel or rock bottoms that are exposed to the wind. Sloping points, islands, reefs, and rock piles close to shore are high-percentage spots to try. Fish them during low-light periods—dawn, dusk, and at night.

A slip-bobber rig baited with a night crawler, leech, or live minnow is a good presentation to use in these areas. Adjust the bobber so the bait is suspended just above bottom. Also, try casting these shallow areas with minnow-tipped jigs or shallow-running crankbaits.

In early summer, walleyes can be caught along weedlines and mid-lake structure, both requiring a boat to properly fish them.

When fishing the weeds, cast a small jig (1/16 or 1/8 ounce) tipped with a minnow right into the edge of the weeds, and then swim it back out. Work slowly along the weedline. Pay special attention to sharp bends in the weedline or areas where the weeds suddenly thin out. (Besides walleye, this technique may also produce bass, crappie, and pike.)

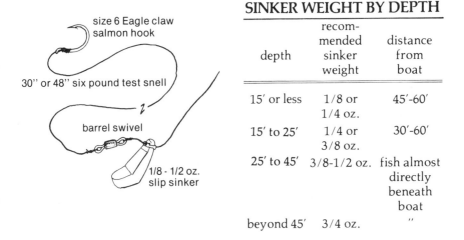

SINKER WEIGHT BY DEPTH

depth	recom-mended sinker weight	distance from boat
15' or less	1/8 or 1/4 oz.	45'-60'
15' to 25'	1/4 or 3/8 oz.	30'-60'
25' to 45'	3/8-1/2 oz.	fish almost directly beneath boat
beyond 45'	3/4 oz.	"

Fishing deep structure can be sort of a needle in a haystack situation, so it's best to stay on the move until you locate fish. If you see other boats clustered in a small area, they're probably fishing productive structure. Go there and try drifting a night crawler on a slip-sinker rig. Move upwind from the other boats, and let line out to the bottom. Then engage your reel and drag the night crawler across bottom as you drift downwind.

A bite will feel like a light tap or bump. Release line immediately, and allow the fish to swim off with the bait. After about 30 seconds of waiting, reel up slack, feel for the fish, and set the hook.

This is the standard way to fish for lake or reservoir walleyes, but there are many other good methods. Bottom-bouncing rigs trailing night crawlers or minnows are great along deep structure or submerged points. This is the same principle as using the slip-sinker rig. Let your line down to bottom, engage the reel, and then simply drag this rig behind you as you drift or troll with an electric motor. A slip-bobber rig drifted across this structure is also a good bet.

As you fish this deep structure, it's a good idea to have a floating marker handy. If you get a bite, throw out the marker, and then come back to this spot after you've landed your fish. Walleyes are school fish, so there are probably more in the same area.

Beginners should try two other simple approaches for walleyes. First, find a rocky shoreline area that slopes off quickly into deep water. Fish this from dusk to around midnight, either with live bait (slip-bobber rig) or by casting floating minnow lures. Second, cast into areas where strong winds are pushing heavy waves into shore. This wave action usually has the water muddied, and walleyes move right up to the banks to feed. Use a jig and minnow; either walk the banks or wade the shallows, casting as you go. Pay special attention to the zone where muddy water borders clear.

White Bass

White bass are fish of open water. During the spring spawning migration, they leave the main lake and swim up tributary streams and creeks. But at any other time, they are usually in the main body of a lake or reservoir, feeding on small baitfish.

The best chance for beginners to catch white bass occurs when they're surface feeding. From early summer through fall, schools of white bass herd baitfish to the surface and then slash through them, feeding savagely on the panic-stricken minnows. When white bass are surface feeding, almost any bright, fast-moving lure cast into this action will get a strike.

White bass normally feed around sunken islands, reefs, flats next to the main channel, or where submerged creeks empty into the main channel. There are two shortcuts to finding these spots: (1) ask the marina operator where you launch where white bass have been surface-feeding, or (2) motor out onto the lake and look for a cluster of boats. Usually white bass will surface feed for a short period, go back down to wait for more baitfish, and then come up again. Wait over known surface feeding areas and then cast fast and furiously when the fish show up.

Be ready with a spoon, in-line spinner, vibrating crankbait or any-thing else that simulates a fleeing minnow. When you see any sign of surface feeding, cast as close as you can and start reeling fast! It's a good idea to have a spare rod rigged and ready. Then, when you land a fish, instead of having to remove the hooks, you can drop that rod, grab the other one, and fire off another cast with little wasted time. When white bass are feeding on the surface, take maximum advantage of the short period they're up.

Another good way to catch white bass in big lakes or reservoirs is to fish at night under lights. Good locations are the ends of points which drop into deep water or under bridges which cross the lake. Position two or more lanterns close to the water. Or buy floating lights powered by batteries. Then use a two-hook panfish rig to fish minnows close to bottom directly under the lights. Lower this rig until it bumps bottom. Then crank up 3 or 4 turns and hold the rig still. Baitfish will be drawn to the lights, and if white bass are in the area, they'll feed on the minnows.

Northern Pike

Pike fishing is best in spring, early summer, and fall, when these fish are in quiet, weedy waters. They are normally very aggressive, attacking

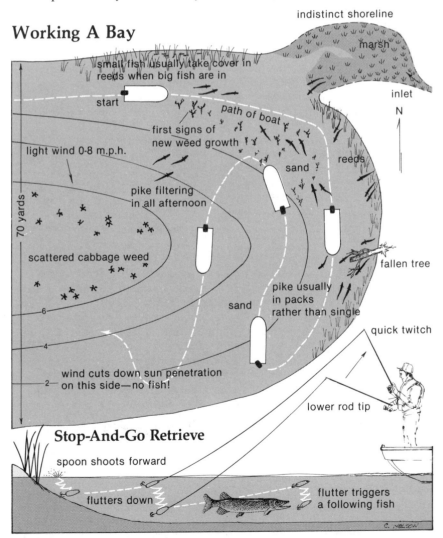

Working A Bay

indistinct shoreline

marsh

small fish usually take cover in reeds when big fish are in

start

inlet

N

first signs of new weed growth

path of boat

light wind 0-8 m.p.h.

sand

reeds

pike filtering in all afternoon

70 yards

scattered cabbage weed

fallen tree

pike usually in packs rather than single

sand

sand

quick twitch

wind cuts down sun penetration on this side—no fish!

6

4

2

lower rod tip

Stop-And-Go Retrieve

spoon shoots forward

flutters down

flutter triggers a following fish

C. NELSON

anything moving that presents a tempting target. This makes pike a prime target for beginning anglers.

Look for pike in bays, sloughs, flats, and coves that have submerged weedbeds, clusters of emergent weeds, logs, or other "hideout" structure. Pike stay fairly shallow in water depths of 3 to 15 feet.

Since pike can get big, and even the small ones are aggressive, use fairly heavy tackle. Many experts use 15- to 20-pound-test line. Also, pike have sharp teeth that can easily cut monofilament. For this reason, always rig with a short steel leader ahead of your lure or bait.

Pike usually hold along the edges of weedbeds or in pockets in vegetation. Find a place where you have access to likely cover. Then cast a large, brightly-colored spoon next to or over this cover. You can cast from the bank or wadefish, staying on the move to cover a lot of water. If you have a boat, motor to the upwind side of a shallow bay and drift slowly downwind, casting to clumps of weeds, weededges, and other high-potential spots. Retrieve the spoon steadily, but if pike don't seem interested, pump the spoon up and down or jerk it erratically to trigger strikes.

Other good lures for pike are large spinnerbaits, in-line spinners, large floating minnows, and wide-wobbling crankbaits.

Live-bait fishing is also extremely effective on pike. A large helpless minnow suspended under a fixed-bobber rig is almost irresistible to these fish. Clip a strong 1/0 or 2/0 hook onto the end of a wire leader. Add a couple split shot above the leader. Then clip on a large round bobber at a depth so the minnow will be up off bottom. The minnow can be hooked either through the back or lips.

Cast this rig to weedlines, pockets, points, or other structure. Then sit back and wait for a bite. When the bobber goes under, give the fish slack as it makes its first run with the bait. Then, when the pike stops, reel in slack line, feel for the fish, and set the hook hard.

Yellow Perch

Yellow perch are widespread and easy to catch. They tend to be small, but what they lack in size, they make up for in numbers and eating quality. Deep-fried perch will knock your socks off!

Yellow perch spawn in early spring when the water temperature climbs into the high 40°F range. They head into a lake's feeder streams or shallows, and during this migration, they are extremely easy to catch.

A fixed- or slip-bobber rig is a good choice for perch. Use light line (4- to 8-pound test) and a #6 long-shank hook. Add a small split shot and bobber, bait with worms or live minnows, and drop the bait into shallow areas around brush, reeds, or other similar cover. If perch are present, one should bite in a few seconds. If you don't get quick action, try somewhere else.

After the spawn, these fish return to main-lake areas where they're more difficult to locate. Smaller fish hold along weedlines, and jump-jigging is a good way to take them. (Refer back to the "Bluegill" part of this section.) But larger perch move onto reefs, ledges, deep points, and other structure, and they hang close to the bottom. They often hold as

134

deep as 40 feet.

Again, ask bait dealers about good deep-water perch spots. When you find one, fish it with a two-hook panfish rig. Bump your bait along bottom to attract strikes. If you catch a fish, unhook it quickly and drop a fresh bait right back into the same spot. Other perch will be drawn by the commotion, and sometimes you can catch them one after another.

HOW TO FISH SMALL STREAMS

While large lakes and reservoirs are North America's most popular fishing spots, streams are the most overlooked. Fish-filled streams flow throughout the continent, yet most receive only a fraction of the fishing pressure that big lakes do. Many anglers ignore streams because they take more effort to find and fish. There are few piers, marinas, tackle stores, boat ramps, or other conveniences to accommodate anglers.

Because streams receive so little pressure, fish in them are naive, and therefore easier to catch. Also, streams are easy to "read" when it comes to determining fish locations. These are two reasons why small rivers and creeks are among my favorite fishing spots.

Streams are divided into two main classifications: warm water and cold water. Warm-water streams harbor typical warm-water species: bass, smaller sunfish, catfish, white bass. Warm-water streams differ in character, ranging from clear, fast-moving, whitewater-and-rock-laced streams to muddy, slow, deep streams.

Cold-water streams are normally found at higher altitudes or in valleys that drain highlands. Their primary gamefish are various trout species. Cold-water streams are usually clean and fairly shallow, and they have medium-to-fast current. Their bottoms are typically rock or sand.

You can fish small streams by either of two methods: wading or floating. In summer, wade in old tennis shoes and blue jeans. In spring and fall, waders or hip boots are necessary to keep out the chill.

When wadefishing, you should work upstream, because you'll continuously stir up silt and debris from the bottom. By fishing upcurrent, this sediment drifts behind you instead of in front of you, so the fish aren't alerted to your presence.

Floating takes more planning and effort than wading, but it may also offer greater rewards. On many streams, floating can take you into semi-virgin fishing territory. When floating, a boat is like a golf cart that carries you over the course. It's a convenience that allows you to cover more territory. I prefer a canoe when float fishing, but jonboats or inflatables also work. An in-depth discussion of the attributes of these boats is found in Chapter 14.

Analyzing Small Streams

Current is *the* primary influence in the life of a stream fish. Current is like liquid wind, "blowing" food downstream and shaping the stream environment. It determines where the fish will find food and cover, two life essentials. This is why stream fishermen must always be aware of current and how it affects fish location. Understanding current and a fish's reaction to it is the key to successful stream fishing.

Basically, fish react to current in one of three ways. (1) They will be out in fast water chasing food. (2) They will position themselves in an eddy right at the edge of current, where they can hold and watch for food without using much energy. (3) They will hold in quiet pools where current is slow. As we'll see in the next section, different species vary in the amount of current they prefer and the places they hold.

The typical stream is made up of series of shallow riffles where current is swift; deep pools where current is slow; and medium-depth runs where current is intermediate. Riffles normally empty into deep pools. Runs usual-

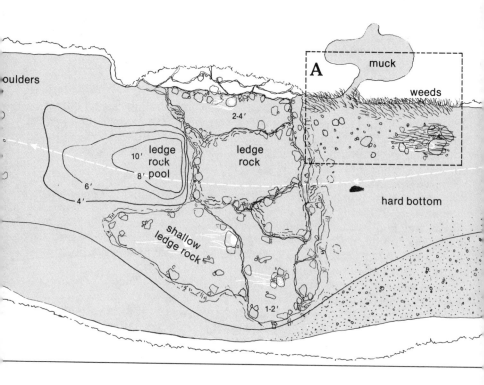

Here's a stretch of river showing many features found in typical, small rivers. Obviously, in order to show as many elements as possible, many features were compressed into this short stretch. Remember, rivers are viewed by stretches, because rarely is a stream the same from beginning to end. Different stretches of the same stream may have different personalities. Consequently, different fish species are present.

River stretches, like area B, consist of alternating riffle/pool/riffle areas. The stream bed is composed of sections of sand, gravel, rocks and some boulders. In addition, ledge rock outcroppings may be present in some rivers.

Rocks provide a current break and cover for the fish. Pools, both shallow and deep, can be located between the riffle areas. Sometimes, humps or even islands can be present and provide another form of current break.

Occasionally, area A, a muck-bottomed bay may be attached to the river, and weeds may grow in adjacent areas at the mouth of the connecting channel. These weedy areas can be an overlooked hot spot.

While the overall depth of the water depends on many factors (rain, melt-water, ect.), the average depth normally ranges from 3 to 10 feet, depending on the river.

Most pools following a rapids are 6 to 10 feet deep and occasionally deeper. Larger, deeper pools may function as a home area throughout the year.

Obviously, not all rivers will have all the features discussed, but the basic principals are the same, Simply read the water!

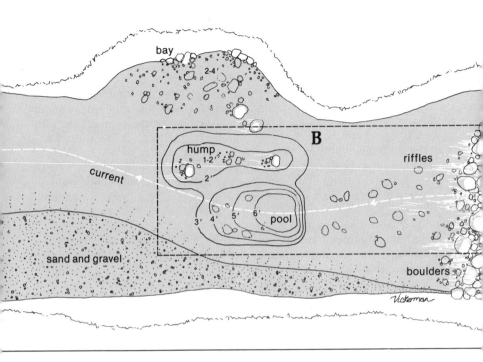

ly drain the downstream ends of these pools, and the runs lead into succeeding riffles. This progression repeats itself over and over as a stream winds through the countryside.

Logs, stumps, rocks, roots, and weeds are examples of attractive stream cover. Many stream fish like to hide under or close to cover and then dart out and grab a crayfish or minnow when the opportunity arises.

So basically, analyzing a stream is a matter of studying the current, water depth, and cover. The more experience you gain at this, the better you'll become at figuring out where stream fish hide. For now, though, remember that stream fish are consistent in the types of places where they hold. Catch one fish from behind a log, and chances are others will be hiding behind other logs further up or downstream.

Techniques for Fishing Small Streams

Information in the previous section involved stream fishing generalities. Now we get specific, learning exactly where to find different species and how to catch them.

In the process, understand that stream fish are more confined than lake or reservoir fish. In big lakes, fish have a lot of room to move around, but in streams, they have to be somewhere along one narrow waterway. Veteran stream anglers can look at a stretch of water and immediately pick out the good places. The only real question is getting the fish to bite. Following are high-percentage methods for doing this.

Bass

Smallmouth bass are found in streams from the Mid-South into southern Canada. These fish are willing biters and hard fighters, and they can immediately offer new anglers some of the greatest pleasures in this sport.

Smallmouth hold in eddies behind or under cover adjacent to fast currents. Typical spots would be behind a rock or a root wad that splits the current; beneath an undercut bank that lies beside a fast run; along edges (and especially ends) of weedbeds; or under a lip or rocky bar at the head of a pool where a riffle empties into it. I always pay special attention to holes gouged out where a stream makes a turn.

Smallmouths prefer shade, not bright sunshine. Any place that offers concealment, quiet water, and immediate access to fast water is a potential smallmouth hot spot. Depth of such locations can vary. I've caught stream smallmouths from a foot of water, and also from 10 feet.

To fish these places, I recommend spinning or spin-cast tackle and 4- to 8-pound-test line. You'll need something fairly light, because most stream smallmouth baits are small.

These fish feed on crayfish, minnows, worms, mature insects, and larvae. The best artificial baits imitate these natural foods. Small crayfish crankbaits are deadly. So are floating minnows, in-line spinners, small jigs, and plastic worms. But my favorite lure for stream smallmouths is a brown 4-inch hollow-bodied tube jig (Fat Gitzit). They have a hard time turning this lure down.

The key with all these baits is to work them close to cover. Cast your lure across or up the current, and work it right through the spot where you think a bass might be holding. I like to swim a Fat Gitzit parallel to a log or a deep-cut bank. I also like to crawl a crayfish crankbait or float a minnow lure over logs, rock, or stumps. I'll cast a jig into the head of a pool, allow it to sink, and then hop it across bottom.

Sometimes stream smallmouths will show a definite preference for one type bait. In early spring, floating minnows or in-line spinners seem to work best. Later on, Gitzits, crayfish baits, and jigs are better. So experiment with different lures to learn what the fish prefer.

One of the secrets to catching stream smallmouth on artificial lures is accurate casting. You've got to get your lure close to the fish. This means sometimes you've got to get close to the fish. So when stream fishing, wear camouflage or natural colors that won't spook fish. Ease in from a downstream or cross-stream position and cast upstream of where the fish should be. Then use the current and your rod tip to steer the bait into the strike zone.

One note on float fishing streams. When I see a place where smallmouth should be, I beach the canoe, get out, and walk around the spot. Then I ease in close from the downstream side and start casting. It's easier to cast accurately while standing stationary instead of floating by the spot. Also, if I hook a fish, I can concentrate on playing it without worrying about controlling the canoe.

Smallmouths can be taken on several different live baits, but crayfish are best. Use a slip-sinker rig (#1 hook) to work crayfish through rocks and heads of pools. Ease them along bottom in likely spots, and set the hook at the first hint of pickup.

Many slower, deeper streams will harbor spotted or largemouth bass instead of smallmouths, while some streams have all three species. Fish for them the way you do for smallmouths. Cast around cover objects. Work the ends and edges of pools, and stay alert for any sign of feeding activity. If you see a bass chasing minnows, cast to that area immediately.

Rock Bass

The rock bass is a small panfish that's plentiful in most warm-water streams. It has many local names: goggle-eye, redeye, black perch. Rock bass almost always hit a lure pulled through their feeding zone, and they're very predictable in location. These two traits make them easy to catch.

Rock bass hold along the sides of quiet pools. They hide in the shadows of large rocks, logs, and stumps. Cast to these cover spots with a small in-line spinner, a Fat Gitzit, or a tiny crayfish crankbait. Any of these lures pulled in front of a rock bass is likely to produce action.

Catfish

Channel and flathead catfish are common in warm-water streams. They usually stay in quiet, deep pools. When feeding, they move to the heads of pools and watch for food washing in from the riffle above.

Try for stream catfish by fishing pools with a bottom rig or fixed-bobber rig and live bait. The weight of these rigs depends on the water depth and current. Don't go too heavy with either one.

Bait with worms, crayfish, fish guts, live minnows, cut bait, or grasshoppers. Cast into the pool, let the bait settle, and wait for a bite. Early and late in the day (or at night), fish at the head of the pool below the riffle. Later on, try the deepest part of the pool. Be patient, and give the fish time to find your bait.

White Bass

White bass spend most of their lives in large lakes, reservoirs, and rivers, but in spring, they make spawning migrations up tributary creeks. During migration, they can be caught by the dozens, and many will be big, egg-heavy females.

This migration occurs as the water temperature approaches 60°F. Huge schools of white bass swim upstream to spawn in shallow riffles. Before and after spawning, these fish hold in eddy pools beside swifter water. They particularly like quiet pockets behind logjams, just below stumps, or at the side of streams.

During this spawning run, white bass are very aggressive, and they'll hit almost any bait pulled by them. In-line spinners, small leadhead jigs, and small crankbaits are top choices. Retrieve them medium-fast, and keep moving until you locate fish. When you find them, slow down and thoroughly work potential spots.

Trout

Trout are found in cold-water streams throughout much of the U.S. and Canada. Some of these fish are native to their home waters. Many more have been raised in hatcheries and stocked into streams where they can survive, but that aren't suitable for spawning. In either case, trout are fun to catch, and they provide a prime opportunity for beginning anglers.

Fly-fishing is a popular, effective method for taking trout, but I don't recommend it for beginners. I suggest sticking with light spinning tackle until you build your angling skills. Then try fly-fishing at some point in the future.

Stream trout are very elusive, skittish fish. Get too close, make too much noise, wear bright clothes, or drop a lure right on their heads, and they'll be gone. Instead, you have to stay back from feeding zones, remain quiet, wear drab-colored clothes, and cast beyond where you think the fish are. Overall, anglers trying for stream trout must exercise more caution than they would when fishing for other species.

Stream trout hold in similar areas as smallmouths. They prefer eddies adjacent to swift water where they can hide and then dart out in the current to grab passing food. During insect hatches, trout also feed in open runs with moderate current.

Since most trout streams are clear, rig with 4- to 6-pound-test line. Then tie on a small in-line spinner, spoon, floating minnow, or crayfish crankbait. Cast these lures around rocks, logs, weeds, and other likely structure bordering swift water. The heads of pools can be especially good early in the morning and late in the afternoon. Also, trout love to feed after dark. This is a prime time to catch big browns.

Natural baits are also effective on stream trout. Night crawlers, salmon eggs, grasshoppers, and minnows are good bets. Canned corn or small marshmallows will take hatchery-raised trout. All of these baits should be fished on the bottom with a very small hook (#12) and a split shot clamped 10 to 12 inches up the line.

HOW TO FISH LARGE RIVERS

Earlier in this chapter, I mentioned that fishing large lakes is like fishing small ponds in terms of basics. The same comparison can be made between small streams and large rivers. Big rivers are just little streams that have grown up. They are more complex, and they present a much broader range of fishing conditions and choices. But the same basics hold true. For this reason, it's best to start fishing in small streams and then graduate to large rivers.

Large rivers are the most diverse of all waters. They contain a wide variety of fishing locations: eddies; bluffs; drop-offs; shallow flats; feeder streams; backwater sloughs; tailwaters of dams; deep and shallow areas; and swift-flowing and calm water. Rivers also hold all species of fish that exist in freshwater. Overall, North America's large rivers offer a smorgasbord of angling opportunity. Pick your fish and try your luck!

As with small streams, large rivers are also divided into two types: warm water and cold water. Most rivers in North America are the warm, deep variety, supporting typical warm-water fisheries—sunfish, bass, white bass, catfish, walleye, etc. Many of these rivers are dammed up into "pools" to provide enough water depth for big-boat navigation. The Mississippi and Ohio rivers are examples.

In contrast, cold-water rivers are characteristically shallow and swift, and they are located in mountainous areas. Cold-water rivers usually contain various trout species.

Large rivers are most often fished from a boat, though you can fish successfully from the bank, especially in tailwaters below dams or in backwater sloughs and oxbows. But whichever method and location you choose, large rivers are topnotch fisheries that beginners and veteran anglers can share and enjoy.

Analyzing Large Rivers

As in small streams, current determines fish locations in large rivers. Therefore, understanding current and being able to read rivers are essential to fishing them successfully.

Current in large rivers may be more difficult to figure out. In small streams you'll see the riffles and swift runs, but in large rivers the current may seem equal from bank to bank. Look closer, though, and you'll find evidence of current breaks. Points of islands, jetties, tailwaters of dams, and mouths of tributary streams are all areas where current is altered, and these are prime spots to catch fish.

Just as in small streams, most fish in large rivers are usually in eddies or slack water. Sometimes they prefer still water bordering strong current where they can rush out and ambush baitfish washing by. Other times they seek out quiet backwater sloughs that are similar to lakes. Besides current, three other variables in large rivers are water level, color, and cover.

Water Level—Rivers continuously rise and fall, depending on the amount of rainfall upstream. The level of the river is referred to as its

High Water (typical spring condition)

20' 10'

wing dam

swift current

eddy

Low Water (typical winter condition)

10'

wing dam

weak current

Here's a clear example of how water level and current flow affects fish position in rivers. Under high water conditions, walleyes are forced to move in close to and behind objects, like wing dams, in order to evade the roaring current. But with low water conditions, walleyes are much more free to move about. The most favorable location might even be completely out and away from the wing dam. The walleyes could be a long distance fram any major change in depth—as long as there's no current to push them around.

144

"stage," and this can have a direct bearing on fish locations. Many times, when a river is rising and its waters are flooding surrounding lowlands, fish move into these freshly-flooded areas to dine on the banquet of worms, crayfish, and other foods suddenly available to them.

Color—Large rivers vary greatly in water clarity. While the main channel areas may be muddy, backwaters may be clear and more attractive to fish. Or entire river systems may be muddy or clear, depending on recent rains. Most fish species feed better in clear water than in muddy water.

Cover—Fish react to cover in rivers the same way they do in other bodies of water. Species such as bass, crappies, and bluegills usually hold in or close to cover. Structure objects provide hiding places and a shield from current.

So when "reading" a large river, be aware of current (especially eddies) river stage, water color, and structure. You will encounter a broad range of combinations of these conditions that may confuse a beginning fisherman. But by following the advice in the remainder of this section, you can be assured that you're on track and that you can, indeed, mine large rivers of their fishing riches.

Techniques for Fishing Large Rivers

Many techniques for fishing large rivers are the same for ponds, lakes, and small streams. Therefore, the key to catching fish from rivers is finding them and then applying the fundamentals of tackle, bait, and fishing methods.

The following is a species-by-species rundown of where to look for fish in large rivers and how to catch them. These certainly aren't the only good ways to fish rivers, but they are the easiest and most reliable methods for a beginner.

Bluegill

Bluegills like quiet water, not current, so look for them in eddies, backwater sloughs, feeder creeks, and other still areas where they concentrate. I've also caught bluegills from bridges, marinas, quarries, gravel pits, tailwaters of dams, and other manmade spots. Remember that bluegills won't stay in strong current very long, so find quiet, deep pools that have some structure, and bluegills will be there.

Then fish for them just like you would in ponds and reservoirs. Use light tackle and small bobber rigs. Bait with worms, crickets, or tiny tube jigs. Toss the bait right beside or into cover and wait for a bite. If bluegills are present, your bobber will soon start dancing. If you don't get a bite in 5 minutes, try somewhere else.

When fishing for bluegills, many beginners get frustrated because they get bites, but can't hook the fish. There are two possible solutions to this problem: (1) Try a smaller hook. Don't use a hook that's too big for the fish to get in its mouth. (2) Wait longer before setting the hook. If your bobber is dancing on the surface, be patient and wait for it to completely go under before setting the hook. Bluegills often nibble at

the bait for a minute or two before finally taking it.

Crappie

Crappies also prefer quiet water. The best places to find river crappies are sloughs, slow-moving tributaries, and similar locations. In addition, these spots should have trees, logs, brush, vegetation, or other cover where fish can feed and hide.

The best times for river crappie fishing are spring and fall, and the easiest way to catch them is to move from one piece of cover to the next. Use a long panfish pole and a fixed-bobber rig to drop a minnow or small crappie jig down beside tree trunks and logs, or into brush and vegetation. If the water is dingy, don't fish too deep. Two to four feet will be deep enough.

This method works best when fishing from a small boat. Use an electric trolling motor or a paddle, and keep moving, looking for crappies. Sometimes you'll fish for awhile with no action, and then you'll move into a good area and load up. Be quiet as you move, and get only as close to structure as you must to reach it with your pole. Work each new object thoroughly, covering all sides of a tree, up and down a log, and all little holes and pockets in a downed tree top or brush pile. Don't neglect areas where driftwood has collected, because sometimes river crappies hide under floating debris. A minnow dropped into a hole in cover is likely to be attacked.

One special time for crappies is when the river is rising and flooding adjacent sloughs and creeks. As the river comes up, crappies move into cover in these areas. If your timing is good, you can work these freshly flooded areas for huge catches. But as soon as the river starts dropping, crappies immediately head back to deep water.

Bass

North America's warm-water rivers harbor abundant largemouth, smallmouth, and spotted bass. These fish receive far less angling pressure than lake and reservoir bass, which often translates into great action for fishermen who put forth the effort to find them.

In spring, look for river bass in quiet, protected waters where current won't disturb their spawning beds. Backwater flats, tributaries, marinas, and quarries are good places to try. Fish these areas the same way you'd fish lakes or reservoirs. Cast to flooded timber, logs, brush, vegetation, riprap banks, etc. Spinnerbaits, buzzbaits, crankbaits, floating minnows, and jigs are good lure choices.

Riverbanks with the right cover hold bass all year. By early summer, however, most of them move out to the main river. This is where the biggest concentrations of baitfish are found. Bass in current breaks can dart out and nail a hapless minnow passing by in the flow.

A wide variety of locations will hold river bass in summer and fall. These include: mouths of feeder creeks or chutes, especially in eddies around the upstream points of the mouths; eddies on the sides and downstream ends of islands or rock piles; points and downstream sides of rock jetties that extend from the bank toward the channel; bridge pilings and riprapped causeways; beneath trees that have washed onto shallow bars or fallen along steep banks; along rock or wood cover on the outside bend of a river; and beside wing walls and riprap banks in tailwater areas. As in small streams, cast wherever the current is deflected by some object or feature of the river.

Lure choices for fishing these spots run the gamut. Minnow-imitating crankbaits are good in eddy pools and along rock piles and jetties. Spinnerbaits are a top choice for working logs and tree tops. Jigs tipped with a pork or plastic trailer will snare bass from tight spots close to cover. Select lures for river fishing just as you would in lakes and reservoirs.

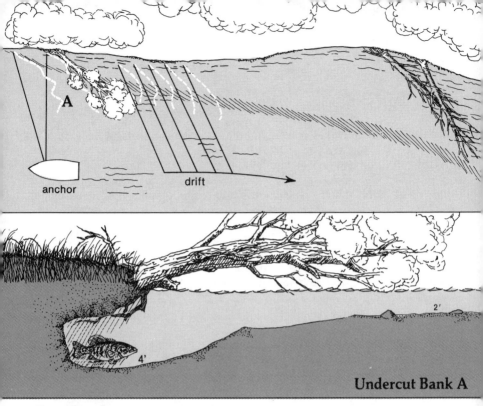

A

anchor | drift

Undercut Bank A

Log Bank

   Note on the cross-sections A, B, and C that the top portion of the bank is deeply under-cut and that this undercut becomes less as the bank comes out of the corner. This is caused because a river does most of its forming during high water levels, and the maximum force of the current strikes the beginning of the river bend.

Position A

   Start fishing at the very top portion of the bank. This is the number-one spot for aggressive fish.

   Allow the boat to drift parallel to the bank and slow enough to allow unhurried presentations. Combine long, thorough, calculated drift over structure extending out from the bank, and thoroughly cover all shoreline targets.

Position B

   In order to facilitate hooking and controlling a hooked fish, stay upstream from the brush piles.

Position C

   After working a brush pile from above, allow the boat to drift below it and work it some more, still focusing on presenting the lure parallel to the cover. Do not overlook the tailing ends of this type of bank. Often where the bank is no longer deeply undercut, it will begin to shallow and form an apron containing scattered logs and brush. These areas can be very significant and may produce several good fish.

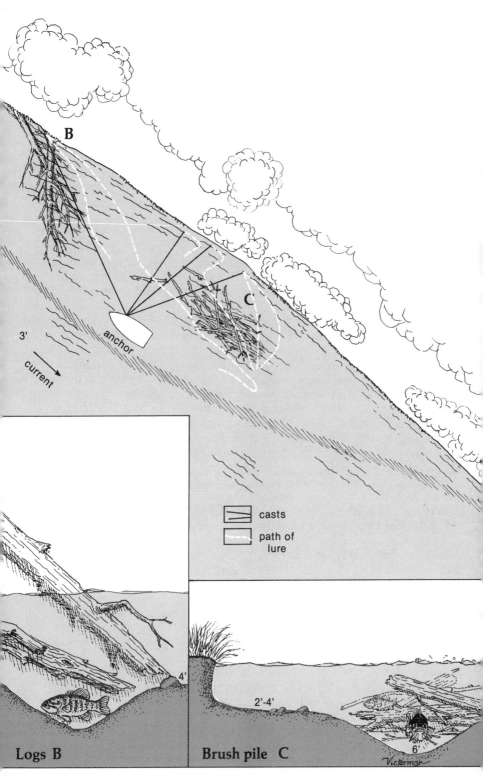

B

C

3'

current

anchor

casts

path of
lure

Logs B

Brush pile C

4'

2'-4'

6'

Vickerman

One special situation occurs when the river is rising and flooding adjacent lowland areas. When this happens, bass move into this new habitat to feed. Look for such areas where the water is fairly clear and current is slack. Fish them with spinnerbaits, topwaters, shallow crankbaits, or plastic worms. But be aware that when the water starts dropping, bass abandon these areas and move back to deeper areas. When the water starts dropping, cast around the downstream end of oxbows, sloughs, and side channels where the water is running out.

Always be conscious of river bass "patterns." If you find fish at the mouth of a feeder creek, chances are the next creek will also hold bass. The same is true of jetties, islands, rocks, etc. Put together a reliable pattern, and you're on your way to a good catch.

Catfish/Bullheads

Catfish and bullheads are plentiful in most large warm-water rivers in North America. In the daytime, catfish stay in deep, slow-moving holes, while bullheads prefer shallower backwaters. At night, both roam actively looking for food.

The best time to try for these fish is just after sundown. Fish for catfish along bluffs, tributary mouths, flats bordering the channel, or the downstream side of jetties. Try for bullheads in mud-bottom sloughs.

For catfish, use stout tackle and a bottom rig. Sinkers should be heavy (2 to 5 ounce, depending on the amount of current), and hooks should be stout and large (1/0 to 3/0 steel). Live minnows, worms, cut bait, or any of several other traditional catfish baits will work. After baiting up, cast the rig and allow it to sink to the bottom. Prop the rod in a forked stick jammed into the mud or sand at the water's edge. Attach a small bell to the rod tip, and then sit back and wait for the action to start. Serious catfish anglers use several rods at once. They will stay in the same spot for several hours, waiting for the fish to begin feeding.

A rock bank during spawning time offers red-hot catfishing, especially if the rocks are out of direct current. Fish these spots with a fixed or slip-bobber rig, adjusting the float so the bait hangs just above the rocks.

River catfishing can also be hot in the tailwater below a major dam— a collection point for catfish. It contains baitfish, current, dissolved oxygen, and bottom structure where fish can hold and feed.

The best way to fish a tailwater is to work eddies close to the swift water that pours through the dam. If you're bank fishing, use a bottom rig and cast into quiet waters behind wing walls, pilings, or the dam face. If the bottom is rough and you keep getting hung up, switch to a slip-float rig adjusted so the bait hangs close to bottom.

A better way to fish tailwaters is from a boat, floating along current breaks while bumping a two-hook panfish rig off the bottom. Use enough weight so your line hangs almost straight under the boat. Make long downstream drifts, up to a quarter-mile or more, before motoring back up to make another float. Don't lay your rod down on the side of the boat. Big catfish strike hard, and they may yank it overboard.

Another special river catfishing opportunity occurs right after a hard rain. Look for gulleys, drain sewers, or other spots where fresh water is rushing into the river. Catfish often move up below these inflows and feed furiously. In this case, use a fixed or slip-bobber rig and dangle a bait only 2 or 3 feet under the surface in the immediate vicinity of the inflow.

Fish bullheads in rivers the same as in large lakes and reservoirs, since you're fishing in quiet backwaters. Light tackle, worms, and a bottom rig or bobber rig are hard to beat.

Walleye/Sauger

Since these fish are so similar, and the techniques to catch them are the same, in this section I will only mention walleyes, though the meth-

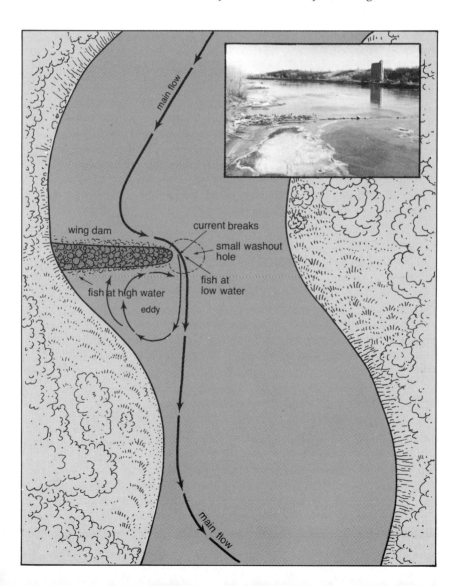

ods apply to both species.

River walleyes gather in fairly predictable places. They spend most of their time out of current, so look for them in islands, rock jetties, eddies behind dams, etc. They usually hold near the edge of the eddy where they can watch for food in adjacent currents.

The best river conditions for catching walleyes are when the water is low, stable, and relatively clear. Walleyes continue feeding when a river is rising, but they may change locations in response to high-water conditions. When the river gets too muddy, or when the water starts dropping again, walleyes generally become inactive and hard to catch.

Tailwaters below dams are the best places for beginners to catch river walleyes. Some fish stay in tailwaters all year long, but the biggest concentrations occur during winter and early spring. Walleyes may hold close to dam faces or behind wingwalls. They especially like to stay along rock ledges, gravel bars, or other structure. But again, the key is reduced flow.

Boats are best for catching river walleyes. Use a jig tipped with a live minnow, matching your jig weight to the amount of current. In slack water, a 1/8-ounce jig is heavy enough to work most tailwater areas. If current is slow to moderate, try a 1/4-ounce jig.

Float or troll through likely walleye locations, vertically jigging off the bottom. Or anchor the boat and cast into eddies, holes, and current breaks. Let the jig sink to the bottom, and work it back with a lift/drop retrieve. At all times, work the bait slowly. Set the hook at the slightest bump or pressure on the line.

If the bottom is fairly clean (snag-free), a slip-sinker rig baited with a minnow or night crawler can be trolled behind the boat. Remember to fish slowly.

A good technique for bank fishermen is casting crankbaits or jigs tipped with minnows along riprap banks in early spring. Walleyes spawn along the rocks downstream from dams when the water temperature climbs into the mid-40°F range. Cast parallel to banks, bump crankbaits off the rocks, or swim jigs just above them.

In summer and fall, look for walleyes farther downstream, along riprap banks, jetties, gravel or rock bars, mouths of tributaries or sloughs, or deep eddy pools at the edge of current. Cast jigs or troll live-bait rigs through deeper areas, or cast crankbaits along rocky shallows.

White Bass/Stripers/Hybrids

These three species of fish share similar river habits and patterns. Since white bass are the most common of the three, I will refer only to them. But be aware that, where stripers and hybrids coexist with white bass, you may catch any of the three. If you're using light tackle for white bass and a big striper hits, you're in for a wild ride!

In the section on how to fish small streams, I mentioned the white bass spawning run. These fish also spawn in tailwaters below dams on large rivers, and at this time fishing is easy and productive. White bass move into tailwaters and feed actively in early spring, when the water temperature rises into the low 50°F range.

One good way to catch them is to cast jigs from the bank. Use 1/8-ounce jigs in light current and 1/4-ounce jigs in strong current. Dress the jigs with plastic curly-tail trailers (white, yellow, or chartreuse). Experiment by fishing in current and in eddies, by allowing your jig to sink to different levels before starting the retrieve, and by varying your retrieve speed. Once you find a good pattern, stick with it. When you find tailwater white bass in early spring, you can catch a stringer full.

After the spawn, white bass move back downstream. In summer and fall, they feed in large open areas of a river, much as they do in a lake. If dams along the river generate electricity, white bass feeding activity may be affected by the generation schedule. When the generators go on and the current kicks up, feeding begins. Some dams publish daily generation schedules, and smart anglers check them to time their trips to coincide with periods of strongest current.

White bass feed where current washes baitfish into shallow or confined areas. Flats on outside bends of a river, upstream points of islands, ends of jetties, sand or gravel bars, or ledges adjacent to tributary mouths are all good locations.

Cast to these areas with jigs, spoons, in-line spinners, chrome-finish vibrating crankbaits, or any lure that simulates a small baitfish. Always be alert for surface feeding; cast into the middle of any surface activity and reel in quickly. Sometimes white bass will come up and froth the surface while chasing minnows. At other times, a single minnow skipping out of the water can signal a school of white bass feeding below the surface.

Northern Pike

Use the same tactics, tackle, and baits for pike in large rivers as you would for fishing large lakes and reservoirs. The only difference is locating these fish within the river system.

The best places to look for river pike are in backwaters. They often hold in sloughs, marshes, tributaries, and oxbows away from main-channel current. Cast to vegetation, logs, brush, or other shallow cover. You can fish from the bank or wadefish, but a boat is better. The more water you cover, the more pike you'll likely contact.

As in lakes and reservoirs, river pike are most active in spring, early summer, and fall. Also, a bonus time to fish for pike is whenever a river is rising and flooding adjacent lowlands. Pike cruise these newly flooded areas in search of food. If you stay on the move and make a lot of casts, you're likely to enjoy some first-rate pike action.

Yellow Perch

Yellow perch aren't sought by many anglers in river systems, though they are often common in rivers. The easiest places to fish are the quieter sloughs and backwaters. Perch can also be caught from tail-waters, slack areas behind jetties, and rock reefs or ledges off the side of the main channel. Perch avoid areas washed by direct current, though they will hold in eddies adjacent to moving water.

Techniques for catching river perch are the same as for perch in lakes and reservoirs. Drop fixed or slip-bobber rigs baited with worms or minnows next to vegetation or other cover. Cast small jigs, spinners, or spoons with light-action spinning gear.

Trout

Many large cold-water rivers offer very good trout fishing, particularly for big fish. Deep runs can harbor lunker browns, rainbows, and cutthroats. These trophy fish are very wary, so they're hard for beginning anglers to catch. However, smaller trout can provide plenty of action for beginners who use basic techniques and are careful not to spook the fish. Once you scare them, you may as well move to another spot.

As in small streams, current is the most important factor in deciding where to try for trout in large rivers. The concept is simple. Current funnels food into predictable areas, and fish hold in or around these areas where the pickings are easy. They'll lie in the shadows and then dart out and grab a morsel as it drifts by.

Pools below riffles or waterfalls are prime feeding locations. So are eddies behind rocks, logs, or anything else that diverts current. Undercut, shaded banks on outside turns of the river are prime hiding places for trout. So are holes just below the mouths of feeder creeks. The trick is to study the current for places next to the flow where trout can lurk and watch for food to wash by.

Fish these spots with the same lures recommended for stream trout: spinners, spoons, floating minnows, and small crankbaits. Always cast upstream and retrieve your lure back with the current. Before casting, decide exactly where you think trout should be; then pull your lure as close to this location as possible.

Use natural bait the same way as in small streams. Worms, minnows, grasshoppers, and salmon eggs will take native trout. Whole kernal corn, cheese, or small marshmallows are good for stocked trout. Fish these baits with a small hook and a split shot crimped a foot above the hook. Make a quartering cast upstream from where the trout should be. Then reel in slack line and feel for a bite as the current carries the bait along bottom. Set the hook at any unnatural bump or pressure.

Summary

In this chapter we've covered a lot of ground, or should we say water. If you've read this whole chapter without trying any of these techniques, you're probably shaking your head and saying, "No way! It's too much." That intimidation factor is setting in again.

But you won't digest fishing by taking big bites. Instead, take little bites, and chew thoroughly. Pick one small part of fishing, one location and species, and learn this before moving on to other species and locations. Then take another bite, and another, and so on until you're an accomplished angler who can match techniques to ever-changing locations and conditions.

Fishing success breeds confidence, and confidence breeds success.

Start simple to build your confidence—like fishing for bluegill from a pier. Then gradually move to other species and more advanced techniques.

One of the greatest pleasures in fishing is catching because you knew what to do and you did it properly, and were not merely "lucky." If you follow the instructions in this chapter and practice them, you'll catch fish, and you'll gain that confidence and sense of accomplishment that veteran anglers enjoy.

Now let's move ahead to Chapter 10 and learn what to do once you get 'em to bite.

PLAYING, LANDING, AND HANDLING FISH

"The more difficult a job is, the more satisfaction it yields when completed successfully."

A heartbreaking moment in fishing, one which all of us experience sooner or later, is having a big one on and then losing it. This is disappointing, but it's a necessary part of the sport. If you *knew* you'd catch every fish you hooked, fishing wouldn't be nearly as much fun. The uncertainty of landing the fish is what provides the excitement and suspense of the fight.

That's not to say that you shouldn't *try* to land every fish you hook. You should, and this is why you need to learn proper playing and landing methods. By practicing the right techniques, you'll become more effective when a fish thrashes on the end of your line.

This chapter will help you understand the following techniques: How to play a fish to keep the odds in your favor; how to land fish when you're fishing either from a boat or from shore; how to handle fish after they're caught, both for your own safety and also the fish's well-being, in case you want to release it alive.

The Fine Art of Playing Fish

"Playing" fish and "fighting" fish are the same. These terms mean tiring a fish and pulling it in close enough to land. Playing small fish is easy, since they lack the strength to put up a difficult fight. But playing big fish, especially with light tackle, can be extremely touchy. If you don't know what you're doing, you'll lose more of these contests than you'll win.

There are two basic ways to play fish. The first is to play them with the main purpose of having fun, of stretching the fight out and giving the fish a maximum chance to get away. Anglers who prefer this type battle frequently use light or ultralight rods, reels, and lines.

It's harder to land fish on light tackle. You can't power them in, so you have to wear them down more. This takes longer, which increases the fish's chances of getting off. But the more difficult a job is, the more satisfaction it yields when completed successfully. This is why many fishermen prefer light tackle and take chances playing their fish.

The second way to play fish is with the sole purpose of landing them the safest and most efficient way possible. These anglers have a saying: "You can play with the fish after you get them into the boat." Tournament anglers or those fishing for food are more likely to use these "power" methods. They normally use heavier rods and stronger line. The primary goal for these anglers is *landing* fish by allowing the least opportunity for them to get away.

Each angler must decide which method suits his preference. Neither is more or less acceptable than the other. They are just different playing styles for different fishing philosophies and purposes.

Pointers for Playing Fish

The following pointers are for playing big, strong fish like trophy bass, muskies, pike, stripers, catfish, and walleyes. When you hook one of these fish, you must play it carefully, or you'll probably lose it.

Once a fish is hooked, you must play the fish until it can be safely landed. Your rod places the pressure on the fish. No rod bend means slack line and often a lost fish.

Rule number one is to keep tension on the line. This is no problem if the fish is pulling against you. But if it's running toward you, reel in line fast enough to avoid slack.

When a fish jumps, keep the line tight and try to control head shakes. It's easier for a fish to throw a hook or lure when line is slack than when it's taut. Many expert anglers try to prevent or control jumps by holding their rod tips low and pulling the fish back down toward the water when it starts up.

During the fight, hold your rod or pole tip high and allow the bend or flex of the rod to wear down the fish. Many experts hold the rod with both hands tight against their chest. This is a very strong fighting position. You may also hold the rod sideways or high over your head for more leverage.

You must adapt your playing technique to the tackle you're using and the spot you're fishing. If you're using light tackle, you obviously can't put as much pressure on fish as you can with heavy tackle. On the other hand, if you're fishing around thick cover (brush, weeds, standing timber), you may have to apply maximum pressure on the fish to keep it from burrowing into the cover and tangling your line. You may consider using heavier tackle and line when fishing around thick vegetation. This will allow you to apply more pressure to turn the fish away from cover.

With big fish, a pump-and-reel playing technique works well. Pump the rod slowly to raise the fish. Then reel in line as you lower the rod back down. Repeating this process will tire a fish quickly. Keep the line tight, however. Many times, while you're pumping and reeling, line will go slack, and that leads to lost fish.

Probably the biggest mistake beginning anglers make when playing fish is hurrying too much. When you reel a fish in too fast, it has a lot of fight left, and you risk breaking your line or pulling out the hook. Instead, unless the fish is swimming toward thick cover, you should play it patiently, without applying unneeded pressure. Simply hold onto the fish while it's fighting; then start reeling in as it begins to tire.

Setting and Using Drag

Drag is one of the most elemental concepts in playing fish, and it's one that all rod-and-reel anglers must learn to use. Basically, drag is a slip-clutch system built into reels which, when used properly, prevents a fighting fish from breaking your line. Drag settings are adjustable, and drag should be set at some point below the breaking strength of whatever line test you're using. Then, when a fish applies this amount of pull, the drag will slip and give line rather than allowing pressure to build to the breaking point.

Let's apply this to a practical fishing situation. Say you're using 6-pound-test line. You might set your drag to slip when 3 pounds of pressure is applied to the line. If you hook a big fish and it makes a strong run, the drag will give before the line snaps. Then, as the fish tires and stops pulling

Drags come in many forms and locations. Star drags on most bait casting reels, front and rear drags on spinning reels and either on closed faced reels. Read the instructions for exact details for setting and use.

drag, you can reel in line and land the fish.

When a fish is pulling out drag, don't crank the reel handle, since this causes line twist in the reel. Instead, hold the reel handle steady until the fish stops running or until it turns back toward you. Then begin cranking to keep tension on the line, and play the fish.

Two Ways to Set Drag

Setting the proper amount of drag can be a very complicated process. Several factors go into knowing how much drag is just right. Strength of the line, weight and strength of the fish, how far the fish is from the rod tip, and the amount of line on the reel spool, all affect how much drag is needed. Also, conditions that determine the optimum drag setting may change rapidly during the fight.

You may use either of two easy methods for presetting drag. First, however, you must decide how much drag pressure to set. A good rule of thumb is half the rated breaking strength of the line. (For 6-pound test, set the drag to slip at 3-pounds pressure.) This may be slightly on the light side, but it provides a good margin for error.

The first method for setting drag is more precise than the second, but it takes more effort. Tie one end of a small fish-weighing scale to a secure object like a post or tree. Then tie your fishing line to the other end. Disengage the reel spool or trip the bail and back away 15 to 20 yards. Then re-engage the spool or bail. Hold the rod at a 90-degree angle to the scale (the angle that you will be fighting a fish), and reel the line tight. Then start pulling on

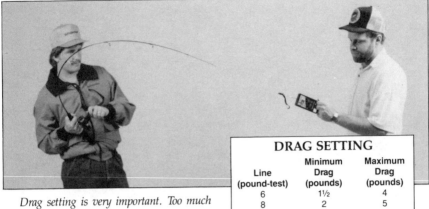

DRAG SETTING		
Line (pound-test)	Minimum Drag (pounds)	Maximum Drag (pounds)
6	1½	4
8	2	5
10	3	6
12	4	8
20	6	12

Drag setting is very important. Too much produces broken line. Too little and you won't be able to set the hook effectively. One way is to run the line through the rod guides and attach to a scale held 15-20 feet away. By placing pressure against the rod bend, set the drag at approximately half the weight of the line test.

the line with the rod while adjusting the drag setting. Have a friend watch the scale and tell you when you're pulling out the desired amount of pressure. Adjust the drag until it slips at this weight. Then it's properly adjusted.

The other method for setting drag, the one used by most fishermen, is the "feels-right" method. You simply run the line through the rod guides. Then hold the rod handle with one hand and pull line off the reel with the other. Adjust the drag setting so the reel slips before the line breaks. This feels-right method of setting drag isn't as accurate as using the scale, but it's faster.

Drags have a tendency to stick when reels haven't been used for long periods of time. When storing your reel, adjust the drag to a very loose setting. Then reset and test it before each new fishing trip. If you follow this advice, you'll catch many more fish in the course of your angling career.

How to Land Fish

Landing a fish is the end result of playing it. This is the actual capture, when you net, grab, or beach the fish. If you know what you're doing, landing is easy.

Regardless of where or how you're fishing, the *number-one* rule in landing is to make sure the fish is tired. Too many anglers try to land fish while they still have some fight left, and the fish escapes in a last-ditch lunge. So play that fish down to the point where it's easier to handle. (The one exception to this is when you intend to release the fish alive. This exception is explained in the next section, "Handling Fish After They Are Landed.")

Always net a fish head first. Fish can be landed by lipping after practice. Don't lip walleyes, pike, muskies, or other fish that have teeth.

If you're fishing from the bank, and the bank slopes gently into the water, simply drag the fish onto land. If the bank is steep, or if you're fishing from a boat, lift the fish out of the water with your rod or pole. To do this, however, the pound-test rating of your line must exceed the weight of the fish. If you try to lift a 6-pound fish with 4-pound line, the line will break.

When beaching or lifting fish, it helps to have the fish's momentum carrying it in the direction you're trying to move it. If the fish is swimming, you can steer it up on the bank or into the shallows where you can grab it. I once used this steering method to beach a 30-pound pike with light spinning tackle and 8-pound-test line.

Nets are great for landing fish from the bank, from a boat, or when you're wading. The netting procedure is always the same. *After* the fish is played down, its head should be lifted out of the water with gentle rod pressure. Then the fish should be led *headfirst* into a stationary net held just below the water's surface. *Never* chase or stab at a fish with the landing net, and never attempt to net a fish tail first. Both mistakes will cause you to lose many fish.

A third common way to land fish is by hand. In doing so, you must be extremely careful. Sharp teeth, fins, spines, and gill plates can inflict injuries. Also, if the fish isn't played down, an ill-timed headshake can embed loose hooks in your hand.

There are two ways to land fish by hand. Bass, stripers and larger panfish (species that don't have teeth) may be grabbed and lifted by the lower jaw. To do this, reel the fish up close and lift its head out of the water with rod pressure. Then stick your thumb in the fish's mouth, clamp the lower jaw between your thumb and forefinger, and lift the fish out of the water.

Species that do have teeth (pike, muskies, walleye) should be grabbed across the back, pinching in firmly on both gill plates, or they may be lifted by placing a hand under the belly. In either case, the fish must be played down beyond resisting before you attempt to land it.

Many anglers also land fish by inserting their fingers into the gills or by squeezing thumb and forefinger into the fish's eye sockets. These methods work, but they are not recommended. Some species have very sharp gill plates that can inflict nasty cuts if the fish flops. Also if the fish is to be released alive, its gills or eyes can be damaged by such rough treatment.

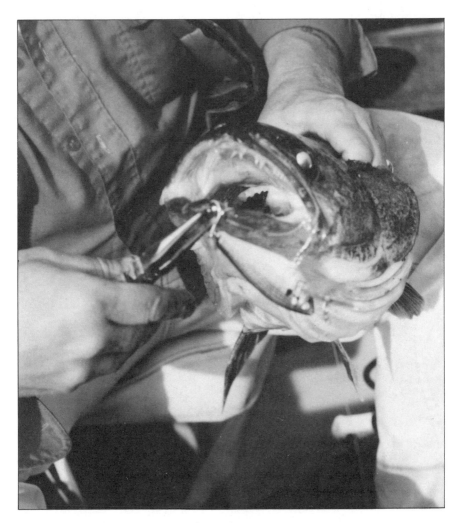

Handling Fish After They are Landed

If fish are to be kept for eating, the only concern in handling them is your own safety. But if they are to be released alive, they must be handled carefully so they can be returned to the water in good shape. (A thorough look at the catch-and-release issue—when it's okay to keep fish, and when they should be released alive—follows in the next chapter.)

In either case, always be alert to possible injury from teeth, fins, spines, or exposed hooks. Maintain a firm grip on the fish as you remove the hooks. I *always* keep a pair of needle-nose pliers handy to remove hooks. You can get a better hold and apply more force to hooks embedded in bony tissue, and pliers keep your hand away from exposed hooks if the fish flops.

Handling Fish for Live Release

If you intend to release your fish alive, special care must start when you're playing it. Land the fish as soon as possible, without completely tiring it. Total exhaustion cuts down on its chances for survival.

After landing the fish, handle it as little as possible, and put it back in the water quickly. Handling removes protective slime from the fish's body, which increases chances for bacterial growth and eventual death. Keeping a fish out of water too long also causes oxygen shortage, which can put fish into shock. It's okay to admire it briefly or snap a picture, but then place it gently back in the water in a swimming position and let go. If the fish rolls belly up instead of swimming off, retrieve it and keep it to eat. It's been injured in the fight and will probably die, so keep and use the fish rather than waste it.

Field Care of Fish for Taxidermy

Many fishermen have trophy fish mounted so they can relive the memory of the catch. When they leave their fish with the taxidermist, they hope to get it back looking as natural as the moment it was caught. How a mount looks will depend on how the angler handles the fish from the time it's pulled from the water.

If you have a camera, take a close-up color picture immediately. This will provide a lifelike guide for the taxidermist when he paints the mount. Then, don't put the fish on a stringer or in a cooler where scales might be knocked off. Instead, wrap the fish in a wet towel or newspapers and place it in a shady, out-of-the-way spot.

When you get home, lay the fish on a plywood board. Wrap it in several tight layers of plastic wrap, and seal it in a plastic garbage bag. Then place the fish in the freezer until it can be transported to the taxidermist. The board will protect the tail and fins from accidental breakage, and the plastic wrap will prevent freezer burn. Your mount is more likely to return looking alive and natural, to provide countless pleasant memories.

SIMPLE METHODS FOR CLEANING AND COOKING FISH

"Besides being fun to catch and tasty to eat, fish are good for you. This is a real case of 'having your cake and eating it too.' "

O ne of my favorite meals is pan-fried walleye fillets cooked over an open fire on the lake shore following a morning of fishing. Activity and clean air guarantee a hearty appetite, and the fish are fresh. If you throw in a skillet of home-fried potatoes and onions, a can of peas, and shredded cabbage with coleslaw dressing, you have a meal that rivals those served in the finest restaurants. Ah, the memories of shore lunches past!

For many anglers, eating fish is the end process and the final reward in fishing. Fish are delicious and more healthful than red meat. So besides being fun to catch and tasty to eat, fish are good for you. This is a real case of "having your cake and eating it too."

For fish to taste their best, though, they must be cleaned and cooked properly. This process starts the moment the fish is landed, and it ends on the serving platter. First, however, let's discuss when to keep fish and when to release them.

To Keep or Release

Catch and release is fishing for fun instead of food. Releasing fish unharmed protects species that may be damaged by heavy angling pressure. When these fish are turned back alive, they can continue spawning, maintaining healthy populations, and providing fun and excitement for other anglers.

So when is it okay to keep fish to eat, and when should you release them alive? There are two sides to this question: legal and moral. Legally, you may keep your catch (1) if you have a license, (2) take your fish by lawful methods, and (3) comply with creel and length limits.

Morally, the question of catch and release is a little more complicated. Some purists feel you should release every fish you catch. On the other end of the spectrum are game hogs who keep everything they can. A practical answer to the catch-and-release question probably lies somewhere between these two extremes.

Basically, you should decide to keep or release your fish according to how plentiful they are and how heavy the fishing pressure is. If fish are plentiful and pressure is light, it's okay to keep your catch. On the other hand, if the fish are scarce or under heavy pressure, anglers should release their catch, with two exceptions: (1) If you catch a wall hanger and you'd like to have it mounted, keep that one fish. (2) Fish that are injured during the fight will probably die. It's good conservation to keep these fish.

Let's use my secret smallmouth stream (Chapter 4) as an example of how to answer the catch-and-release question. This stream holds a healthy population of bass, and I've never seen another angler on it. I fish it only twice a year so I have no qualms about keeping enough fish for a couple meals. The removal of this small number of bass has no effect on the overall number of smallmouth in this stream.

But let's say the stream was suddenly discovered by other anglers and fishing pressure became heavy. Then, if everyone kept his catch, the stream would soon be fished out. If I saw evidence of angling pressure hurting the smallmouth population, I would immediately start releasing all my fish alive, and I would encourage other anglers to do likewise.

As a general guideline, sunfish, crappies, perch, bullheads, catfish, and white bass are rarely hurt by fishing pressure; so it's usually acceptable to keep these species. It's the bass, walleye, trout, muskies, and other trophy fish that suffer the most from fishing pressure. Depending on population and pressure in each situation, these are the species that should be considered for live release.

If you do choose to keep fish to eat, keep only what you need for your personal use; release the rest. Even when fish are plentiful, don't be wasteful.

Caring For Your Catch

When you keep fish to eat, be sure they stay fresh. This guarantees they will be delicious. If fish aren't kept fresh, the flesh becomes mushy, strong-tasting, and spoiled.

There are two ways to ensure freshness: Keep fish alive, or keep them cold. Fish may be kept alive in a fish basket, a large plastic bucket, or the livewell of a boat if the water is cool. Or they may be killed and placed on ice as soon as they're caught.

When you fish from the bank, a simple rope or chain stringer is the easiest way to keep your catch. Punch the point of the stringer up through the soft skin which forms the flat bottom side of the fish's mouth; then pull the stringer through the open mouth. Don't string fish through the gills. This makes it hard for them to breathe, and they might die. In hot weather, it's better to put fish on ice rather than trying to keep them alive in the water.

Dead fish that aren't iced will spoil quickly. Check the eyes and gill color to determine freshness. If the eyes look clear and the gills are dark red, the fish are fresh. But if the eyes are cloudy and the gills have turned pinkish-white, the fish are spoiled.

Before putting fish in a cooler, give them a sharp rap with a blunt object (pliers, knife handle, etc.) on the spine just behind the eyes. This kills them, which keeps them from flopping around and bruising the meat. Then place the fish on top of a bed of crushed ice in the cooler.

Keep excess water drained away as the ice melts, because fish flesh gets mushy when soaked in water for an extended time.

Many anglers prefer to field dress their fish before placing them on ice. This is done by cutting the gills and guts away with a small knife. These are the organs that spoil first, so this additional step helps ensure freshness.

Simple Methods for Cleaning Fish

Cleaning should be done as soon as possible. Don't leave fish in a cooler overnight. Clean and refrigerate them immediately. They will taste better, and you'll be glad you don't have to face this cleaning chore the next day.

There are a number of ways to clean fish. They can be scaled or skinned with the bones left intact, or they can be filleted (meat cut away from the bones). Smaller panfish (sunfish, perch, crappies) are usually scaled, though they may be filleted. Larger fish are usually filleted.

Tools for Cleaning Fish

Any fish-cleaning method requires a sharp knife. I recommend one of the fillet knives sold in sporting goods stores. These knives have thin, sharp, flexible blades for faster and easier cleaning. A knife with a 7-inch blade is best for cleaning most panfish and gamefish.

An inexpensive metal scaler with pointed teeth makes scaling fish much easier, but scaling can also be done with a metal spoon or a stout, short-bladed kitchen knife. A fish-cleaning glove is optional; it protects your hand from nicks. A piece of plywood makes a good cleaning platform, and you'll need two pans or buckets: one for the cleaned fish, and the other for discarded remains.

Fishermen also need "tools" for removing the fish smell from their hands once the cleaning job is finished. Commercial soaps for this purpose are available, but toothpaste will also remove fish smell. Rubbing your hands with lemon juice adds a refreshing scent.

Scaling

Scaling involves scraping the scales off the fish and then removing the head and guts. The skin is left on, and all bones remain intact. Smaller sunfish, perch, crappie, walleye, black bass, and white bass can all be scaled and cooked whole.

For Panfish Too Small to Fillet

Remove dorsal and anal fins by running knife point along each side of base and pulling free. This removes many tiny bones from flesh. Scale fish, then behead, by cutting body at an angle behind the gills. This eliminates most of the rib cage and viscera. Finally, cut off the tail with two slanting incisions to remove many fine bones.

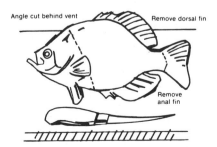

Angle cut behind vent

Remove dorsal fin

Remove anal fin

To scale a fish, lay it on its side. Hold the head with one hand and then scrape off the scales with the scaler, spoon, or knife. Scrape from the tail toward the head. The sides are easy to scale. The hard spots are along the back and stomach and close to the fins, so pay special attention to these areas.

After scaling, cut off the head just behind the gills. Then slice the belly open back to the first fin and remove the guts. The tail and major fins may be cut off if desired. Finally, wash the fish thoroughly to remove loose scales and blood. (Scaling should usually be done outdoors. Flying scales make a mess in the kitchen or garage.)

Filleting

Many anglers prefer to fillet their fish for meat with no bones. These fillets are easier to cook, and they're a pleasure to eat. Also, when

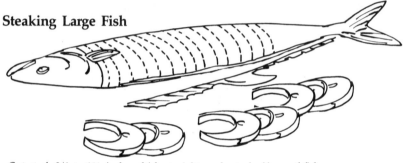

Steaking Large Fish

Cut steak 3/4 to 1½ inches thick at right angles to backbone of fish.

For Fish With Heavy Rib Structure: Large Bass, Pike or Salt Water Species

1. Holding head of fish firmly, make first cut at angle indicated, down to but not severing the backbone. Run knife at angle along backbone without cutting through rib cage, to point just behind vent. Push blade all the way through and, with blade flat against backbone, run knife all the way to tail.

2. Holding up free flap of meat, carefully separate fillet from rib cage. Penetrate thin stomach skin to free fillet; turn fish over and repeat process. Now remove skin from outside fillets.

172

filleting is mastered, it's faster than scaling. Experts can fillet a fish in less than a minute. The only drawback is losing a small amount of meat in the filleting process. Very little meat is wasted, however, if the knife is close to the backbone during the long cuts down the fish's body.

To fillet a fish, place it on its side and hold the head with one hand. Cut through to the backbone just behind the pectoral fin (the fin behind the gill plate). Then turn the knife and slice with a sawing motion along the backbone toward the tail. You'll be cutting through the ribs, separating the whole side of meat from the body. Make sure to keep the knife close to the backbone during these long cuts down the fish's body.

Cut all the way to the tail, but stop just before cutting through, leaving the fillet attached to the skin at the base of the tail. Then lay the fillet back over the tail with the skin side lying flat against the cleaning board. Now cut through the meat at the base of the fillet, but don't cut through the skin. Instead, hold the knife blade parallel to, or at a slight angle to the board. With a pulling-sawing motion, work the length of the fillet to separate the meat from the skin.

Now you have a side of meat with the skin removed, but the rib bones are still in the fillet. The last step is to cut around the rib section with the point of the knife to remove it from the fillet. Each side of the fish is filleted in this manner. The end result will be two boneless slabs of meat, which should be washed and refrigerated immediately.

Skinning

Catfish and bullheads are covered by slick skin instead of scales. Small catfish and bullheads may be filleted, but larger catfish should be skinned and cut into steaks.

To do this, lay the fish on its stomach. Grip the head firmly with one hand; make sure to avoid painful puncture wounds from the side and

Skinning Techniques With Use of Special Board

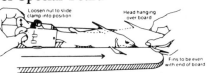

Lossen knurled nut and slide into channel, keeping cone-shaped piece on top-side of groove. Use knurled nut to loosen and tighten for proper length of fish.

1. Place skin-type fish (catfish or bullhead) on board, placing tail in clamp. Adjust for length of fish by loosening knurled nut on top of clamp and slide in slot until head of fish hangs over the end of the board and front fins (pectoral) are even with end of board. Then tighten knurled nut.

2. Start cut just behind rear dorsal fin at clamp and continue a shallow cut along the top of the fish to the back of the head.

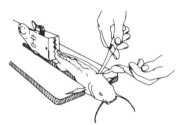

3. Turn the blade and cut downwards to the backbone, being careful not to cut through it.

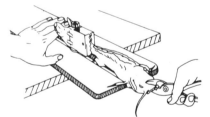

4. Place the board over the edge of table. Use a plier and grip the outside of the head. With the other hand, hold the board firmly.

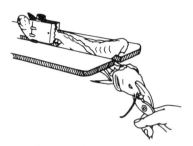

5. Pull down on pliers, forcing the head below the board; and, as you pull, gently twist the head from side to side to keep skin separating evenly.

6. The head and skin will start to separate from the body, taking with it the entrails and unedible parts of the fish. After skin is removed, fish is taken from clamp and tail is cut off.

The skin on catfish and bullheads will vary in thickness. This could cause the skin to tear prematurely. If this happens, it can be removed with pliers.

top spines. Slit the skin down both sides just behind the pectoral spines. Then slice the skin from the back of the head along both sides of the dorsal (top) fin to the point where the fin ends. Still holding the head, use pliers to grasp the skin at the point where these two cuts meet, and peel the skin back down the body and over the tail. Skin the other side the same way. Then cut off the head and remove the guts.

For steaking, place the fish on its side and slice it as you would a roll of bologna. Cut sections approximately 3/4 inch thick. Wash and refrigerate.

Other Cleaning Methods

Trout are cleaned by simply removing the head and guts. Trout scales are very fine and soft, so they don't need to be removed. Pike, muskies, and pickerel have rows of Y-shaped bones down the sides of their bodies. These bones aren't removed during standard filleting. They can either be cut away from fillets before cooking, or they may be removed after cooking.

Storing Fish for Cooking

Fish can be kept in the refrigerator 2 to 3 days without losing much freshness. If longer storage is desired, they should be frozen.

To keep whole fish, fillets, or steaks in the refrigerator, blot the fish dry with paper towels. Then place them on a plate covered with paper towels and wrap them tightly with plastic wrap.

Use milk cartons or plastic frozen food containers for freezing fish. Place the fish in a container and completely cover them with water. Tap the sides of the container to release trapped air. Use masking tape to label the container with the type fish and the date they were caught. Then freeze. Fish frozen in this manner will keep 6 months or longer without losing their fresh flavor.

To thaw, run tap water over the container until the block of frozen fish can be removed. Place this frozen block in a colander or a dish drainer so melting water can drain. Thaw fish at room temperature and cook them as soon as they're thawed.

Simple Tips for Cooking Fish

I find real pleasure in cooking and serving fish. This is the end result of the harvesting process. It provides me with the same satisfaction that other people get by growing gardens. They wouldn't go hungry if they didn't have gardens. They could buy vegetables at the grocery. But they gain a sense of fulfillment in growing and harvesting them by their own effort. I think this is so because man has a basic provider instinct. Some people satisfy this instinct by raising gardens. Others do so by fishing or hunting.

Frying

Frying is probably the most popular way to cook fish. Fish can be fried whole or in steaks or fillets. I prefer to fry fillets, and I cut fillets from big fish into chunks no bigger than a cassette tape.

Bread the fish before frying. Crushed saltines or corn flakes, bread crumbs, pancake mix, biscuit mix, and commercial fish breadings are all good. The most popular breading, however, is corn meal. Corn meal fries to a thin, golden-brown crust that doesn't overpower the taste of the fish.

I make a special breading by "jazzing up" my corn meal with several

Shore lunch is a custom in the northern part of the country. Nothing beats the fresh air, open fire and excellent food.

spices. I use 2 cups of yellow corn meal, 2 Tbsp. flour, 1 tsp. garlic powder, 1/2 tsp. paprika, 1 tsp. dill weed, 1/2 tsp. salt and 1/4 tsp. pepper. I mix these ingredients together in a double-layered paper sack.

Then I roll my fillets in a mixture of 2 beaten eggs and 2 Tbsp. milk. Next I drop the fish into the breading sack and shake vigorously for an overall coating.

I deep-fry fish in peanut oil, in a cast-iron Dutch oven. Fish can also be fried in a skillet containing 1/2 inch of vegetable oil or melted shortening.

Regardless of which method you use, the secret to delicious, crispy fish is having the grease hot enough before you drop the fish in, and then keeping it hot as you cook. The ideal temperature for frying fish is 375^0. If you don't have a thermometer or a temperature control, test hot oil with a drop of water. If the oil spatters and bubbles, it's hot enough.

If the fillets are thin, they don't take long to cook. Whole fish will take longer. When deep-frying, individual pieces are done when they float to the top of the bubbling oil. When pan-frying, cook the fish until they are golden brown; flip them over and cook them the same length of time on the other side. Test for flakiness with a fork. When they are done, place them on a platter covered with a paper towel and serve immediately, because fried fish are best when they're almost too hot to chew.

To make a simple tartar sauce, stir together equal portions of salad dressing and tomato catsup. Then mix in a heaping spoonful of sweet pickle relish.

Baking

Baking is an almost foolproof method for cooking fish. Lightly grease the bottom of the baking dish. (I use butter or olive oil). Arrange whole fish, fillets, or steaks in the dish. I brush them with a mixture of melted butter and lemon juice. To add variety, you might also add seasoned salt, garlic powder, Italian dressing, or soy sauce. Put the lid on the dish, or seal it with aluminum foil and place in a 375⁰ preheated oven.

A standard-size baking dish of fish will take 15 to 25 minutes to cook, depending on the size and thickness of the pieces. Baste the fish with the lemon-butter mixture at least twice while they're baking. Test for doneness by inserting a fork into the thickest part of the fish to check for flakiness. Do not overbake fish; they'll dry out and flavor will be damaged. When the fish are ready to serve, baste them once more with the hot lemon-butter and serve immediately.

Microwaving

Microwaved fish taste like baked fish, and preparation is similar. Arrange fish the same as for baking. Add whatever seasonings you wish and seal tightly with a lid or plastic wrap.

Follow your microwave's instructions on how long to cook fish and which setting to use. (Usually, cook lean fish 3 to 4 minutes per pound on high setting. Cook fatty or oily fish 7 to 8 minutes per pound on medium setting.) Turn the dish halfway through the cooking period. It may be necessary to rearrange the fish if outer pieces are cooking faster than inner pieces. Again, don't overcook fish in the microwave. Keep a close watch during the last couple minutes of cooking, and remove the fish if they start to dry out.

Charcoaling

More and more anglers are discovering the ease and good taste of charcoal-smoked fish. This simple cooking method doesn't take long, and it leaves little mess to clean up. It does require a grill with a hood or top to hold in smoke and regulate temperature.

I prefer fillets of larger fish for charcoaling, and I leave the skin on the outer side of the fillet. Whole fish may also be charcoaled.

Light the charcoal and wait for the briquettes to burn down to an ash-grey color. Then add water-soaked hickory chips for a smoky flavor.

When the fire is ready, spread heavy-duty aluminum foil over just enough of the grill to hold the fillets. Then place the fillets skin-side down on the foil. Baste them with lemon-butter, barbecue sauce, Italian dressing, or any other desired seasoning. Lower the top over the grill and regulate the air control so the charcoal will smolder and smoke at a low temperature. Baste the fish at intervals until they're done. Do not turn fillets. Leave them with the skin down. Test for doneness by inserting a fork into the thickest part of the fish, and twist to see if the meat is flaky. Do not overcook. Cooking time will vary, depending on the size of fish and heat of the fire. (For whole fish, do not use foil. Place the fish directly on the grill.) Turn whole fish, cooking equal time on each side.

Summary

There are many other ways to prepare fish for the table. They can be used in soups, stews, or gumbos; pickled; flaked and used in cold salads; stuffed; served in casseroles; or embellished with a wide variety of sauces and garnishes.

Dozens of excellent fish cook books are available for anglers who would like to try more involved recipes. One that I use frequently and highly recommend is "Cleaning and Cooking Fish," available from the Hunting and Fishing Library, Minnetonka, Minnesota.

Overall, fish are good for the angler's body and soul. They are truly a health food, and they are great fun to catch and prepare. That's why anglers who don't cook their catch should learn to do so. Through cooking and sharing your fish dishes with others, you will discover still another way to gain pleasure from this most rewarding sport.

WHAT TO DO WHEN FISH WON'T BITE

"For my money, being skillful is far better than being lucky when it comes to getting reluctant fish to bite."

Sometimes, despite all your best efforts, the fish just won't bite. You try where you think they should be with the right bait and technique (remember the F+L+P formula?), but you don't get a nibble. What next? Give up and go home, or try something different to stir up action?

Don't get frustrated over this lack of action. Feeding patterns may change from day to day or even hour to hour. I've seen times when fish were "jumping in the boat" and then suddenly quit biting. I knew they were still around. I could see them on my depthfinder. But due to some change in their mood, environment, or whatever, they went from very active to inactive in a few minutes. Maybe they just finished their meal?

I've also had the opposite happen. The fish had lockjaw and then suddenly started eating everything in sight. Something triggered a feeding spree. If I'd gone home half an hour earlier, I'd have missed all the fun!

Even when fish aren't actively feeding, there are usually a few around that'll still bite. It's like a fraternity house. Right after mealtime, somebody's snacking on leftovers. If you keep looking for fish, you can find a few hungry ones. Also, in many cases, you'll learn more about fishing when action's slow than you will when they're attacking the bait.

The point is, if you're not catching, don't give up. Instead, start experimenting with other baits, methods, and locations. By changing tactics, you might find the right combination. But you won't catch anything or learn anything if you stop fishing.

In this chapter we'll look at the different factors that cause fish to bite, or not to bite. Then I'll offer suggestions on what to try when the fish are playing hard to get.

Factors That Affect Fish Behavior

The fish's world is an ever-shifting one. There's always something going on beneath the surface. Weather, water, and food conditions are constantly changing, and this alters the fish's mood and activity level.

This is why fishermen must be versatile. They must analyze conditions when they get to their fishing area and then make a decision about where the fish are and what they will bite (once again, the F+L+P formula). Veteran fishermen are good at this. They have a wealth of experience to help them make good decisions. As a beginner, you don't have this "data base," but you must start somewhere. In the years ahead, you'll add to your knowledge and learn to make the right moves faster.

Meanwhile, following are factors that affect fish's activity (feeding) levels. These are *general* guidelines, because in fishing, there are exceptions to every rule. But for most fish, most of the time, the following rules apply.

How Weather Affects Fish

Every fishing trip you'll ever take will be affected by weather of some sort. Sometimes weather will help you; other times it'll hurt you. Smart anglers recognize and take advantage of good conditions, and they learn to work around unfavorable ones.

From a fish's perspective, weather consists of several elements. Air temperature can be warm or cold. The sky can be sunny, cloudy, or somewhere in between. It can be raining (snowing) or dry. The wind can be blowing, or it can be calm.

Fish are very sensitive to *changes* in weather, such as the passing of a cold front, rising or falling barometric pressure, wind shifts, etc. These are the things you must notice and figure into your fishing plan.

Now let's look at how fish react to specific weather stimuli.

Air Temperature—The warmer the air, the warmer the water, and vice versa. Since fish are cold-blooded, their activity levels are controlled by water temperature. In warm water, fish use up their food faster, so they have to feed more. The exception to this rule is that in *very* warm water, fish sometimes slip into a semiactive state. In cold water, they don't need to eat as much or as often. So usually, fishing for most species is better in warm months than in cold months.

Sky Condition—Is the sky cloudy or sunny? Sky condition determines where fish are located. On cloudy days fish are more likely to be in the

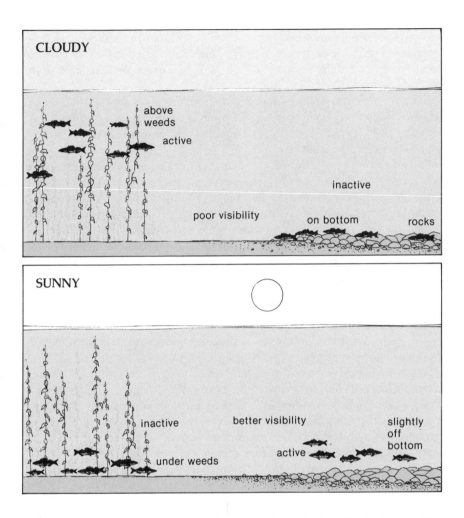

shallows and holding on the outside edges of weeds, brush, docks, etc. But when bright, midday sunshine penetrates the water, fish will usually slide deeper, or they'll move into shade—burrow into weeds, brush, or under docks. Rarely do fish stay in shallow, open water during bright-light conditions.

Precipitation—It's an old saying that fish bite better in the rain. I think this is true if the rain is light to moderate, but not pouring. With a medium rain, you have several positives: cloudy sky; runoff washing new food into the water; new "color" added to clear water from mud washing into the water; in hot weather, a cooling of water temperature; and a fresh oxygen supply. All these things cause fish to feed.

Wind—Wind may make fishing more difficult, but it usually causes fish to be more active. Wind forms waves that push baitfish into feeding areas. These waves also stir up mud or silt along the shoreline, adding color and dislodging crawfish, insects, and other foods. It breaks the surface of the water, which dissipates sunlight and allows fish to move shallow. And it replenishes the water's oxygen supply, which makes fish feel friskier. These are all reasons why the windy side of a lake often offers better fishing than the sheltered side.

Barometric Pressure Change—Barometric pressure plays a *major* role in fish behavior. Fish are usually more active when the barometer is dropping, or when it's been high and steady for a couple days. They are least active following a sharp barometric rise.

One of the very best times to go fishing is right before a storm or cold front passes. In these situations, the barometer may drop rapidly. Fish can sense this, and they go on a feeding binge. Then, after the front passes and the barometer starts back up, the fish usually quit feeding. In this situation, it may take two to three days for the barometer to stabilize and for the majority of fish to resume normal feeding. However, by using techniques I'll describe later in this chapter, you can still catch some fish on the heels of a cold front.

How Water Conditions Affect Fish

Water conditions include: water clarity (clear, dingy, muddy); water temperature; water level; currents; and amount of dissolved oxygen. All of these conditions are linked directly or indirectly to weather.

Following is how each of these water conditions affects fish.

Water Clarity—When fishermen talk about water color, they mean water clarity. Some lakes, reservoirs, and streams are clear, while others are dingy or even muddy. Also, clear or dingy lakes may become muddy after heavy rain or strong winds. Or certain areas of a lake may become muddy (wind-swept banks), while other areas may remain clear or dingy.

Fish in clear water usually hold deeper or in heavier cover than fish in dingy or muddy water. Also, fish in clear water are spookier since visibility is better, and they're more vulnerable to predators.

The Three Basic Degrees of Water Color

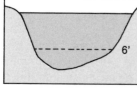 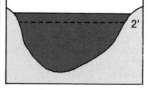

Clear Water
lure disappears at 6 ft. plus

Stained Water
lure disappears at 2-6 ft.

Dark Water
lure disappears at 0-2 ft.

Lower a white lure into the water. Note the depth at which it disappears. This gives you a general idea of fish behavior and the relative importance of sight vs. sound.

As a rule of thumb, the *best* water to fish is slightly to moderately dingy. The fish will be shallower and not so spooky, yet visibility is still good enough for them to see their prey and your bait. Many experts start a day of fishing by searching a clear lake or reservoir for an area that has some color.

Extremely muddy water is not good, however, since it almost eliminates a fish's ability to see food. Only scent-feeding species like catfish and bullheads are active in muddy conditions.

Water Temperature—Fish seek water temperatures that are most comfortable to them; this "comfort zone" varies from species to species. Warmwater fish (bass, crappie, sunfish, white bass, catfish, bullheads) prefer a range of 70°F to 80°F. Cool-water species (walleye, pike, perch, muskies) prefer a range of 60°F to 70°F. And cold water species (trout, salmon) prefer a range of 50°F to 60°F.

Note that these are *preferences*. Depending on time of year and prevailing water temperatures, fish are often found and caught outside their preferred temperature ranges. However, they're usually more active when they're in their preferred range.

Water near the surface changes temperature faster than deeper water. Surface water warms faster during bright sunlight, and it cools faster at night.

So how does this help you find fish? Say you're a bass fisherman on a lake in the heat of summer. The local fishing report has the surface temperature at 80°F. You would expect most fish to be in deep water or thick cover, since these areas would be cooler and more comfortable. But at night, as the surface temperature cools, bass might move up shallow or out of cover, where they're more accessible to the angler. In this case, night fishing would probably be more productive than daytime fishing.

Another example applies during early spring. On a sunny morning, shallow, wind-protected flats in a lake may warm several degrees. The fish may find this warmer water more comfortable, and they'll move into it and feed in the midday. But by late afternoon, these shallows will begin cooling rapidly, and the fish will return to their deep holding areas.

Many expert anglers use water thermometers to check temperature. As a beginner, you probably shouldn't worry about this until you gain more experience. But you should be aware that water temperature plays a big role in where fish are and how active they'll be. You can usually find water temperatures for specific fishing areas in the newspaper, at the bait store, etc. These should be used as an overall guide. Actual water temperature in different areas of a lake may vary several degrees on the same day, due to depth, wind, water color, air temperature, and other factors.

Water Level—Water levels in lakes, reservoirs, or rivers may rise or fall, depending on rain, water discharges, and seasonal fluctuations. As a general rule, fish bite better when water is rising, and they're less likely to feed when it's falling.

Rising water means either of two things: (1) In lakes and reservoirs, rising water covers new areas, making new food sources available. Many times fish scatter into newly flooded flats to feed. (2) In streams and rivers, rising water washes new food downstream, and stronger currents steer the food into predictable zones. So when the water starts rising, stream fish often move to feeding locations.

Dropping water has just the opposite effect. Fish pull back into or near deep areas. If the water drop is gradual, they may continue with near-normal feeding habits. But if the drop is fast, they will usually quit feeding until the level stabilizes.

Current—As we've seen in Chapter 9, current is like liquid wind. It blows food in the direction it's flowing. Predator fish know this, and they rely on current to carry food to them.

Currents in rivers and creeks are steady, although they may get stronger after heavy rains or weaker during prolonged dry periods. On the other hand, currents in tailwaters and power-generation reservoirs are highly variable. Currents may be slow or nonexistant, but when power generators are turned on, currents pick up. When this happens, fish usually get very active, since moving water means better feeding conditions.

How the Moon Affects Fishing

Many newspapers, magazines, and TV and radio fishing reports list "feeding times" or "solunar periods" for fishing. These are based on how the moon's gravitational pull affects the earth's waters.

Here's the theory. The moon's gravity causes tides in the oceans, and saltwater fishermen know that when the tides are running, fish normally bite better. The same happens in freshwater lakes and reservoirs. Tides aren't noticeable here because these bodies of water are so small in comparison to the oceans. But many experts believe freshwater fish can still feel the moon's gravity changes, and these influence the fish's feeding moods. Matching the tides, the charts usually list two "major feeding periods" and two "minor feeding periods" each day.

Many anglers swear by these feeding times, while others ignore them. I think they have some merit, and I check them before each fishing trip. I believe "moon times" may be secondary to other influences that affect fish behavior, namely, changing weather or water conditions. But day in and day out, I think fish feed better during the charted periods than they do between these periods. Too many times I've seen them turn on for no apparent reason other than the beginning of a feeding period.

Fishing records also show that during the four-day period around the full moon, big fish are definitely more active. The four-day period around the new moon is the second best time for fishing. And the times of the month between the full and new moons are usually the least productive.

How do I use this information? I still fish just as hard between feeding periods or the full and new moons as I do during them. But say I've got one

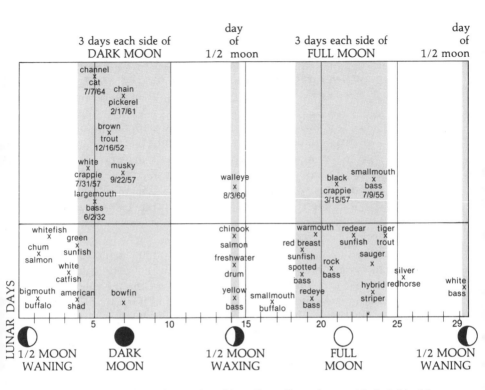

Selected world-record gamefish catches. (Note: Since all records are not included in this group, it is intended only to represent individual records and not to show a complete picture.)

spot I'm really counting on. I might plan to be at that particular location during the major feeding period. Or if I can only go fishing a couple times a month, I'll try to plan my trips around the full or new moons.

Tricks to Try for Inactive Fish

Hopefully you now understand why fish sometimes bite, and why they sometimes don't. You also have an idea about fish locations during varying weather and water conditions. So let's go back to the original question. What should you do when you can't get fish to bite?

Change your presentation. Rework the F+L+P formula and try to figure out *why* the fish aren't biting and what it'll take to get them to hit. Then start experimenting with different locations, baits, and retrieves. Here are suggestions for various things to try.

Change locations—If you're not catching fish in one spot, go somewhere else. And try a different *type* spot, not another like the one that just failed to produce. If you've been trying open water, fish around cover. If you've been fishing around cover, fish *in* the cover. If you've been fishing in shallow water, try deeper water. Remember that inactive fish are likely to be in thick cover or deep water. Choose your fishing location to match weather and water conditions.

Change baits—If you're fishing with artificial lures, you might switch to live bait. Or if live bait isn't handy, change to a lure that has a more subtle action. Also, go to a smaller lure. Inactive fish are more likely to take a small bite than a big one.

Many years ago Charlie Brewer of the Slider Lure Company told me a story that makes this point. He said to imagine that I'd just polished off a steak dinner and settled into an easy chair for a nap. If somebody brought me another steak, I'd refuse it. But if that same person passed a small dish of ice cream under my nose, I'd probably take a bite. Charlie says it's the same with fish. After a feeding spree, they rest. If a large bait swims by, they'll probably ignore it. But if a small "dessert bait" glides right under their nose, they're likely to suck it in.

Slow the retrieve—This goes along with changing to the subtler, smaller baits. Active fish will attack a fast-moving lure. But when feeding is over, these fish aren't in the mood for a chase, and they'll ignore the speedy lures. But if a slow, lazy bait comes drifting along, and they don't have to expend much effort to catch it, they might still bite it.

Change lure colors—I think color is one of the least important factors in whether or not fish will bite. Still, sometimes changing lure color will make a difference. The only way to find out is to try another color.

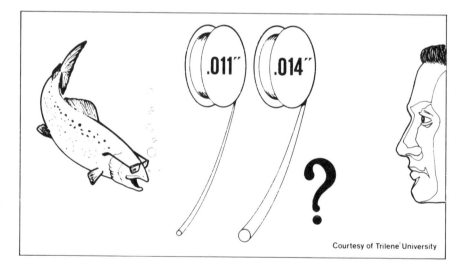

Courtesy of Trilene University

Switch to lighter line—Lighter line is harder for spooky fish to see. It also allows you to cast smaller baits, and it gives lures a freer, more lifelike action. (Switching to lighter line may be impractical when using a spincast or casting reel. But with a spinning reel, all you have to do is change spools. It takes less than a minute to change spools and retie bait.)

Be more careful in your approach—Sometimes simple carelessness is why fish won't bite. Don't let them see you. Don't get too close to them. Don't bang on the boat. Don't cast a bait or lure directly on top of them. Instead, cast beyond where you think they are (weeds, brushpile, etc.) and ease the bait into them. Overall, be alert to and avoid things that tip off your presence to the fish.

Fish at a different time—This may be the best of all tips. If you're fishing in the middle of a bright, hot summer day, you're more likely to catch fish at

dawn, dusk, or during the night. Come back. The fish have to feed sooner or later.

Also, watch the weather and try to anticipate feeding sprees. We know that fish are more likely to bite under cloudy conditions, like right before a front passes. If you go fishing when fish are *more likely* to bite, you increase your chances of catching them.

Try for another species—If the bass aren't biting, try for bluegill. Don't be "species stubborn." Sometimes one species will be more active or available than another. Don't be reluctant to switch to another type fishing. As I've said before, catching *anything* is preferable to getting skunked.

Summary

Success in fishing like any other sport comes from building on fundamentals. We laid our "foundation" for fishing in earlier chapters. Now, in this chapter, we've introduced a new and advanced plateau of fishing knowledge. By understanding how fish react to different stimuli, and by figuring these reactions into your fishing strategy, you're refining fundamentals. The more you refine, the better angler you'll be.

The best way to *learn* these refinements is simply by going fishing often and gaining as much experience as you can. Try new things. Put the information in this chapter to the test. Then your skills will increase, and you'll catch fish more often than before. For my money, being skillful is far better than being lucky, when it comes to getting reluctant fish to bite.

HOW TO INCREASE YOUR FISHING SKILLS

"One common thread binds fishermen with other athletes: The more they practice, the better they become."

Several years ago I fished the famed Manistee River in north-central Michigan, one of the very best brown trout and brook trout streams in the Upper Midwest. My host was a local guide who knew all the tricks for catching these fish, even in tough conditions when they don't cooperate. On this particular day, they weren't cooperative.

We were fly-fishing, and our delicate dry flies had tempted only a few small brookies. The bigger browns were sulking deep in holes.

My guide wasn't stymied, however. When dry flies didn't produce, he poked around in his fly-box and came out with an ugly looking wet fly named the Skunk. After tying it on, he started picking up brown trout by casting upstream from logjams and root wads and then allowing the fly to sink back under the cover.

It didn't take me long to bum a Skunk from him and start copying his "dead float" presentation. Regardless of its ugly appearance, this fly was the perfect imitation of "dinner" served to the fish, and it changed a slow day into one punctuated by fast action and bully-size trout.

What's the moral? You won't ever know it all! You'll never be too smart to pick up new information or tricks that'll help you catch more fish, regardless of species. Savvy fishermen are those who continually add to their knowledge and skills, who master new techniques, and who dare to try new waters and various species. Learning to fish should be a never-ending process for beginners and experts. Beginners just have *more* to learn. After you've mastered the basics, it's time to expand your knowledge of the sport. The following information will serve as a guideline to help you do this.

Practice, Practice, Practice

Fishermen are athletes, even though their sport doesn't demand the strength of football players or the stamina of long-distance runners. Fishing requires a unique combination of mental and physical skills, plus a measure of finesse. One common thread binds fishermen with other athletes: The more they practice, the better they become. If you fish a dozen times a year, you'll be better than if you fish only twice.

Fishing practice does two things. First, it increases your mental sharpness. You learn from your mistakes—which you'll make. And practicing allows you to experiment with various baits and techniques, to build a storehouse of spots, baits, and methods that have produced fish in the past.

Secondly, practice develops the physical coordination and "feel" you need to be an effective angler. You'll learn to be more comfortable with your tackle, more able to tell when you're getting a bite. You'll also know when to set the hook, and you'll be more in tune with the total fishing environment. This all combines to improve your consistency in making good catches.

Casting Practice

Over the years I've fished with many of North America's top fishing pros, and I've asked them, "What do average anglers need to work on most?" The answer has almost always been, "casting accuracy." In many fishing situations, success depends on being able to drop a lure or bait in exactly the right spot—not two feet to the side, back, or front.

That's why beginning fishermen should spend extra time learning to cast accurately. You can do this in your spare time by casting practice in your backyard. Set up a bucket, a garbage can top, or any other similar-sized target. Next, tie a practice plug onto the end of your line. (Practice plugs are plastic, teardrop-shaped weights without hooks. They're available in most tackle stores.) Back away 10 yards from your target and cast to it, over and over again. When you're able to hit the target consistently, move back to 15 yards, then 20, then 25.

Begin casting by holding your rod in front of your nose. Line it up with your target, and make your cast. When you're comfortable with this style, add sidearm and backhand casting. You'll sometimes need to make such close-to-the-water casts to get your lure under boat docks, overhanging tree

limbs, and other similar spots where fish may be hiding.

Practice casting as often as possible, but limit practice sessions to around 15 minutes. Concentrate on making smooth casts, allowing rod action to propel the plug. Don't overpower it. Accurate casting is a matter of easy coordination rather than strength.

Attend Fishing Seminars

Fishing seminars are held throughout the country, usually in late winter and early spring. Most seminars are either small, informal gatherings in tackle shops, or large formal affairs at sport shows, colleges, or similar sites.

Some are no-charge, while others require an entry fee. These seminars feature experts who can give you pointers on local fishing. When you attend, take notes, ask questions, collect available literature, and analyze how the tips apply to your fishing spots and methods. Watch for seminar notices in tackle stores, on your newspaper's outdoor page, and in magazines and other advertising outlets.

Fishing with a Guide

Another way to add to your fishing knowledge is to hire a guide. This is better, though more expensive, than attending seminars. In this case, the "classroom" is a lake or river, and the fishing is a "hands-on" experience. A guide will answer your questions and show you proven spots and techniques. Overall, this one-on-one session can be the greatest shortcut to fishing success that you ever can take.

Hiring a professional guide will average $75 to $150 per day. If this is too much, consider hiring him for half a day or find a partner to split the cost.

Go with the specific objective of learning about fishing. Ask your guide how he finds fish, why he fishes the way he does, and what tips are most important. You've employed a fishing tutor, and it's up to you to learn as much as you can from him. If you catch fish and have fun, that's a bonus. But your main objective should be to gain as much practical fishing information as possible.

Fish in a Tournament

You can also get on-the-water instruction by entering a fishing tourna-

ment. (Tournament age requirements often limit anyone under 16 or 18 years of age from participating.) Specifically, I'm referring to "draw" tournaments, where contestants are paired by drawing names out of a hat. In this case, your tournament entry fee is similar to money paid for a guide. It's your cost for sharing the boat and observing an experienced angler performing at his best.

There are risks. You're taking a chance that you may not draw a good partner, though most tournament contestants will be seasoned veterans. You won't be able to quiz your partner like you would a guide. But you'll be able to study how he fishes, and most partners won't mind offering an explanation of what they're doing.

If the idea of entering a tournament appeals to you, don't be shy about following through. Just explain to your partner that you've entered as a learning experience, and that you're willing to try whatever tournament tactics he wishes. Chances are, he'll be happy not to draw a partner who may want to go somewhere else or try something different.

Books, Magazines, Videos

Anglers who want to increase their knowledge of the sport can buy, subscribe to, rent, or borrow instructional books, magazines, or videos. Unfortunately, many of these are too technical to benefit beginners. But hopefully, you are now beyond the novice stage, and you've progressed to where you can take advantage of these teaching aids.

You can be selective because there are so many different books, magazines, and video's on the market. There are publications and videos specifically about fishing for bass, crappie, walleye, trout, etc. Choose those which offer details about catching the fish you've selected as your target species. Also, don't overlook your public library. All libraries have fishing books and a variety of fishing and outdoor magazines.

Join a Fishing Club

Many towns and cities have fishing clubs, and most welcome new members. By joining, you'll make new friends who share your interest in fishing, and you can learn a lot from other members. If you don't know how to contact local fishing clubs, call your newspaper's outdoor writer, your game warden, or tackle store, and ask how to get in touch with club members.

Keep a Fishing Log

Fishing may seem like an always-changing sport to beginners. Fish move from place to place. They prefer different foods at different times. One day they're active and biting anything that moves; the next day they're inactive, and they refuse to hit even the most attractive baits.

Over the years, though, you'll learn that fishing has definite patterns. At a certain time of year, under certain combinations of weather and water conditions, the fish will be very predictable in terms of location, lure preference, etc.

Anglers learn to recognize these conditions and predict fish behavior in

two ways: (1) through years of fishing experience and making mental notes, and (2) by keeping a written log and referring to it before each new outing.

The second method is more accurate, and it's also the faster way for beginning fishermen to put together a body of facts for reference. I recommend that all fishermen (beginners and vet erans) maintain a log and update it after each fishing trip. Some tackle stores and mail-order houses sell fishing logs, or you can make your own. Simply record dates; locations; weather and water conditions; methods, baits, and tackle used; fish caught; and other pertinent details.

If you have a favorite body of water, keep updated on it with a map showing the location of fish caught by yourself and others. During the seasons, you'll soon realize locations where fish are caught and also where successful anglers fish.

Keeping a log takes effort, but it will help you recognize patterns for choosing the right spots and methods. Also, in years to come, it will re-kindle warm memories of enjoyable trips in the past.

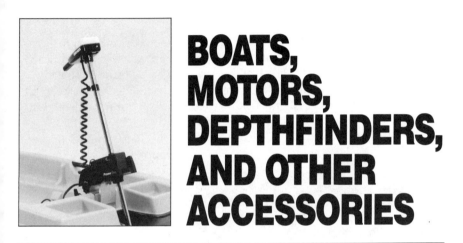

BOATS, MOTORS, DEPTHFINDERS, AND OTHER ACCESSORIES

"You'll have access to your chosen lake, river, or stream's entire angling menu."

I learned to fish as a small boy on the back seat of my dad's homemade wooden jonboat. It was by no means a fancy craft, but it allowed us to fish the deep areas of the lake where the big schools of crappie roamed. I remember days when we completely filled our cooler and had fish scattered along the boat floor.

Not many beginners will have the same learning opportunities. Most will start fishing from the bank, dock, pier, bridge, etc. But sooner or later, as your skills increase, you'll probably want to broaden your horizons by moving out from shore.

It's not that you can't make good catches around the banks. You certainly can, as you've learned in earlier chapters. But by owning a boat, you'll step up to another level in fishing. A boat will allow you to try more spots, fish deeper water, and be more versatile in your overall approach to the sport. In other words, a boat opens many new fishing opportunities, and it allows you to increase your knowledge and fun.

Types of Boats

Fishing boats come in a broad range of designs and prices. On the high end are bass boats that cost more than $20,000. On the low end are inflatables that start at around $30. The expensive rigs are highly technical and functional, and someday you may decide to buy one. But with this book's theme of keeping fishing simple, we'll stick to the fundamental, less expensive, easier-to-maintain models that beginners are more likely to buy.

Boats in this category include: jonboats, semi-Vs, canoes, mini bass boats, inflatables, and tube floats. Following are looks at each of these types, the waters where they work best, and their advantages and disadvantages.

Jonboats

The aluminum jonboat may be the best all-purpose fishing boat for beginners. It has a flat bottom and square front, is very stable, and draws only a few inches of water, which allows it to ride easily through shallow areas. Jonboats were designed for streams, but a deep-sided, wide-beamed jonboat also adapts to large open lakes. These boats perform well with outboard motors.

Jonboats vary in length from 8 to over 20 feet. The 14-foot model is most

popular. It's light enough to be car-topped and carried to the water by two anglers. This means you can use a jonboat wherever you can drive within a short distance of the stream bank or lake shore.

Jonboats have three minor disadvantages: (1) The flat hull provides a rough ride in choppy water. (2) Jonboats are clumsy to paddle. And (3) because of their all-metal construction, they are noisy when objects are dropped on the floor or banged against the sides.

Many anglers buy basic jonboats and customize them with seats, livewell, carpeting (to quiet noise), rod holders, etc. These make very practical, inexpensive fishing boats.

Semi-V

The semi-V is the workhorse of fishing boats. It's called "semi-V" because it has a pointed V-shape bow that tapers back to a flat hull. This design allows the semi-V to slice through waves, giving a smoother, safer ride in rough water.

Semi-Vs are made of aluminum and fiberglass. Fiberglass boats are

heavier, and they provide a smoother ride in chop. Most popular semi-V sizes run 12 to 18 feet in length. These boats are routinely fitted with outboard motors ranging up to 60 horsepower.

One disadvantage of the semi-V is that it's heavier than other boats, which means it's less portable. Smaller models may be car-topped, but larger semi-Vs require trailers, and they must be launched from ramps. Also, semi-Vs are awkward to paddle, but they maneuver well with an electric motor.

These boats are the standard on big water, so they should be strongly considered by anglers who will fish mostly on larger lakes and rivers. As with jonboats, fishermen often customize semi-Vs to suit their specific likes and needs. Also, many companies offer models with all these conveniences built in. Because they require more material to construct, semi-Vs are more expensive than jonboats.

Canoes

Canoes suffer an image problem. Inexperienced canoeists believe they are too tippy for fishing. The truth is, certain models are very stable, and they're excellent fishing boats for a wide range of waters. With only a small amount of practice, beginners can learn to handle a canoe and fish confidently from it.

Canoes offer several advantages to anglers. They are extremely portable. They can be car-topped and carried to lakes or streams far off the beaten path. They are also ideal for small urban lakes where bigger boats are impractical. Canoes draw only a few inches of water; they glide easily through shallow riffles or bays; and they paddle easier and maneuver better than any other boat.

Canoes are made from four different materials: Royalex/ABS, polyethylene, aluminum, and fiberglass. They come in square stern and double-end models. Square-stern canoes accept electric motors or small outboards, but they don't paddle as efficiently as double-ends. Motors can be used on double-end canoes via a side-mount bracket that attaches near the stern.

Fishermen shopping for a canoe should strongly consider a 16- or 17-foot model that has a wide beam and a flat bottom. These features offer the greatest stability and versatility. Beware of buying a "cheapie" canoe that is poorly designed and constructed. A high-quality canoe is a bargain, considering the service and pleasure it will provide.

Mini Bass Boats

Despite this boat's name, it can be used for many different species. It is a rectangular, hard plastic casting platform supported by flotation arms runing beneath both sides. Mini bass boats come in one and two-man models, ranging up to 10 feet in length. Most have molded-in seats, rod wells, battery compartments, etc. An electric trolling motor is used on these boats, and most accept a small outboard.

Mini bass boats are mainly used on small, protected waters such as ponds, sloughs, strip mine pits, and arms of larger lakes. Since they're small, they're highly maneuverable in standing timber, brush, or other cover. On the other hand, mini bass boats should not be used on large lakes or rivers with high waves or strong current.

Mini bass boats are bulky, which means they aren't very portable. They must be hauled in the back of a pickup or on a small trailer. Also, they cannot be used to cover long distances of water.

Inflatables

Inflatables are like rubber rafts, except today these boats are made mostly from PVC plastic. They come in sizes to carry from two to six or more people. They can be carried in small automobiles or backpacked to out-of-the-way waters and inflated on the spot. Portability is this boat's strongest advantage.

Inflatables have several disadvantages, however. They are more a simple means of water transportation than a true fishing boat. Their soft sides and bottom make them unstable for stand-up casting. (Certain models come with plywood floors, but this feature lessens their portability.) Inflatables are subject to puncture from sharp objects, though most are sold with easy-to-use repair kits. They are unwieldy to paddle, but a special motor-mount bracket allows the use of small outboards on larger inflatables.

One of the most attractive features of inflatables is price. They are very inexpensive compared to other boats. Two-man models start at around $30.

Tube Floats

The tube float (also called "belly boat") isn't a standard boat like the others mentioned in this chapter. The tube float is an inner tube with a sewn-on seat and leg holes. An angler carries it to his fishing site, steps in, pulls it up around his waist, and walks into the water. When he's deep enough for the tube to support his weight, he propels himself by kicking with swim fins or special paddles attached to his boots. Also, float-tube anglers usually wear waders, though they're not necessary if the water is warm.

Float tubes are used to fish along the shore or spots immediately adjacent to it. They're very maneuverable, but they're slow. They can be used only to cover small areas. They're good for fishing in flooded brush, timber, patches of reeds or cattails, or other similar spots that are hard to reach by boat. Also, since float tubes are very quiet, they're especially good for slipping up on spooky fish.

Be careful *not* to use float tubes in strong-wind/deep-water situations. High waves can flip you upside down, and float tubes can sometimes be difficult to right. These "boats" should be confined to quiet, close-to-shore fishing.

Tube floats come in basic or deluxe models. Deluxe models feature such conveniences as zippered tackle compartments, shoulder straps, an inflatable backrest, and a Velcro rod holder.

Motors

Motors aren't absolutely necessary for fishing, but in many cases they certainly make the job easier. You must decide if you need a motor by the type boat you have and the water where you plan to fish. If you'll be using a little boat on remote streams, small ponds or lakes, paddles may be all the power you need. But if you'll be on larger waters where you'll have to cover more distance, or where winds or currents can be strong, a larger boat and a motor will be more practical and efficient.

Fishing motors come in two varieties: outboard and electric. Outboard (gas-powered) motors are more powerful and are used mainly for running long distances. Electric (battery-powered) motors are less powerful and much quieter. Their job is to ease the boat through the target area while the angler fishes. An electric motor may also be used as the main power source for smaller boats on lakes where outboards are banned.

Outboard Motors

New outboard motors are expensive. Often they cost more than the boat they power. But fishermen should view outboards as a long-term investment. Modern outboards are dependable and easy to operate. They will last many years if cared for properly.

Outboards range from 1.5 to 250-plus horsepower. Smaller motors are lightweight and portable. They attach to the boat's stern with clamp mounts. Larger motors are heavy, and they're permanently bolted onto the stern.

The main consideration when buying a motor is not to overpower the boat. All boats list maximum horsepower ratings either on a stern plate or in the owner's instructions. Never exceed these ratings, since overpowered boats are unsafe to operate.

Electric Motors

Electric motors are divided into two categories: 12 volt and 24 volt. Twelve-volt motors are powered by one 12-volt battery. Twenty-four volt motors are powered by two 12-volt batteries hooked together. The obvious difference between the two is power, which is measured in "pounds of

thrust." The 24-volt motor is much stronger and faster than the 12 volt. Twenty-four volt motors are normally used on big boats that may operate in high waves or strong currents. On smaller boats and quiet waters, a 12-volt motor is adequate.

Electric motors have different types of mounts and methods of operation. Some motors have "clamp-on" mounts with screws to tighten down on the sides or transom of the boat. Others have bow mounts that attach permanently on the front of the boat. Also, some electric motors are operated by hand, while others have foot controls that allow the user to run the motor while keeping his hands free to fish. Some companies now offer remote-control and radio-control electric motors. These may be the future trend as technological advances improve electric motors and make them more "user friendly."

It's much more efficient for an electric motor to pull a boat rather than push it. A boat with an electric motor mounted on or near the bow is easier to propel and steer than one with an electric motor on the transom.

When shopping for an electric motor, you'll find models with many options and power ratings. My recommendation for a beginner's first electric is a 12-volt, clamp-on model with 20- to 35-pounds thrust. Remember that the heavier your boat, the more power you'll need to push or pull it. Also, electric motor shafts come in different lengths. Owners of jonboats, canoes, and mini bass boats will probably need motors with shafts that are 30 or 36 inches long. Owners of semi-Vs may need a motor with a 42-inch shaft, since these boats have higher sides and are more likely used in rough water. Boat dealers can provide guidelines for choosing the right shaft length.

Depthfinders

A depthfinder is truly a fisherman's "eyes under the water." Its basic function is reading the bottom, which is an important safety feature. But beyond this, depthfinders can show submerged structure: drop-offs, sunken channels, stumps, brush, rocks, weeds, etc. Depthfinders can even tell whether the bottom is hard or soft, and they can pinpoint concentrations of baitfish and gamefish. However, being able to read depthfinders with this expertise takes a combination of following the manufacturer's instructions and many hours of on-the-water experience.

Even though depthfinders require considerable investments of money and time, they are still considered an indispensable tool by serious anglers. I strongly recommend that all beginners who will be fishing away from shore on lakes and large rivers buy a depthfinder and learn to use it.

A depthfinder is a sonar unit. It sends out sound waves that strike underwater objects. Then the depthfinder measures how long it takes the echoes to bounce back to the sending unit. The deeper the object is in the water, the longer the time required for this roundtrip. The depthfinder then translates this time into a distance display, showing bottom depth and objects between the surface and bottom.

Different types of depthfinders show this information in various ways. Flashers display lighted readings on a circular depth scale. Chart recorders draw pictures of structure and fish on paper, which rolls across the recorder plate. Liquid crystal depthfinders show chart-like pictures on a liquid crystal (LC) display. And video recorders show chart-like images on a video screen.

Each type of depthfinder offers certain advantages. Chart recorders show the most detailed and accurate information. They are "fish finders" in the truest sense, but they're more expensive. Flashers provide detailed information in the least expensive package, but they're harder to interpret than other models.

Liquid crystal units are relatively new. They don't offer as much detail as chart recorders or flashers, but they're being improved rapidly. Video scanners are also relatively new in freshwater fishing. They show fine detail. Many models have multi-color displays, which help distinguish bottom features. On the negative side, video scanners are expensive, and their technology is less perfected than other units.

For my money, the flasher depthfinder still offers the best dollar value for beginning anglers. With a little study and practice, anyone can learn to read one. But regardless of which depthfinder you choose, this is an essential item for successful deep-water fishermen.

Boat Accessories

The boat, motor, and depthfinder make up the core of the fishing rig, but several other accessories are needed to complete the package. State and federal laws require certain safety equipment on all boats. Boats under 16 feet long must carry a Coast Guard approved flotation device for each passenger, some type of sound signal (whistle, air horn, etc.), running lights if the boat is to be used at night, and a fire extinguisher if gas is kept in an enclosed compartment. Boats 16 feet and longer must meet these same requirements, plus the flotation devices must be wearable life preservers, and the boat must also have a throwable flotation device (cushion, safety ring, etc.). For a full explanation of these requirements, contact your state water-safety office.

Beyond these required items, you may consider a broad array of boat

206

accessories: batteries and battery boxes, battery charger, landing net, paddle, anchor and rope, seats, fish basket, bilge pump, rod holders, and marker floats. These and other accessories will complete your boat package and make your fishing easier.

There are two types of marine batteries: "deep cycle", and "quick start." Deep-cycle batteries release small amounts of electricity over a long time. They are used primarily with electric motors. Quick-start batteries provide short, powerful bursts of electricity. They are intended for starting outboards and also for running electric accessories, other than the electric motor.

Remember three tips for battery maintenance. First, always recharge your batteries immediately after using them; don't allow them to sit discharged for long periods. Second, don't overcharge your batteries. If your batteries don't have charge indicators, as you charge them, periodically check the charge with a simple hydrometer (available in auto-parts stores). Stop charging as soon as the hydrometer shows "full charge." And third, during winter, *don't* set boat batteries next to a heater to keep them warm. Charge them fully and store them in a cool, dry place.

One tip applies to battery chargers: Consider buying one with an automatic shutoff. This feature prevents overcharging.

Buying Your Fishing Rig

It's obvious by now that, even with a simple fishing rig, you're looking at a sizeable investment. When it's time to go shopping, check around for a package deal. By buying boat, motor, trailer, depthfinder, and accessories from one dealer, you have a better bargaining position for a discount.

Don't buy a rig before shopping around. Ask dealers for advice on what boat, motor, and accessories you'll need for where you'll be fishing. Check prices, collect literature, study it, and decide for sure what you want before making any purchase commitment.

Boat dealers generally offer their best deals in late summer or fall, toward the end of the fishing season. At this time you're also in a good position to bargain and wait for them to come down on their price. Don't be in a hurry to buy your fishing rig. This is a big step, and you should take it slowly and carefully.

Once you *do* take the step, however, you'll have graduated up to fishing's "high school." You'll have access to your chosen lake, river, or stream's entire angling menu. No longer will you have to fish from shore and watch the boats go by. Now you can join them. The door will suddenly open to many new fishing challenges and pleasures, more than you can experience in a lifetime.

CHAPTER 15

SAFETY IN FISHING

"An ounce of prevention is worth a pound of cure."

One of the worst scares I ever had while fishing came several years ago on my home lake. I was in my boat alone, casting for bass around shoreline on the far side of the lake. I'd noticed the storm clouds building, but the fish were biting, and I just wanted to catch one more.

I finally decided to dash back to the boat ramp, but I'd waited too long. About a third of the way across the lake a fierce wind struck, and it seemed as though my small boat and I were alone in the North Atlantic. Waves were higher than my head. Spray drenched me, and the boat started taking water.

I cinched my life vest tight. My only hope of not swamping the boat was to turn downwind and run with the waves. After an anxious 15-minute ride, I beached on a desolate stretch of shoreline, where I was stuck for two hours while the storm passed. Rain poured and lightning popped. I sat huddled in a gully, soaked and miserable, but at least I was safe.

That night on the news I heard that another fisherman farther down the lake had drowned in the storm.

Overall, fishing is a safe sport, but it can involve hazards. Some of these may be life-threatening, others only discomforting. The old adage, "an ounce of prevention is worth a pound of cure," applies. If I'd started back to the boat ramp 15 minutes earlier, I wouldn't have been miserable. If the angler down the lake had done the same, he'd probably be alive today.

Following is a look at the safety aspects of fishing, at dangers which may arise and how to avoid or cure them. We'll take them in order of seriousness: life-threatening, first; discomforting, second.

Weather Perils of Fishing

Lightning—Because fishing is an outdoor sport, you will experience different types of weather. This means that sooner or later you'll be exposed to one of the most dangerous of all natural killers, lightning. Lightning doesn't get the scare publicity that tornadoes, hurricanes, and other sensational weather phenomena do. But each year lightning claims more lives than all other weather-related accidents combined. Invariably some of these victims are fishermen.

Kids learn at an early age that lightning strikes tall objects. Tallness is relative. A fisherman in a boat on a lake is tall in comparison to what's around him. So is somebody standing on a flat, barren shoreline. In either case, if the fisherman is using a rod (particularly graphite), he's holding a ready made lightning rod, and he's inviting disaster.

The cardinal rule is to never allow yourself to get caught where lightning is likely to strike. If you see a storm coming, get off the water or away from high areas or tall objects. The safest place to be is inside a house or vehicle. Don't stand under isolated trees, poles, etc. If you get caught outside in an electrical storm, wait it out in the lowest spot you can find, and keep a low profile. (Notice in the introduction that I sought shelter in a gully.) If you get caught on the water, and you can't make it to shore, stow your rods and lie down in the boat.

Again, lightning is a killer; don't tempt it. "Catching one more" is a feeble excuse for risking your life.

High Winds—High winds are another weather peril for fishermen in boats. Small boats and big waves make bad company. If you think the waves are too high, don't go out. If you *are* out and see a storm coming, head in. If you get caught out in high waves and start taking on water, forget about trying to get back to the dock or ramp. Turn and go with the wind. Let the waves take you where they may. As in my case, it's far better to be stranded for a few hours than to jeopardize your boat and possibly your life.

Fog—Sometimes you may be tempted to head out onto a foggy lake. My advice is don't go. You can't see where you're going, so you risk running into something or getting lost. Stay at the ramp or dock until the fog lifts. You won't miss much fishing time, and you won't be taking unnecessary chances.

Also, I carry a small compass in my tackle box in case I'm on the lake and a fog bank rolls in. Fog causes you to lose all sense of direction, and a compass will help you find your way back to the launch site.

Hypothermia—"Hypothermia," the medical term for loss of body heat, can be extremely serious. It's not only a winter problem. It can occur in other seasons, too. It's usually caused by a combination of cool air, wind, and wet clothes. Evaporation of moisture from clothing causes a rapid heat loss, and this leads to a drop in body temperature.

Hypothermia is the greatest danger in water activites. Cold water drops the body temperature to extremely low levels very fast.

The first sign of hypothermia is mild shivering. This is the body's way of trying to warm itself, and it's also a warning signal. If something isn't done to reverse this situation, the shivering can become uncontrollable, and the victim starts losing feeling in his arms and legs. His speech becomes slurred and his thinking turns fuzzy. If his body temperature continues to drop (75°F to 80°F), he will slip into a coma and probably die.

If you or a fishing buddy start shivering, don't ignore this signal. It's time to take action. There are two things to do: (1) Remove the cause of cooling (wet clothes); and (2) rebuild body heat. This can be done by replacing wet clothes with dry ones (especially a dry cap), by drinking warm fluids (tea, coffee, etc.), and by eating energy-rich foods (candy). Build a fire. Get to a warm place. Stop the loss of body heat and restore it to normal. If the symptoms progress to uncontrollable shivering, get medical help fast. Remember, hypothermia is a killer.

Frostbite—Frostbite is a threat to winter fishermen. In essence, this is a burn which occurs when skin is exposed to a combination of very cold air, moisture, and wind. Circulation drops. The flesh becomes numb and freezes. Frostbitten toes or fingers turn white, and they're very cold to touch.

Frostbite can be avoided by moving around, replacing wet gloves or socks with dry ones, holding numb fingers under your armpit, or holding a warm hand over an exposed ear, nose, or cheek.

If frostbite does occur, don't rub it. Instead, place the frostbitten area against warm skin, and leave it there to thaw. Seek medical attention.

The Danger of Drowning

Drowning is a constant danger to fishermen. Each year we hear tragic stories of fishermen who have fallen out of boats or off the bank and lost their lives. Yet, like lightning, this danger is easily avoided. Following are common sense rules for making sure you won't become a drowning victim.

Wear a Life Preserver: Using a life preserver is the "ounce of prevention" I mentioned earlier. Very few anglers drown while wearing a Coast Guard-approved wrap-around life preserver. Whenever you're in a boat, you're required to have such a preserver with you. You're not required to wear it, however, and this gets many fishermen in trouble.

Accidents happen when you least expect them, and they happen fast. If you're not wearing your life preserver, and your boat suddenly overturns, you probably won't have a chance to put your preserver on. Always wear your life preserver when the boat's running, and zip it up or tie it. Also, it's a good idea to wear it even when the boat's not running, especially if you're a poor swimmer. A vest-type preserver isn't bulky. It's comfortable, and it won't interfere with your fishing.

Bank fishermen should also consider wearing life preservers. If you're fishing along steep banks, tailraces, docks, bridges, or similar spots, you could fall in and be in serious trouble. Children should never be allowed close to such spots without wearing a securely fastened life preserver.

Don't Overload the Boat: One of the worst incidents in my life was watching a duck hunter drown. Four grown men and a retriever were in a small jonboat motoring across the lake where my partners and I were hunting. Suddenly the boat capsized, and the men were in the water. One couldn't swim. He sank in deep water before my hunting partners and I could rescue him.

The first mistake these men made was in not wearing the life preservers they had in their boat. Their second mistake was putting too much load into too small a boat. Little boats aren't meant for heavy loads and high waves.

This lesson absolutely applies to fishermen and all other boaters. If you're going out on a big lake or river, be certain your boat is seaworthy enough to endure rough water. Sure, you don't intend to get caught in a blow, but unexpected storms can lead to disaster.

All boats are rated for maximum loads. Before you leave shore, figure the total weight that'll be in the boat, and don't overload it.

Finally, distribute the weight evenly through the boat. Don't concentrate the weight in one area.

Don't Drink and Boat: Statistics tell the story. A majority of boating accidents involve the consumption of alcohol. Drinking and boating is just as serious as drinking and driving. Don't drink and boat, and don't ride with a boat operator who's been drinking.

Avoid Known Danger Areas: Tailwaters, dam intakes, rapids, waterfalls, and other areas with strong currents pose special dangers to fishermen. Yet, some people fish these spots despite warnings to the contrary. Invariably some of them get into trouble. Never fish where posted warnings or your own common sense tells you it's unsafe. Be alert to sudden water releases when fishing below dams. After a hard rain, avoid streams prone to flash flooding.

The Danger in Ice Fishing: Each season a few anglers go out on new ice too early. Or they try to stretch the season by fishing on ice that is thawing and rotten. Both groups are pressing their luck, and inevitably some press too far. Incidents of fishermen breaking through thin ice and drowning are all too common and could be avoided if anglers would exercise more caution.

Here's the rule of thumb: Two inches of new, clean ice is safe to walk on. Anything less is dangerous. Also, don't walk on ice when you see air bubbles or cracks. When walking on new ice, take a long-handled chisel and tap in front of you to make sure it's solid. But again, if there's any reasonable question that the ice is unsafe, don't go out on it!

Beyond these guidelines, veteran ice fishermen follow other safety rules in the early and late season. They wear life preservers. They go fishing with a buddy, one walking several yards ahead of the other. The second angler carries a safety rope coiled up in a bucket, or he may carry a long pole. Either may be used to pull his partner out if he breaks through the ice.

And as a last safety measure, ice fishermen should carry long nails or pointed dowels in a handy pocket. If you're alone and you break through, these can be used to bite into ice at the edge of the hole to pull yourself out of the water.

The Danger of Sunburn

Sunburn rides the fence between "discomforting" and "life threatening." A sunburn is certainly uncomfortable, though the pain is only temporary. Now, though, doctors are learning that overexposure to the sun's rays may eventually cause skin cancer, and this can be deadly.

Pro fishermen used to wear shorts and fish without shirts. They had beautiful tans, and they looked macho. Today, though, many pros have gotten the message. They wear long pants, long-sleeved shirts, and caps with flaps to shade their ears and necks. On skin areas still exposed to the sun (backs of hands, nose, cheeks) they apply a strong sunscreen.

You may not be outdoors as often as the pros, and you may not go to the extremes they do to protect yourself from the sun's radiation, but you should, especially if you're fair-skinned! *Always* apply sunscreen to exposed skin areas. This sunscreen should have an SPF (Sun Protection Factor) rating of at least 15.

The Danger of Flying Hooks

There are three times when hooks "fly:" (1) When you're casting; (2) when you snatch a hung-up lure out of a shoreside limb; and (3) when you're fishing with a surface lure, and you set the hook. In any of these cases, "flying" hooks can be hazardous to anglers who happen to be in their path.

I once fished a stream in Arkansas with a friend who buried a treble hook into his scalp while making a cast. I've yanked a lure free from a limb and had it stick into my cap bill. It's easy to tell people not to do dumb things like this, but they'll probably happen anyway. Just be alert when *you're* casting and also when *others* are casting. If you cast into the bushes, don't get impatient and yank. Try to flip your bait out, and if it won't come, go get it.

Sunglasses or clear safety glasses will protect your eyes from flying hooks. I wear sunglasses during daytime fishing, and I wear safety glasses when night fishing. I particularly enjoy night fishing for bass with topwater baits. Most strikes, however, are heard instead of seen. If the fish misses and you rear back with your rod, you'll have a hook-studded missile flying at you through the darkness. The danger is obvious. I've never been hit, but that first time could cause serious eye injury.

How to Remove Embedded Hooks

Despite all good intentions, sooner or later you or your partner will probably be on the receiving end of a flying hook, or you'll sit on an exposed hook. When this happens, you have a choice. You can go to a doctor and have it cut out, or you can pull the hook out yourself by the following simple, fairly painless method.

You'll need two 18-inch pieces of strong twine. (Monofilament doubled over works well.) Run one piece through the eye (hole) of the hook, and hold it snug against the skin. With the other hand, run the other piece of string through the bend of the hook, between the skin and the hook, and get a strong grip. If you're doing this properly, the two pieces of string will be pulling in opposite directions.

Now, hold the hook eye firmly in place next to the skin. With the other string, yank up and away very suddenly and forcefully. The barb will pop cleanly out of the skin. Wash the puncture wound, treat it with an antiseptic and apply a Band-Aid. Watch closely the next few days for sign of infection, and if any appears, seek medical attention.

step 1

First remove hook from lure or attached line, then make a loop from 20-pound-test line and tie the ends securely together. Place the loop around the back of your wrist and out between the thumb and forefinger.

barb buried in   line around wrist

step 2

Place the loop over the eye of the hook and center it in the middle of the curved part of the hook. With the thumb of the other hand, press down firmly on the eye of the hook and steady it from wobbling.

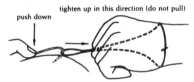

push down | tighten up in this direction (do not pull)

By pusing down on the eye of the hook and tightening up slightly on the loop, the wound spreads open a bit and the barb is in such a position that it has very little bite.

step 3

Now while applying downward pressure on the eye of the hook, give a sharp jerk on the loop. This will pop the hook out in the direction it entered.

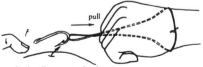

pull

hook will pop up in this direction

215

FISHING ETHICS AND ETIQUETTE

"Always consider fishing as a gift instead of a right. Be thankful for your opportunity to enjoy it, and do your part to preserve it."

Several years ago, I traveled into a neighboring state to write a magazine story about a 77-year-old man who had fished streams all his life. He was still active and got outdoors frequently, so we drove to a creek near his farm to wade and cast for smallmouth bass.

He parked his pickup by an old country bridge, and we gathered our tackle and hiked down a path to the water. It was obvious that someone had been there ahead of us. An empty worm box, food wrappers, and soft drink cans littered the bank.

My friend didn't say anything about the litter as we went on fishing. In the next two hours he caught and released a half dozen or so nice bass while I took the photographs I needed for my story. Finally we decided to head in before an approaching thunderstorm doused us.

But before we walked back up the path to the truck, the aged angler stopped and quietly picked up the cans and paper and stuffed them in his pockets. When we left, the spot was no longer marred by the leftovers of someone's thoughtlessness.

The lesson in this story is a little more complicated than it may first seem. Of course, litter spoils the natural beauty of the outdoors, and no one should leave trash on the landscape. But beyond this, the man's attitude and example of picking up someone else's mess conveyed that he was a sportsman in the truest sense. He cared enough to get involved. Even though he didn't cause the problem, it was still there, and he rectified it.

Hopefully you have this same attitude, not just about litter, but about looking after the fishing resource. Always consider fishing as a gift instead of a right. Be thankful for your opportunity to enjoy it, and do your part to preserve it. If you do this, you'll help maintain the fishery and beauty of the outdoors. You will also gain self-respect by doing what's right. When you maintain good fishing ethics, you feel better about yourself and gain more pleasure from the sport.

Obeying Fish and Game Laws

Good ethics begins with obeying fish and game laws. These laws are designed to protect fish and game populations and also to make sure that everybody has an equal chance to enjoy them.

Always buy required fishing licenses. Money from these licenses goes back to maintain and improve fishing. When you buy a license, you're actually paying your fish and wildlife agency to provide you with better fishing. When people fish without a license (if they are required to have one), they're cheating honest fishermen who buy licenses.

Be familiar with creel and length limits and always follow them. Never take more fish or smaller fish than you're supposed to. Again, limits are set to protect fish populations. If limits are exceeded, fish populations can actually be hurt beyond recovery.

Never use prohibited means of taking fish. Some methods are so effective they don't give fish a chance, and they can be taken in large numbers. This can lead to overharvest, which is why these methods are outlawed.

And finally, if you observe others breaking fish and game laws, report them to your local wildlife officer. By doing so, you're not a snitch. Instead, you're living up to your responsibility to protect fish and game. If you saw someone breaking into a house, you'd have no qualms about calling the police. Likewise, people who break game laws are fish and wildlife thieves, and they're stealing from you and all honest sportsmen. It's your duty to report them.

Obeying Other Laws

Besides obeying fish and game laws, obey all other laws that relate directly or indirectly to fishing. Littering is the prime example. I feel littering is almost an unpardonable sin. *Never* leave trash on the shore; never toss it out of the boat or car window. Don't sink cans in the water. Don't strip old line off your reel and toss it down. Don't sail twist-off bottle caps into the bushes. Don't leave *anything* behind after a day's fishing. If you bring it with

you, take it when you leave. If everybody did this, our lakes and rivers would be much cleaner and prettier. Of course, you can't control the actions of others, but you can control your own behavior, and littering is taboo.

Never go onto private land without permission. You wouldn't want somebody trespassing on your property. Instead, if you find a place you'd like to fish, ask the landowner if he'd allow you to try it. Many times he'll grant permission. But when he doesn't, respect his wishes and find another spot.

Never drive automobiles or off-road vehicles in areas where they're prohibited. These vehicles aren't allowed on many areas in order to protect fragile environments. Don't camp, cut trees, or build fires unless you're sure it's okay to do so.

Obey all boating laws. These laws are designed to protect you and other boaters. Make sure to observe "No Wake" zones. Also, while it's not a law, it's common courtesy not to run your boat too close to a non-moving boat or to anglers fishing from the bank. Steer a wide course so your wake won't upset the other boat or stir up the bank angler's waters.

Other Ethical Considerations

Observing fishing, litter, trespass, and boating laws is only the minimum in good ethics. Beyond this is a higher level of ethical behavior, one not re-quired by law, but which separates true sportsmen from those who are ethical only when they have to be.

This is hard to define in words. The elderly angler at the beginning of this chapter didn't have to pick up someone else's litter, but he did. It may be legal to keep your limit of fish on each trip, but it's unethical to keep more than you need or to take too many fish from one small area. You should especially consider releasing trophy fish alive, unless you want to keep one for mounting. I know anglers who keep all their big fish so they can get their picture in the newspaper each week. They're more interested in building reputations as expert fishermen than in helping preserve the fishery.

Garbage belongs in its' place, not along our waterways.

This doesn't mean that you shouldn't keep some fish to eat. (We've already covered when to keep fish and when to release them in Chapter 11.) Nor is it wrong to keep that occasional trophy for mounting or for shar-ing with family and friends. But there are bounds beyond which keeping fish and showing off trophies is unethical. The difference has to do with ex-cess and with placing your own considerations before those of the fishery.

This is my personal fishing philosophy, and others may disagree with it. But I think it's important to keep man's impact on nature within well confined limits. As a fisherman, you do this by not being wasteful of fish and by not spoiling the outdoor setting.

Angling Etiquette

Part of good ethics is having good manners toward other fishermen, or in other words, maintaining good "angling etiquette."

The Golden Rule applies in fishing just as it does any other time. To paraphrase, "Do unto other anglers as you would have them do unto you." Simply be considerate of other fishermen, and try to avoid interfering with their pursuits and pleasures.

Specifically, don't crowd another angler who got to a spot first. If somebody is already fishing where you wanted to fish, let him enjoy it. Find another spot, or at least don't fish so close that you get in his way. This applies when fishing either from the bank or a boat.

Two special rules apply to boat fishermen. One, if another angler is casting his way down a shoreline, don't circle and move ahead of him. This is like breaking line at a movie theater. Instead, leave that spot and find another bank that's vacant of fishermen. And two, if you're in a boat fishing along a bank and get close to someone fishing from shore, make a wide circle around his spot without fishing it. He only has that one small area to fish. You have the rest of the lake.

If you're fishing in a crowd (on the bank, fishing pier, boat), avoid casting over another angler's line. If someone else hooks a fish, reel your line in so he can play the fish without tangling.

If you're launching a boat, and other fishermen are waiting in line behind you, be ready when it's your turn on the ramp. Put all your gear into the boat and undo the tie-down straps. Then you can launch the boat quickly, and you won't keep others waiting longer than necessary.

Summary on Angling Ethics and Etiquette

Being an ethical, considerate fisherman has nothing to do with how many fish you catch. In fact, I've known a few fishermen who are extremely good at catching fish, but extremely lacking in ethics. They pay little attention to fellow anglers' rights. In a word, they're selfish.

As you grow in fishing, strive to stay out of the trap of letting the end justify the means. Successful fishing entails a lot more than the number of fish you catch. It includes "how" as well as "how many." In a nutshell, fish hard, but at the same time fish honorably and always with consideration for the resource and the rights of other anglers. If you do this, you'll be a beneficial addition to the fraternity of fishermen, and you'll set a good example for others to follow.

CHAPTER 17

PLANNING A FISHING VACATION

"There's nothing quite so enjoyable as a fishing vacation where your plans work out and the fish cooperate."

Through my years of outdoor writing and broadcasting, I've traveled to many of North America's great fishing spots. I've waded for salmon in remote Alaskan streams and stalked largemouth bass in shallow Florida lakes. I've gone after walleye in Saskatchewan, catfish in Mississippi, trout in Montana, crappie in Kentucky, and muskies in Minnesota. The list goes on and on.

During many trips, the fish almost jumped into the boat. I've also had several duds, where the only things biting were insects, and I was the bait! There's nothing quite as enjoyable as a fishing vacation where your plans work out and the fish cooperate. On the other hand, there's nothing quite as disappointing as a promising trip which turns into a bust.

Millions of anglers take fishing vacations each year. Some spend a lot of money getting to remote areas, while others head to not-too-distant lakes over long weekends. Exotic or simple, fishermen take these trips for the same reasons: to test their skills on different waters; to enjoy better fishing than they can find close to home; to catch different species; to try for trophy fish; to spend quality time with family or friends.

Consider taking your own fishing vacation. This is a perfect way to reward yourself for your efforts to date and also to learn even more about the sport. It's fun to research new places, to plan trips, and then to put those plans into action.

You must plan carefully, however, to experience that trip of your daydreams. Without careful planning, your vacation could turn into one of the busts I mentioned above. Traveling a long distance and spending a lot of money is no guarantee for success. You still won't catch many fish if you go at a poor time or use the wrong methods. Planning a successful trip means doing your homework and arranging details so all the odds are in your favor.

Following is how to plan a successful, enjoyable fishing vacation. It's the guide I now use as a professional outdoor writer. It's certainly not fail-safe, but it's as close as I can come. It takes everything into account but the weather, and I'm still trying to figure out how to control that.

Picking a Target Species

"Picking a target species" means deciding which fish to try for. This is the first step in planning a fishing vacation. Choose a fish; then find good places to catch it. Many anglers make the mistake of first picking a location, and then deciding what to fish for. This is "putting the cart before the horse," and it can lead to problems.

My advice for your first trip is not to pick a fish that's too challenging. Regardless of such benefits as scenery, relaxation, or sharing the outdoors with friends, the main focus of a fishing trip is catching *something*! If you don't, despite all the other positive aspects of the trip, you'll go home with a hollow feeling.

So don't plan your first trip around muskies, trophy brown trout, or some other species that you may cast for all day and not get even one strike. Instead, center your trip around panfish, bass, pike, walleyes, or other fish that are plentiful and more likely to bite. This way you're starting with a much higher chance of success.

Selecting Your Vacation Site

Next you must select an actual vacation site, a lake, reservoir, river, or other body of water that offers good fishing for the species you've chosen. Several factors go into this decision: how far you can travel; how much money you can spend; how much time you have; what type facilities you desire. You should decide these things before researching potential vacation sites.

Then make a list of sites that meet your requirements. There are several sources for finding them: magazines, newspaper outdoor pages, TV fishing shows, boat and tackle shows, state travel bureaus, and word-of-mouth from other fishermen. Don't stop when you learn of one place that sounds attrac-

tive. Remember back in Chapter 4 when you became a detective to find close-to-home fishing spots? The same applies when planning a vacation, except the distances are farther. Draw up a list of *several* possible locations, and then investigate each to see which sounds best.

Drawing up this list and checking out each spot takes time, so plan ahead. I start planning a fishing vacation at least six months in advance, and a year's better. To get a reservation at a popular fishing lodge or campground, you'll need an early jump.

When making your list of fishing sites, use the magazines, newspapers, TV shows, etc. *only* as an initial reference. Follow up by contacting lodge or marina operators at the sites and asking for names of customers who have been there. Then write or call them and ask their opinion of the fishing, accommodations, etc. I've learned that other fishermen are the best sources of factual information on potential vacation spots. They'll provide you with a true picture of what you can expect if you go there.

Also, write to the state fish and wildlife agency, and more specifically, to a fisheries biologist who manages the waters you're considering as your vacation site. Ask a few basic questions like: How would you rate fishing here? When is the best time to go? How deep will the fish be at this time? Is any certain area better than others?

Leave a short space after each question for the biologist to write his answer. Also, include a self-addressed, stamped envelope. If you follow this advice, you should receive a speedy response. But if you ask long, detailed questions that the biologist must answer on a separate sheet of paper, and you don't include a self-addressed, stamped envelope, your letter may not be answered for a long time.

Going at the Right Time

This is where many fishing-vacation planners go wrong. Each lake and species have particular times of the year when fishing is best. If you plan your trip to coincide with one of these times, you'll probably catch plenty of fish. But if you go at the wrong time, you may strike out. *When* is almost as important as *where* when planning fishing vacations.

There are peak times of the year for fishing. Species vary and locations change. The best time makes the difference between a full or empty stringer.

Again, this is a simple matter of research. Ask everybody you contact when is the best time for your trip, and plan accordingly.

Also, check moon phases when considering dates for your vacation. The best fishing usually occurs during the periods around the full and new moons. If possible, plan your vacation to coincide with the full moon (best choice) or the new moon (second best).

Staying Long Enough

Invariably, sometime during your vacation a cold front will blow through, and the fish will get lockjaw. This seems to happen every time I go somewhere! So I plan my trips long enough for the weather to stabilize and the fish to start biting again.

If time allows, plan for at least three days of fishing, and five is better. Out of three days, you'll average one poor day, one medium day, and one excellent day. If you're lucky, you may hit three good days in a row; if you're unlucky, you could hit three slow days. The longer you stay, the better your odds are of being there when the fish are biting. Persistence pays big dividends in this sport, both during vacations and on regular day trips close to home.

Hiring a Guide

This is *the* one most important tip I can offer vacationing fishermen. Hire a local guide the first day of your trip, and ask him to show you how and where you can catch fish during your stay. This gets you started off right, and it cuts down on wasted time. It also gives you instant confidence in the spot. If you *know* you can catch fish, you'll try harder when you're on your

Guides can be very helpful and worth the expense. Being on the water every day, they have the knowledge of fish activity, movements, and location.

own. When I travel to a new spot, I always go with a guide the first day.

Many anglers are reluctant to hire guides because of the expense. Most guides charge $75 to $200 for a full-day's fishing. But this amount is minimal compared to costs of travel, lodging, food, and licenses. By tacking on the guide's fee, you take a giant shortcut toward a successful trip, so figure in this amount when you start planning. It'll probably be the best vacation investment you'll make.

Packing for Your Fishing Vacation

Successful planning includes taking essential items and leaving unneeded items at home.

Take all your basic tackle, including rods, reels, tackle box, and accessories. Be prepared, however, to buy some new lures or baits when you get to your destination. I've never been to a new lake where there wasn't a hot lure that all the locals were using. Buy a couple of these lures. There's probably a reason they're producing.

Pack clothes for varying weather conditions. Even if it's summer, take warm outer wear. Early mornings and strange lakes always seem to produce chill factors that are much lower than expected. Also, don't forget the raingear. If you're on a local fishing trip and it starts raining, you can head in. But if you've traveled a long distance and your time's short, you'll probably want to fish right through the showers.

If you've picked a remote vacation site (a fly-in lake, for instance), be very thorough when making your list of things to take. Remember, there won't

be tackle stores where you're going. Ask your outfitter what type lures and tackle you should bring. Also, don't overlook items like insect repellant (100% DEET is best), lip balm, camera, film, etc. If you wear glasses, *always* take a spare pair. I've been on more than one trip where lost or broken glasses spoiled the vision and the vacation of anglers who forgot spares.

Give yourself time to pack. Start laying things out a week before you leave, and cross items off your list as you go. By not rushing, hopefully you won't forget anything.

If you're traveling other than by car, or if you're taking a fly-in or paddle-in vacation, pack as light as possible. But if you're going in your car and staying in a resort or motel, take everything but the kitchen sink! In this case, there's no reason to leave items at home that *might* be needed.

Classic North American Fishing Vacations

Webster's Dictionary defines the word "classic" as "traditional, enduring, serving as a standard of excellence." With these guidelines in mind, there are many classic fishing-vacation areas throughout North America, places that offer top-quality action from year to year. Most are well known and heavily fished. But for some combination of location, size, fertility, or whatever, they keep producing both plentiful numbers and big fish.

Following is a short list of classic North American fishing-vacation spots. I've fished several of these myself and can recommend them firsthand. I list others on the recommendation of fishing friends whose judgement I fully trust. A trip to any of these places should result in a memorable, fun vacation that's worthy of the classic title.

Southwest Alaska

Why not start with the ultimate? Fly-in lodges in southwest Alaska offer perhaps the best, most pristine fishing on the continent. Salmon, trout, arctic grayling, pike, and other species offer almost nonstop action in a spectacular setting. Fishing in Alaska is true adventure! It's also extremely expensive, but every angler who loves the sport should treat himself at least once to the joys of Alaskan wilderness fishing. Late June through August is the best time to go.

Lake Okeechobee, Florida

This large, shallow lake is one of the best largemouth bass fishing spots on the continent. Because of south Florida's semitropical climate, bass grow almost year-round, so they reach huge size. Facilities are good. A guide is a must, at least to get you started. The best time for largemouth is February through April.

Boundary Waters Canoe Area, Minnesota

This watery maze along the Minnesota/Ontario border is a designated wilderness area. Local outfitters (mostly in Ely, Minnesota) rent canoes and camping equipment to anglers who desire a true back-to-nature experience. You can paddle and portage into remote lakes where you're not likely to see another human. Fishing for smallmouth bass, walleye, and pike is great. Time to go is June through September.

Lake of the Woods, Ontario

This giant lake sprawls over the corner where Ontario, Manitoba, and Minnesota join. Lake of the Woods literally teems with smallmouth bass, walleye, muskie, pike, black crappie, and bluegill. If one species isn't biting, another usually will be. Facilities range from modern lodges to rustic campsites. Fishing is good all summer, but September is an excellent time to go here for a mixed bag.

Land Between the Lakes, Kentucky

The Land Between the Lakes is a large recreation area between Kentucky

Lake and Barkley Lake, two of the best warm-water reservoirs in the U.S. This area claims to be the "Crappie Capital of the World," and with good reason. Each spring these lakes produce hundreds of thousands of these tasty panfish, many that top the two-pound mark. Largemouth bass fishing is also extremely good. For crappie, plan a trip the middle two weeks in April. For bass, the time to go is mid-May through early June.

Ozark Streams, Arkansas

For family fun, nothing beats an old-fashioned guided stream float in the Ozarks for smallmouth bass or rainbow trout. Fishing is almost always good. Scenery is spectacular. The guide takes care of getting you on fish, handling the boat, making camp, and cooking—meals on these stream floats are legendary! One-day floats are available, but two- or three-day trips are best. Plan to go late April through June or during the last two weeks in October.

Thousand Islands, New York

The Thousand Islands region lies at the eastern end of Lake Ontario, where the St. Lawrence River divides New York and Ontario. The Thousand Islands consists of the river channel, a maze of adjacent islands, and quiet backwater sloughs. These waters are filled with largemouth and smallmouth bass, walleye, muskie, and pike. This beautiful, underfished area offers peak action in June and September.

High Country lakes, Western U.S.

The Rocky Mountains are sprinkled with high, remote lakes loaded with cutthroat trout. The main way to get to them is on horseback or by hiking. Outfitters in several mountain states specialize in pack-in fishing trips to these lakes. They offer fast action, beautiful surroundings, and a tranquility found only in high, far away places. This is another great fishing opportunity for families who like to rough it. Summer months are best.

Summary

In the years ahead, you may fish around the world, or no farther than your own neighborhood. You may try for the most elusive, most difficult gamefish, or you may be content with the smallest, easiest panfish. You may get into high-tech fishing, with all the gadgets and sophistication of our modern age. Or you might prefer the simplest tackle and techniques to escape, at least for awhile, such modern sophistication.

Wherever and however you fish, I urge you never to get too far away from the basic joys and challenges in this sport. Even when fishing for trophies or in tournaments, your main focus should be that one-on-one contest between you and the fish, not some reward or glory you'll receive if you land a big one or win the tournament. I urge you to respect the fish, and always be a good caretaker of God's gifts of pure waters and the

creatures that inhabit them. Use them, but don't abuse them.

Perhaps some day we'll meet on a lake or stream bank, and we'll share a few tales. We'll talk about the weather and what the fish are hitting. Our conversation won't get very serious or philosophical, but we'll understand each other because we have a common bond. We share the same pleasures, so we're brothers and sisters in one of the greatest sports in the world.

Until we meet, I wish you good fishing. Let your worries blow away with the wind or flow downstream with the currents. This is the real gift of fishing, the gift of inner peace, and I pass it along to you.

GLOSSARY
OF SIMPLE
FISHING TERMS

Following is a list of fishing terms used in *FISHING FUNDAMEN-TALS* that will help beginning anglers understand the concepts and techniques explained in this book.

Artificial lures—Manufactured lures designed to attract strikes by simulating natural bait or by appealing to a fish's aggressive or curious instincts.

Appetite moods—The three basic attitudes of fish toward feeding. See "positive," "neutral," and "negative" feeding moods.

Backwater—Normally, a shallow-water area off a river.

Basic nature—A species' inherent make-up or tendencies that determine its niche or place in its environment.

Basic needs—The three basic survival requirements of any fish species: reproduction, suitable habitat, and food. A favorable environment fulfills these needs.

Bay—A major indentation in the shoreline, particularly in a lake.

Bottom content—Make-up of the bottom, i.e., gravel, sand, mud, etc.

Biting—The feeding action of fish.

Breakline—The point in a body of water where there is a definite change in depth—either deeper or shallower—or a change in a weedline or brushline; a change in bottom composition.

Color of the water—Clarity of the water—clear, dingy, muddy, etc.

Comfort zone—The area offering conditions in which a fish feels comfortable and seeks out. These may include water temperature, water clarity, light level, and other conditions.

Competitive species—The relationship of different species within a body of water, particularly for available food, habitat, and spawning areas.

Controls—How anglers vary the depth and speed of lures or baits.

Countdown method—A method to determine the retrieve depth of a sinking lure and achieve depth consistency during repeated casts and retrieves.

Cove—A major indentation in the shoreline of a lake or reservoir.

Creel limit—The number of fish an angler can keep as set by local or state regulations.

Current break—The location or area where current is altered or blocked by some structure or topography in a stream or river bottom. Also, the zone where current is bordered by calm water.

Dorsal fin—The prominent, main fin on a fish's back.

Drop-off—A point of definite increase in depth; where a lake or river bottom takes a sudden downward turn.

Eddy—A slack-water area in a stream or river, usually bordering strong currents.

Fish attractors—Brushpiles, stake beds, mats, tires, or other cover put into the water to attract fish.

Fishing pressure—Intensity of fishing on a body of water, including the number of fishermen and the effectiveness of their approach.

Flats—Areas of lakes, reservoirs, or rivers characterized by little or no change in depth.

Front—A weather system that moves cross-country and causes changes in temperature, sky cover, precipitation, winds, and barometric pressure, therefore affecting fish location and activity levels.

Holding area—A specific location where fish spend much of their time.

Hook eye—The small circle or loop in a hook where the line is tied.

Impoundment—A confined area where water accumulates as a result of damming a river or stream.

Jetty—A line of large rocks extending from a riverbank toward the channel, for the purpose of directing current and steering the course of the river.

Lake—A confined area where water accumulates naturally.

Length limit—A specified length range of fish limits. (Most length limits are "minimum" limits, though "maximum" or "slot" limits are sometimes imposed on certain species.)

Light penetration—The amount of light and the distance it penetrates a given body of water, normally determined by sky condition and water clarity.

Location—Where, why, and how a fish positions itself in response to its environment.

Migration—The movement of fish from one area to another. Migrations generally occur on a seasonal basis, such as from winter habitat to spawning areas.

Movement—The locational shift of fish from one area to another, generally on a daily or even hourly basis. Also fish changing from a neutral to a positive feeding mood, with a resulting shift of only a few feet from a resting to a feeding position.

Mudline—The zone where muddy water borders clear or dingy water, with the two appearing distinctly different in color.

Natural bait—Bait that occurs in nature or is made from organic substances.

Negative feeding mood—An appetite mood of inactive fish not interested in feeding.

Neutral feeding mood—An appetite mood when fish aren't actively feeding, but could be tempted by a refined presentation.

Oxbow—A lake formed by a change in the course of a river channel; a section of river channel cut off from the main river by a change in the river's path.

Panfish—Small, easy-to-catch fish that are sought more for food than for challenge.

Pattern—Any set of location and presentation conditions that consistently produce fish from a lake, reservoir, or river.

Playing a fish—The process of tiring a fish so it can be landed.

Point—A finger of land that juts out into the water; also, a finger of submerged reeds, timber, grass, etc. that extends from the main body of cover.

Pond—Small natural or artificial body of water.

Population density—The number of fish species occupying a certain area. For example, the number of bass per acre in a lake or reservoir.

Position—The spot from which an angler fishes a particular location.

Positive feeding mood—The appetite mood of actively feeding fish.

Pound test—System for measuring the strength of fishing line; the stress point at which a given line will break.

Preferred food—Food or forage best suited to a species' liking and basic needs.

Presentation—The combination of bait, method, and timing used to catch fish.

Prespawn period—The period of the fish cycle immediately before spawning when fish position themselves near their spawning grounds.

Reservoir—An impoundment; a manmade lake.

Riffle—A shallow, swift area of a stream.

Rig—The combination of hooks, sinkers, floats, snaps, swivels, leaders, and knots used to hold a bait (live or artificial) for presentation to fish; also a fishing boat.

Riprap—Large rocks placed on a shoreline, dam face, causeway, or other exposed areas to prevent erosion from wave action or current.

River (or creek) channel—The original river or creek bed that was flooded when a reservoir was formed.

Rod action—Rod stiffness.

Root wad—A washed-out stump with its root system intact, normally lying in a stream or river.

Seasonal movements—Fish movements from one area of a body of water to another, often in response to spawning urge or changing food conditions.

Skulling—Quietly paddling a boat with a small paddle.

Slough—A creek arm or indentation in the shoreline of a reservoir.

Solunar periods—Daily best-fishing times, based on the moon's gravitational pull on water (tides).

Spawn—A fish's reproductive process.

Species interaction—How various species react to each other in terms of feeding, population density, and competition among species.

Sportfish—Any fish sought by anglers.

Stocking—Releasing hatchery-raised fish into a body of water.

Striking—A fish's act of hitting or taking a bait or lure.

Structure—Physical features of a body of water.

Suspended fish—Fish in open water hovering considerably above bottom.

Tailwaters—The area on the immediate downstream side of a dam.

Target species—The species an angler is trying to catch.

Terminal rig—The combination of hooks, sinkers, floats, snaps, swivels, leaders, and knots used to hold a bait for presentation to fish.

Terminal tackle—Tackle components that make up a terminal rig.

Trailer—A plastic skirt, grub, pork rind, or live bait attached to hooks of lures to entice fish.

Triggers—Lure or bait characteristics (action, color, size, shape, scent, sound, vibration, texture) designed to appeal to a fish's sensory organs.

Trolling—Pulling a lure or bait by moving the boat, as opposed to taking up line with the reel. Trolling speeds are normally slow and powered by an outboard or electric motor.

Undercut bank—An area along a stream or riverbank where currents have washed dirt from under the edge of the bank, providing a shady hiding place for fish.

Weedline—The edge of a mass of weeds.

Wing wall—A large concrete wall running out from a dam to deflect and steer tailwater currents.

Working method—The aspect of presentation that involves triggers, controls, gear selection, and technique.